PRAISE FOR *MANAGING COACHING AT WORK*

"This is a must-have book if you want to gain a greater understanding of coaching and it will give you all the guidance you need to set up an internal coaching programme in your organization. The information provided is invaluable as it offers a variety of tools and techniques to use for planning the future."

Hyacinth Daly, Coaching and Mentoring, Leadership and Learning Directorate in Human Resources at London Metropolitan Police Service

"As CIPD's 2011 learning survey shows coaching is becoming more widespread... However, with quantity we need quality and business coaching needs system, structure and outcomes if its real value is to be realized. Crammed with practical insights, tools and techniques, and grounded in theory and evidence, this vital book helps practitioners reflect and act on every aspect of coaching. Rich in case examples, it explains everything from how coaching takes hold to how it should be held to account. The authors bring their rich pragmatism and wide experience of the workplace and coaching to bear in a guide which I would recommend to every coaching practitioner. Linked to a rich online treasury of resources, it should energize and enable those involved in coaching delivery and design, learning and HR practitioners as well as students and coaches themselves."

Dr John McGurk, Adviser: Learning and Talent Development, HR: Practice Development Team, Chartered Institute of Personnel and Development

"I found this book to be an incredibly useful resource for anyone who is looking into expanding the impact of coaching inside an organization. I wish I'd had this ten years ago, because it brings together critical business thinking, real-life examples and the soft side of coaching into an integrated whole. Before you invest in creating a coaching program from scratch, read this book and learn how it's done from the leaders in this area."

Carl Dierschow, Small Fish Business Coach

"This is a thorough, thought provoking guide for anyone wanting to introduce a coaching program in their organization that facilitates new ways of thinking and brings out the best in their people."

Chris Sier, Professional Certified Coach (PCC), Executive Potential Plus, author of *100+ Tips Taking the Busyness out of Business: Doing the Right Things, Not Everything*

"Keddy and Johnson have done it again, producing a comprehensive handbook – this time into the world of coaching. I wish that this had been published when I was introducing a strategic coaching programme at VT Group. The book is full of advice on how to establish a business case for coaching, implement a coaching initiative and maintain the momentum. The book and website gives useful templates – in particular evaluation tools and coaching role profiles will save the busy HR/OD professional a lot of time and effort. The case studies are interesting and they do help to keep your personal motivation up – which will be sorely tested at times."

Jo Robbins Chief Executive Path2Profit, Talent Management Specialist and Executive Coach with CPS. Ex Group HR Director of VT Group Plc, a FTSE 250 company

"Keddy and Johnson manage to do what is often considered impossible: to define and describe coaching and its role in Executive Development, as well as how and why it works, in a way that is both understandable and relevant."

David Kaiser, PhD, Executive Coach at Dark Matter Consulting

"Having been involved in executive, performance and development coaching as well as coach training for many years, I have a major regret: that *Managing Coaching at Work* had not been written years ago! Had it been, my work when developing leader coach training programs, sustaining and reinforcing coaching, and delivering coaching would have been much, much easier. The content, tips and tools included are invaluable whether considering, designing or overseeing a coaching program at work."

Ed Nottingham, PhD, Clinical & Consulting Psychologist, Leadership Coach, author of *It's Not as Bad as It Seems: A Thinking Straight Approach to Happiness*

"This single volume captures vast swathes of learning since the inception of coaching and distils it into an easily readable format. Coaching is presented in a realistic and balanced way that provides useful information and real life experience. This aids the corporate reader in assessing the need, or actually implementing coaching, in their organization from a much more informed perspective. It addresses the full life cycle of the coaching process. This is the book that coaches in organizations and organizations looking at coaching have been waiting for."

Robert Nogue, Manager Organization Development, Well Construction Services, Weatherford International Limited

Managing Coaching at Work

Developing, evaluating and sustaining coaching in organizations

Jackie Keddy and
Clive Johnson

KoganPage

LONDON PHILADELPHIA NEW DELHI

Publisher's note

Every possible effort has been made to ensure that the information contained in this book is accurate at the time of going to press, and the publishers and authors cannot accept responsibility for any errors or omissions, however caused. No responsibility for loss or damage occasioned to any person acting, or refraining from action, as a result of the material in this publication can be accepted by the editor, the publisher or any of the authors.

First published in Great Britain and the United States in 2011 by Kogan Page Limited

120 Pentonville Road
London N1 9JN
United Kingdom
www.koganpage.com

1518 Walnut Street, Suite 1100
Philadelphia PA 19102
USA

4737/23 Ansari Road
Daryaganj
New Delhi 110002
India

© Jackie Keddy and Clive Johnson, 2011

ISBN   978 0 7494 6136 2
E-ISBN   978 0 7494 6137 9

British Library Cataloguing-in-Publication Data

A CIP record for this book is available from the British Library.

Library of Congress Cataloging-in-Publication Data

Keddy, Jackie.
   Managing coaching at work : understanding, delivering and assessing coaching in organizations / Jackie Keddy, Clive Johnson.
       p. cm.
   Includes bibliographical references and index.
   ISBN 978-0-7494-6136-2 – ISBN 978-0-7494-6137-9 1. Employees–Coaching of. 2. Personnel management. I. Johnson, Clive, 1962- II. Title.
   HF5549.5.C53K43 2011
   658.3'124–dc22
                                        2011009258

Typeset by Saxon Graphics Ltd, Derby
Printed and bound in India by Replika Press Pvt Ltd

CONTENTS

10   Learnings, change and new directions 211

LIST OF CASE STUDIES

By the same authors: *Managing Conflict at Work*

ACKNOWLEDGEMENTS

We are indebted to many people for their part in making this book happen. The case studies that have so illuminated our research and insights that have enriched our learning owe much to those with whom we consulted, and especially: Alan Kay (The Glasgow Group, Toronto, www. glasgrp.com), Alex Fedorcio, Andrea Wood, Bill Griffiths (former Director of Leadership Academy, Metropolitan Police Service), Carl Dierschow (Small Fish Business Coaching, www.smallfish.us), Carla Johns, Coral Ingleton, Deborah Huisken (Dancing Star, www.dancingstar.com), Ian Gibson, Jaclyn Smith, Judi Heaton, Karen Tweedie (KT Consulting Pty Ltd, www. knewtechnologies.com), Katherine Pope (UK ICF, www.coachfederation. org.uk), Lindsay Wittenberg (www.lindsaywittenberg.co.uk), Lisa Atkinson-Browne, Lise Lewis (Blue Sky International Ltd, www.blueskyinternational. com), Liz Hall, Liz Macann, Luke Shinnors, Margaret Eaton, Marilena Beuses (4 Total Success, Inc., www.4totalsuccess.com), Mark Rowland, Martin Tiplady (HR Director, Metropolitan Police Service) Masayuki Uenishi, Matt Becker, Michael Fahie (Point Ahead, www.pointahead.com. au), Michelle Duval (Equilibro, www.equilibrio.com.au), Paddy Stapleton, Polly Gavins (Acorn Business Consulting Ltd, www.acornbusinessconsulting. co.uk), Serena Cunningham, Shaun Lincoln, Shawna Corden, Shilpa Solanki, Stacey Radin (Corporate EQ, www.corporateeq.com), Susie Linder-Pelz (Good Decisions, www.gooddecisions.com.au), Trayton Vance (Coaching Focus, www.coaching-focus.com) and Yasuteru Aoki (Solution Focus Consulting Inc. Japan, www.solutionfocus.jp).

At Kogan Page, thanks are due to Hannah, Lara, Martina, Matthew, Cary, Noemi, Helen, Kasia, Kim, Taryn and Sarah, and we are grateful too to our publicist Helen (www.bookedpr.com), to David and Sue at Hale Farm, and our advisers, indexers, illustrators and proof-readers, all of whom have offered valuable expertise, wisdom and creativity.

From Jackie: A huge thank you to everyone mentioned, but especially to Clive, a remarkable ambassador for coaching, a kindred coaching spirit and a dear friend.

From Clive: My thanks are due to everyone mentioned above, but so too to Jackie, a superstar amongst those who champion coaching and a privilege to call a friend.

PART ONE
Contexts

What is coaching?

Introduction

This book is about the task of sustaining, managing and growing an existing coaching initiative as much as introducing it for the first time. It concerns using coaching as a tactical or strategic means for achieving a beneficial purpose within an organization.

We'll pay attention to circumstances where it may be necessary to revitalize a flagging initiative as well as to situations in which setting a new direction is needed to keep pace with changes occurring within the business. We'll examine the challenges involved in evaluating the effectiveness and impacts of coaching and suggest what can be done to limit these. Finally, we'll consider how the collective experience of individuals who manage, deliver or receive coaching across an organization can position it to better direct opportunities for coaching to drive both people and business performance.

The tips, techniques and guidance that we suggest draw heavily on the insights of others as well as from our own experiences. We are indebted to those who generously gave their time to contribute case studies specifically for this book, but also to many others who took part in consultations to relate lessons from their own coaching programmes.

Their experiences, described in the feature boxes peppered throughout the book, cover widely different applications and interpretations of coaching, and feature case studies from the smallest of organizations to the largest of multinationals. Public, private and third sector organizations are all represented, the shared insights relate to experiences of coaching practice from organizations around the world.

Our own learnings have come out of acting both as consultants and trainers to individuals responsible for developing coaching capabilities within their own organizations and in Jackie's case as a former 'staffo' (staff officer), responsible for leading a project to roll out a brand-new coaching practice in the London Metropolitan Police Service too.

One of the difficulties of writing a text such as this is that the needs of each organization and so the operating context for every coaching project are different, even if many similar challenges may be faced by those who are at similar stages in their coaching implementations.

We can't promise a single, prescriptive 'one size fits all' approach to making coaching work either, but rather we hope that by highlighting the wide range of considerations that any leader of any coaching initiative may want to concern themselves with and by providing a comprehensive range of templates to draw upon, this book will serve as a valuable reference to help them with their task. We can't promise that making coaching an everyday practice from top-to-bottom in any organization will be an easy task, and we aim to give realistic guidance for those who may find themselves as lone voices, attempting to further the coaching cause with limited budgets and having little more than lip-service support from senior-level sponsors.

Checklists of topics that project leaders might find useful are brought together at the end of the book (Appendix B). These are intended to include full 'shopping lists', even if some items are optional considerations and others don't apply to every type of coaching project. Some degree of discretion is therefore needed to choose which items are relevant and practical for your particular needs.

The book is organized into three main parts:

- **Part One** considers the organizational contexts for using coaching, exploring the concept of setting an agenda to align coaching applications with business needs and discussing the relevance of choosing between different levels of aspiration in deciding how to focus a coaching project. The potential need to identify different interpretations of what 'coaching' is and factors that might indicate why coaching may be preferred over other interventions such as training and mentoring are considered in Chapters 1 and 2.

- **Part Two** provides guidance on implementing a coaching initiative – not just where coaching is being introduced for the first time, but also where concerted action is needed to set a fresh direction. The tasks of operating an ongoing coaching service are considered, as is the challenge of sustaining and developing coaching as a management style.

- **Part Three** puts the spotlight on capitalizing on what is learnt through coaching, emphasizing especially the role of audit and evaluation. A method for assessing the effectiveness and impact of coaching is described and a means for ensuring that a coaching practice remains fit for purpose is also outlined.

Readers who have already embarked upon a coaching programme or who are well acquainted with the principles of coaching may find that there's much that will be familiar to them in the first two chapters. Even though just a skim read of these opening pages may be appropriate for such readers, we suggest that it will be worth at least reconsidering what is meant by coaching and why coaching may be a preferable intervention for addressing particular needs over others.

Defining coaching

Before we can start considering how to implement coaching, we might start by asking: *What is coaching?*

Unfortunately, for many, finding an answer to this question has proved to be quite an elusive task: put 10 coaches in a room, and the chances are that you'll be offered 10 different versions of what coaching actually is! Indeed, there are possibly as many definitions of what coaching is as there are coaches, though hopefully there'll be a fair degree of common ground between these!

A quick glance at the myriad of attempts to create a Rubicon definition that can be accepted by all illustrates the dilemma that many have encountered. Michael Jay offers us: 'in the simplest terms, the coach is someone who uses coaching knowledge, skills and abilities without responsibility, accountability or authority over the outcomes of the person being coached while seeking to co-generate well-being, purpose, competence and awareness as a result of a coaching interaction' (Jay, 1999).

Meantime, Richard Kilburg weighs in with a definition for executive coaching: 'a helping relationship formed between a client who has managerial authority and responsibility in an organization and a consultant who uses a wide variety of behavioural techniques and methods to help clients achieve a mutually identified set of goals to improve his or her professional performance and personal satisfaction and, consequently, to improve the effectiveness of the client's organization within a formally defined coaching agreement' (Kilburg, 1996). Next, Loehr and Emerson (2008) give us '[helping] another person reach higher performance by creating a dialogue that leads to awareness and action'.

Dig a little deeper, and the definitions become more elaborate still – and so too, more and more perplexing for a newcomer to fathom.

Eric Parsloe is amongst the body of coaching commentators who prefer to avoid seeking a definitive explanation of what coaching is, although he offers a preferred version: 'coaching is a process that enables learning and development to occur and thus performance to improve. To be successful, a coach requires a knowledge and understanding of the processes as well as the variety of styles, skills and techniques that are appropriate to the context in which the coaching takes place' (Parsloe, 1999).

Another thoughtful definition comes from Whitmore: 'coaching is unlocking a person's potential to maximize their own performance. It is helping them to learn rather than teaching them' (Whitmore, 2002). Perhaps more simply, we might adopt a view that 'coaching is [about] the conversation, not the tool'.

What is useful about these offerings is that they begin to pick out the bones of what gives coaching its power, or what it is that makes coaching work for many people.

We might also talk about 'life coaching' ('a purposeful conversation that inspires you to create the life you want' (Burn, 2007)), 'executive coaching' ('the art and science of facilitating the personal development, learning and performance of an executive' (Dembkowski, 2006)), 'leadership coaching', 'performance coaching' and 'transformational coaching', to name just a few. Then there are differing coaching practices to consider as well – 'solutions focus coaching', 'cognitive-behavioural coaching' and 'appreciative coaching' amongst them.

Our own favourite choice of words is offered by *Naked Leader* author David Taylor in his own take on organizational coaching, *The Naked Coach*: '[business coaching is] any and every intervention that enables people, teams and organizations to be their very best' (Taylor, 2007).

For the coaching purist, Taylor's somewhat blunt explanation may be lacking substance. On its own, this definition doesn't distinguish coaching from 'mentoring', 'counselling', 'training' and a variety of other interventions.

We believe that his offering at least encourages us to get to the heart of what coaching is meant to be about – helping people move forward, and in a way that taps into their inner personal resources and self-potential. This is where coaching often has an edge over other approaches: it gives insight and inspiration, challenging people to search inside for answers and to gain satisfaction and increased motivation when they find them. This is also why coaching has built up such a strong fan base within organizations – it really offers the power to change people in both the short and the long term, both for their own good and for the good of their organization.

So you may be wondering what our own contribution to the lexicon of coaching definitions might be! While not wanting to be deliberately evasive, we prefer to concur with some commentators that the best definition of coaching is *the one that works for you and your organization*. As we'll see later, the ways in which organizations have applied their meaning of coaching have taken widely differing starting points. It's not for us to say whose choice of words is right or wrong.

Nevertheless, it's helpful to consider the telltale signs that characterize most people's definition:

- Coaching is *non-directive* – it's for a coachee to set the agenda, not the coach.
- Coaching focuses on helping a coachee to reach their objectives.
- Coaching causes individuals to dig deep, reflect, think through options clearly and determine courses of action that they feel motivated to follow.
- Coaching is for a purpose – it's not about having a cosy chat about 'anything and everything'; it has a definite start and an ending.

- Coaching invites an individual to stretch out of their comfort zone and helps them to explore more of their potential.

Taken alone, some of these characteristics might easily be applied to a variety of managerial interventions and communication styles, such as transformational leadership training, for example. Again, it's a question of the context in which the activity is being described and any definition adopted by the organization that matters when comparing one thing with another. In practice, coaching overlaps and integrates with a range of other disciplines; for example, it typically plays an important part in mentoring conversations.

None of these criteria is the mutually exclusive domain of coaching. Arguably all management interventions should have a clear beginning and ending; various activities may focus on helping an individual to achieve their objectives, while many teaching methods adopted in classroom training are non-directive. Some in our list might also be challenged. In the workplace, for example, coaching is often aimed at achieving organizational goals as much as ones set by an individual. However, this merely serves to illustrate the tangled web we weave when trying to establish a universal definition for coaching: what one person or organization understands isn't necessarily the interpretation of another.

One further reason that we prefer to avoid offering a single definition of 'coaching' is that the term is often used to refer to a *management style* as much as to an ongoing process in a committed relationship, whether the coach is a professional in their field or not, and whether or not they are able to act as an independent party to their coachee's management line.

A research team commissioned by the UK's Chartered Institute of Personnel and Development (CIPD) to explore the factors that are likely to encourage coaching on the front line would seem to concur with our view. In summarizing their approach to their study, the Portsmouth University team suggest that '[the] line manager as a coach role is better understood as a coaching style of management, integrated within a move from a command and control approach to a more participative style of management' (Anderson *et al*, 2009).

CASE STUDY
Onward and upward: the rise and rise of CareSource

Now with a workforce of more than 900 staff, Dayton, Ohio-based healthcare management provider CareSource has seen its staff base triple in size in almost as many years. As others that have faced similar growth have discovered, growth brings its own challenges. Not least, new managers and leaders need to become quickly effective in their posts, while career development needs to be managed carefully.

There was then an obvious role for coaching when the organization launched its coaching programme, having earlier launched a successful mentoring programme. Coaching is offered to all new managers and directors as part of a structured process by the organization's Coaching and Consulting faculty, one of four schools of the CareSource University (CSU). New manager and director coaching typically comprises 12 sessions spread over a six-month period and includes formal contracting and evaluation activities.

While career and leadership development is an important focus for coaching, this doesn't have an exclusive call on the services offered by CSU. Interpersonal issues are also popular amongst the themes that are brought for coaching.

This mix of process and clear communication has helped foster an openness amongst newcomers to coaching to engage with it, for example by excluding individuals whose current performance isn't in good standing from being eligible to take up the service. From the outset of the programme, CareSource were careful to promote coaching as being a positive intervention, rather than one that might be seen as having remedial overtones.

Matt Becker, CareSource's coaching and mentoring manager, explains that steady growth was important when establishing the practice, which initially launched on an informal basis and with an individual-centred focus. Later, the programme was developed in a small manageable way, remaining capable of matching demand with the supply of available qualified coaches and developing a reputation for trust along the way.

Potential candidates for coaching must satisfy key eligibility criteria, and appreciate the differing contexts for using coaching and mentoring. The latter recognizes that a mentee is likely to receive a higher level of direct guidance, direction and advice than they might expect from a coach, while the former is positioned to support 'improving [an] individual's self-awareness, discovering possibilities for themselves and how to handle various situations'.

Becker also remarks that making sure that no one is ever coerced into coaching has played an important part in creating a successful practice, while CareSource's focused use of coaching has enabled it to align closely with organizational development priorities.

Jaclyn Smith, director of CSU, adds that the ability to build on the early success stories of individuals who had sought out coaching and at the same time tying the role of coaching to other development strategies (eg when on-boarding new managers) allowed a much stronger case for fully investing in coaching to be made than might otherwise have been the case.

The organization has paid special attention to evaluating coaching, to the point of assessing impacts and even (where relevant) attaching these to monetary values.

The coaching practice has shown that it can not only keep step with the needs of an organization that is on a fast-track expansion, but help to facilitate an easy transition through this critical period too. Now with a strong body of leaders whose own careers have been helped through coaching and who are able to see why coaching matters, there's every reason to believe that CSU's coaches will have an equally important part to play in the company's next period of development.

Perhaps some organizations shy away from taking steps to 'implement coaching' because they believe that too much is involved in training all managers to a minimum standard of coaching proficiency, making time available for coach and coachee to meet regularly in private, and not really being sure that it's all worthwhile. Another common objection (as Jackie was once informed) is "We don't do emotions round here, just delivering the job." It doesn't have to be this way: basic awareness training can deliver positive returns, even where a minority of managers are ready to take a coaching mindset into their everyday management repertoire.

So within a single organization, it's possible to talk about coaching in a variety of contexts and with differing meanings. Perhaps this is why many have struggled to pin down a perfect definition. In the parlance used in this book, we'll therefore use the term 'coaching' quite loosely, making clear when distinguishing one type of coaching application (such as implementing a programme to develop in-house coaches) from another (eg sourcing executive coaches).

In starting implementation or deciding where to take a coaching initiative that's already been put into practice, it's therefore important to decide what type of coaching to target. At one extreme, there is what we might for convenience call 'pure' coaching.

At the other extreme, 'coaching' may simply refer to a style of communicating – a way of interacting with another person that aims to help them think, find realization and then act.

Contracting external coaches is most popular for meeting executives' needs, although this doesn't mean that the coaches they engage need to possess a radically different skill set from any other coach. An exception is perhaps the ability to relate to the types of issues, language and context that their clients most commonly want to discuss.

Coaches brought in from outside an organization or peer-level coaches drawn from other organizations are generally preferred by executives for the simple reason that many amongst the top brass don't feel comfortable opening up on what may often be personal or commercially sensitive matters with their peers or more junior personnel.

However, this is by no means a universal reality that can be seen in every organization. We have encountered several examples of in-house coaches being successfully matched with clients[1] who rank several levels higher than themselves within their organization. From what was at first a surprising discovery for us, we learned that coachees often preferred this arrangement over being coached by a heavyweight in their organization who they felt might be inclined to judge them or increase pressure on them to perform – or by an outsider who found it hard to relate to the situations they described.

What goes on behind the closed doors of an executive's office is often more mundane than might be assumed. Rather than poring over key strategic decisions and reflecting on how to become a better leader, many executives' concerns often focus around feelings of isolation in their role or being troubled over how to interact with a fellow director. That's not to play down the importance of such concerns; of course, a fair bit of character building and high-level creative and strategic thinking does flow out of executive coaching sessions too. The beneficial impacts for the organization that result can often be far-reaching.

Of course, in between these extremes lies a wide range of variations, such as the *in-house programme*, designed to up-skill a cohort of coaches from amongst an organization's own staff base at a level no different from that which might be expected of an external coach (Figure 1.1).

FIGURE 1.1 Meaning of coaching. Coaching may mean different things to different people or organizations, characterized by a number of variables or 'sliding scales'

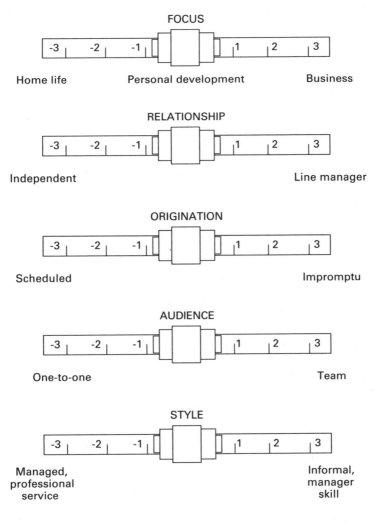

What coaching *isn't*

As much as we might try to pin down what coaching is, it's possibly helpful also to consider what it *isn't*. For a start, as it's often used within workplace contexts 'coaching' doesn't normally have the same connotation as it does when used in sports environments. In recent years, coaching has emerged as a discipline on the back of a practice that was found to work in sporting contexts; however, it's often the case today that the notion of a 'national coach' of (say) a hockey or baseball team bears little resemblance to the type of coach that an organization may wish to engage with, and even less with the wonderful character known as 'Coach', who some might recall used to clean glasses behind the bar in the popular TV series *Cheers!* Of course, that's not to say that these types of coach don't have a valuable role to play too.

Sports coaches may well deploy very similar techniques to achieve the best from their teams, to encourage and support. However, they are also often seen as the people who are key decision makers in planning game strategy, hiring and firing players, and being the object of endless criticism in the back pages of our newspapers. These are not typical role models for the type of coach that we have in mind.

In our view, coaching isn't quite the same as mentoring either, although both often go hand-in-hand and mentoring typically involves using a coaching style. Some might want to under-stress a distinction between the two, including Bob Garvey, Professor in the Centre for Individual and Organization Development at Sheffield Hallam University. From his exploration of the origins of coaching and mentoring, Garvey reports that he '[has] found that there isn't a difference in the skills and processes of coaching and mentoring but in timescales and context' (Garvey, 2008). Perhaps this highlights a difference in the way that coaching and mentoring are often used.

As with coaching, mentoring aims to help an individual move forward in some way. Often – but not always – this takes a longer-term, career-focused view. But for us, the key question in a mentee's mind is usually 'How do I achieve…?' or perhaps 'What is it that I need to do to become…?'

A mentor may bring wisdom, knowledge and an appreciation of the political and organizational structures within which a mentee works. He or she may offer suggestions and act as a source of information and reference point for contacts. But the mentor's greatest contribution is to help a mentee develop their own understanding of their potential and to identify the pitfalls and the opportunities they may face – often through coaching.

Both coaching and mentoring involve good listening skills, working to an individual's goals, and should be non-judgemental and free of assumption. Both rely on trust, confidence and openness and should offer an opportunity for the individual to speak, clarify thoughts and put things in perspective. Both are mutually compatible and as communication styles are often used together.

As there is both a blurring and a distinction between coaching and mentoring that most people would recognize, so too can comparisons be made between coaching and other types of intervention. We'll consider some of these later in this chapter.

One further popular misconception of coaching is the idea that it offers no more than an opportunity for a busy person to shut off from their frantic schedule once or twice a month for half an hour or so, to unburden whatever's on their mind with someone who's not going to give them a hard time. As those who coach or who receive coaching will know, this is a fallacy. In fact, a good coach may occasionally raise the strength of a challenge put to a coachee, and most practical coaching sessions usually end with a coachee resolving to carry through a series of actions. As Jackie likes to put it, coaching isn't just for those who like to retreat to 'a darkened room and drape a wet flannel across their forehead'.

This isn't to say that the opportunity to take a brief break from normal activity isn't useful, nor that the discipline of sounding out with another person isn't valuable either. In one sense, a coach *may well* be thought of as a 'professional friend'. However, as we hope may be becoming clear, their role extends far beyond this.

In practice, we've found that most organizations aim to encourage coaching in a variety of forms. Informal coaching is usually no less important than a formal, contracted coaching relationship, and especially if a significant proportion of managers are ready to take coaching on board as a basic skill, used without ceremony in everyday conversation.

Our definition of 'workplace coaching implementation' is therefore equally broad. This potentially includes a programme of mixed activities to provide an internal pool of coaches, a managers' training course or coaching awareness initiative, or standardizing on criteria for offering coaching and hiring coaches.

Similarly, when we refer to 'coaching', we may speak about the *coaching* that is offered to teams rather than individuals, in particular circumstances only, or as ambitious a purpose as its sponsors want it to be. To come back to the point we made earlier, it's the *outcomes* of coaching rather than the precise nature of the practice itself that really matters. For organizations that are often resource-strapped, outcomes need to have a clear business value.

Role of the coach

Our foregoing discussion of what coaching is should shed a light on the role of a coach. As we've already mentioned, a coach should be a powerful ally for a coachee, someone who is more than a mere sounding board or 'second brain'. Rather, a coach helps an individual to make sense of a particular topic or situation and to work through their response to this.

A coach then needs to be an exceptionally good listener, able to give the space and time needed for a coachee to form their thoughts and draw their own conclusions, in their own time. Coaches must be able to frame their comments and pose the deep questions that will prompt coachees to set about probing self-searching, and they must be able to play back what they hear and offer further suggestions for reflection when relevant to help a coachee pull together their developing insights. At the same time, they must be ready to challenge their clients and encourage them to move out of their comfort zones.

As basic as this may seem, the ability to genuinely listen to what an individual is saying and to form questions that don't presume an answer is considerably more difficult for most of us than we might like to admit. The temptation to jump in and offer opinions of our own as well as to cut short another person as soon as we believe that we've understood the point that they are making is just irresistible for many of us!

Depending on the context of the work they perform and their preferred personal styles, many managers fall into this trap. In environments where the onus is on 'getting the job done', it's perhaps understandable that cutting to the chase with bold instruction is the management style of choice for many. When this becomes entrenched as a normal means of interacting, to suddenly change into a coaching mode is a tall order. Not only may the skills demanded of a good coach not be readily practised, but the whole psychological contract that exists between managers and members of their teams ('I'm the boss' and 'This is the way we do things around here') is difficult for some managers to set aside.

But there are other challenges too. A coach's role requires that they can be perfectly trusted with virtually any personal confidence. In order for an individual to talk through their feelings and to open up on their inner thoughts, as is often necessary for coaching to do its work, both coach and coachee must feel fully comfortable about sharing these feelings and thoughts.

Of course, some individuals will feel perfectly at ease opening up in this way with their line manager or another colleague with whom they interact on a day-to-day basis. However, for most, this is to expect a great deal, not least because it assumes that individuals will set aside the usual *modus operandi* in their relationship with their manager.

It's then perhaps not surprising that some believe that coaches need to be independent of an individual's network of everyday working relationships and management line. But managers can and do coach, and a common objective for many organizations' coaching initiatives is to encourage this practice as the norm. We'll have a little more to say on this in the next section.

Ultimately, coaching is typically about changing mindsets and behaviour, very often being transformational in nature – in other words, having a lasting, positive effect. For us, this is usually what is most exciting to witness as a coach – an individual really 'unlocking their potential' and breaking through personal comfort zones to discover hidden talents and ways of playing to their natural strengths. To observe a transformation is almost like witnessing a miracle, and there's something very special in seeing a fellow human being experience such a breakthrough. Of course, since a coach and coachee work together to achieve a coachee's objectives, there's a sense of shared achievement in this (although a coach shouldn't forget that the real work has been undertaken by the coachee).

The manager as coach

If the role of a coach is relatively easy for most people to agree upon, then the notion of the 'manager as coach' is altogether more difficult to discern. Once again, we start with a potential conflict of definitions: are we referring to a standard coaching relationship in which the only variation is that the coach and coachee have a line management relationship with each other, to a style of managing, or perhaps to both of these? Since managers are often the key target for coaching training, it's worthwhile spending a moment or two considering the part that coaching can play in a management role.

Conversations with different organizations quickly reveal that one of two outcomes is usually expected of manager coach initiatives. One intention is to equip those responsible for managing staff with the knowledge, skill and will routinely sit down with each of their charges and just coach, no less diligently than as if a professional coach had been contracted for the task. Such coaching typically focuses on staff performance, remedial or skill-building objectives.

Line managers may be seen as being well placed to develop and motivate their staff, since not only are these an integral part of their role, but they are usually also able to observe and offer feedback to coachees when appropriate. What's more, managers can help coachees put their objectives in context not only with what matters for them, but with what's important for their team and wider organization as well. Of course, there are also disadvantages for line managers taking on a coach's role, as we'll see in just a moment.

A second common intention of putting managers through a coaching programme is to provide them with an appreciation of how and why coaching is effective in helping staff, and to equip them with basic coaching skills to use at their discretion. The expectation here is not that managers will start scheduling in monthly 'one-to-ones' with all their staff, but will regularly adopt a coaching style in the briefest of everyday conversations. So too, coaching of teams is increasingly being promoted as a powerful manager skill-set, and one that is distinct from facilitation, with the former tending to be 'more goal-focused than the process-orientation of group facilitation and the roles of coach and facilitator [being] subtly different' (Brown and Grant, 2010).

A wider hope might be that managers' mindsets and approaches to working with staff might change if there's a groundswell of enthusiasm for coaching – in short, when managers feel more ready to get in touch with their 'helping side'.

This second objective for manager coach programmes seems to be the one most organizations expect to achieve. According to respondents to a recent learning and development survey by the CIPD (CIPD, 2008), 36 per cent of the organizations questioned identified responsibility for coaching as lying with line managers and 79 per cent reported that coaching is used for 'general development'.

But while the skill-sets and mindsets needed for both intended outcomes are the same, each requires different treatment to implement effectively. We should then consider each of the two intentions separately.

The question of whether a line manager can or should be a coach is itself controversial, setting the stage for an engaging debate hosted by the Association for Coaching in London some years ago[2] with the differing positions represented by Carole Wilson and Philip Ferrar, then a consultant with Momenta Consulting. Ferrar argued that it's implausible to expect all managers to adopt a coaching mindset all of the time, citing findings from his postgraduate research into the topic. He argued that there are inherent aspects of a manager's role which often get in the way of their becoming a good coach: a manager's mindset tends towards thinking in terms of completing tasks rather than seeing staff as 'clients', while the relationship that managers and subordinates have with each other often acts against openness, trust and shared confidence where reputations, concerns for career progression and managers' perceptions of their power zone come into play.

Opponents of this argument might respond that coaching can often make life easier for managers, producing better-thinking individuals, more cooperative teams and more effective ways of completing tasks. While this might often be so, a problem facing those who promote manager coach programmes is how to get this message across in a way that convinces managers to invest a little time to try out what's on offer, to show that coaching isn't a 'pink and fluffy' distraction.

Coaching as a management style

We return to considering the aim of integrating coaching as an everyday management style, by which we mean an approach to managing, an attitude and an application of skill.

Janice Caplan puts it as follows: 'a coaching style of management is one where the manager uses coaching techniques in discussions and dealings with staff. By using these techniques, the manager encourages the employee to identify options and seek his or her own solutions to problems' (Caplan, 2003). She continues, 'This style is in direct contrast to a directive one where the manager has the answer and tells employees how it should be done.' This may be a hackneyed definition for coaching purists: brief, ad hoc conversations are rarely transformational, they might say, while giving relatively little focus to the coaching relationship.

However, using a coaching style in everyday management and perhaps occasional one-to-one meetings such as personal development planning is not without value. What's more, this may have the best chance of being permanently taken up by a majority of managers over plans to establish regular coaching sessions, and especially if coaching is offered as an option for managers to use at their discretion rather than by decree. It's not just managers either who may benefit from adopting a coaching approach in conversation – indeed, anyone can usefully get in on the act. We should note, however, that it is possible to over-coach or coach at inappropriate times.

Most of the anecdotal success stories of 'manager as coach' programmes cited by coaching sponsors are of this type: the major UK retail store Selfridges has seen rising customer satisfaction scores following sales-floor staff coaching, a dramatic jump in National Vocational Qualification (NVQ) skill levels was seen by train staff of the railway company First Great Western, and happy cohorts of staff have responded to coaching interventions at John Lewis Partnership, to name just a few.[3]

Angela Vint *et al* suggest that one benefit of adopting coaching as a management style is that it can be a powerful way to influence others: 'the coaching director makes time on a regular basis to talk to the person concerned about themselves, rather than just about the task. [She/he] recognizes, respects and encourages the person to include total life responsibilities in work.' They continue: 'the coaching director provides the context for the people to come up with the right answers for themselves and the business by setting the direction, giving support and then asking questions and listening to the answers... [their] aim is to inspire people, to get the best out of them and create an atmosphere that allows them to succeed' (Vint *et al*, 1998).

Coaching's role amongst the 'helping skills'

As a management style, coaching might be thought of as one of a number of approaches – though not to say one of the more important – that managers might use when offering support for an individual's development and learning, or when encouraging them to perform at their best. Amongst the other 'helping skills' are those shown in Figure 1.2. There's a close overlap between many of these styles, and switching back and forth between different interventions can occur quickly within a single conversation.

These skills may be broadly categorized according to the degree to which an individual knows the answer and the degree to which it is appropriate ask questions or give answers.

Considering the alternatives, the primary concerns for a manager are then: *What will most help the individual move forward, getting them from 'A to B'? Which is the style that is most likely to be effective given the current need?* and *When is it appropriate to involve a specialist?*

A possible approach when choosing which style to adopt is to consider the situation an individual is in. The well-known model for 'Situational Leadership' developed by Paul Hersey and Ken Blanchard (Hersey and Blanchard, 1977) offers help here. This presents a mix of possible management interventions, which adopt, to a greater or lesser degree, supportive or directive styles (Figure 1.3). The argument underpinning the model is that the choice of style that is most appropriate to use in different circumstances should be driven by both an individual's ability *and* their motivation. Coaching might be recommended where an individual has some ability but lacks commitment, although it may also be relevant where their competency level is high.

FIGURE 1.2 Management styles

Counsellor	Coach
'You do it; I'll be a reflecting board'	'What do you want to achieve?' 'How will you achieve this?' 'What will you do?' 'How committed are you to seeing this through?'
Facilitator	**Teacher or Trainer**
'You make the decisions; I'll help smooth the process'	'Here are some hints and techniques you can use for this task'
Reflective observer	**Adviser**
'You try; I'll observe and reflect back what I see'	'I'll answer any questions when you hit a problem'
Mentor	**Collaborator or Partner**
'First, tell me what you think. If you wish, I'll then offer suggestions based on my experience'	'We'll try this together and learn from each other'
Hands-on expert	**Modeller**
'I'll do the task; I'll tell you how to do this'	'You watch me demonstrate. Learn from me'

FIGURE 1.3 Choice of management approach according to situation (after Hersey and Blanchard (1977))

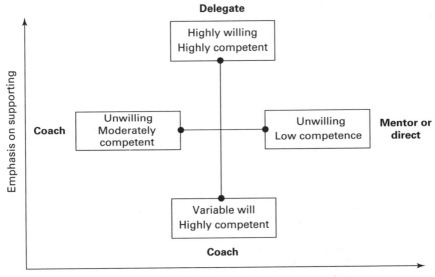

But motivation and ability aren't the only concerns for coaching. A coachee's knowledge must also be taken into account. There's little use continuing to probe for answers when a coachee has genuinely exhausted the bounds of their knowledge – 'knowing what they don't know' or 'not knowing what they don't know', to borrow a line from another concept familiar in training circles.

An initial consideration is that an individual may choose not to declare what they do not know to a coach or manager, a boundary which of course any good coach worth their salt needs to respect. Furthermore, both coach and coachee may be in the dark about some topics, in which case coaching is a logical style for a manager to adopt.

But where a coachee is knowledgeable, a variation of the Johari Window and 'conscious consciousness' model[4] comes into play for selecting the appropriate management style (see Figure 1.4). Here, coaching or mentoring is the preferred choice.

The Situational Leadership model takes us back to another way of classifying styles according to two main variables – the extent to which an individual knows an answer, and the extent to which they are asked questions. Figure 1.5 suggests how alternative styles might be plotted against these two axes.

Of course, all of this is mere guidance. Managers shouldn't need to struggle over which style to use at every turn, but rather be able to move naturally from one to another, even when they may be less practised or prefer some less than others. Encouraging this 'portfolio' ability is perhaps one key objective for much coaching training offered to managers.

FIGURE 1.4 Management intervention according to knowledge

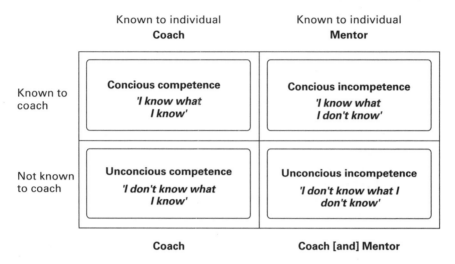

FIGURE 1.5 The 'helping skills'

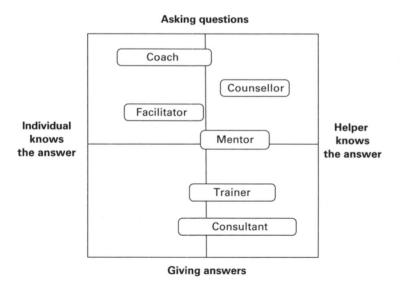

'Coaching culture'

Accepting the role qualifications that might be expected of a coach described above and the contexts in which many managers operate, it's perhaps not surprising that the notion of achieving a 'coaching culture' is a tall order for many organizations. This isn't to say that this isn't achievable, but as we'll see in the next chapter, in some cases it isn't always desirable either.

The term 'coaching culture' is referred to very regularly, but – guess what? – there are more than a few different ideas of what this actually means. A recent conversation between Clive and an organization development (OD) director of a large public service organization during a break at a conference illustrates the point.

The jocular senior officer had been expounding his pride at what had been achieved within his organization some two to three years after introducing coaching. 'All of our top guys are heavily into this coaching thing', he explained. 'You see it all the time. There's a definite coaching culture right across the business now.'

At that moment, his mobile phone rang and, making his apologies, he retreated into a nearby corner to take the call. Left alone with half a glass of apple juice and a half-eaten piece of quiche, Clive couldn't avoid overhearing most of what was quite a loud and expressive conversation. 'Haven't I told you a thousand times not to do that!... Tell him to get off his !!@&*! butt and do what I say!... No, we're not doing that!'

Phone call completed, the OD supremo returned to his conversation with Clive, beaming about the joys of having a coaching culture.

Of course, it's not necessary for coaching to be a part of every single conversation for an organization to feel that coaching is an important part of its culture. The OD director may well have been right about the change in perspective or an intention to coach when it's appropriate being widespread within his organization, and his apparently off beat phone conversation might simply have been one of those moments when a strong directive style was called for. However, it's possible that his perception of what constitutes a coaching culture may be different from others. Certainly, coaching is not just an add-on to what's practised already, although in our experience some organizations seem to view it this way, if not as a 'light and woolly bolt-on' at that!

For some, just the fact that a coaching programme exists or that some coaching takes place is enough to suggest that an organization has adopted a coaching ethos. Recruit a coach for every executive and let them proclaim the benefits of coaching for others, and some may say that you're already one step away from being in coaching culture heaven.

The leader of a coaching programme in a large UK retail organization offered another interpretation: 'For me, it's about being able to walk around this building and eavesdrop on lots of small coaching conversations going on – by the water-cooler, in the cafeteria, across a desk. I'd like to think that most people – not just managers – are constantly thinking "Is this a good opportunity for me to coach?" and not thinking twice to take action when they see that it is.'

This seems to us to be quite a common aim for coaching initiatives – to instil coaching as a pervasive style right across an organization, and in the process, changing the way in which colleagues interact with each other from a situation in which direction is the normal mode of communicating to one in which supporting each other's development and quality of thinking is at the forefront.

We might add another view of what a coaching culture is: one in which everyone who wants to be coached and when it's appropriate and practical is offered coaching (possibly by a manager or other close working colleague).

Of course there are clear situations where using a coaching style may not be preferred. For example, when a fire breaks out, it wouldn't be very bright for a Manager to launch into a stream of questions about the situation, such as: "What colour are the flames?", "How warm are you feeling?", "What options are available to stop you getting burned?" and the like!

We've encountered a relatively small number of organizations that currently operate this policy, although as we'll see later, the growth in popularity of in-house coaching programmes makes this more of a practical reality for many more.

What this all means for implementing workplace coaching

Enough for some starting definitions. We hope that we may have at least highlighted the importance of being clear about where coaching implementation starts and where it ends, and we'll keep the various distinctions that are often made in mind as we continue through the following chapters.

However, first we should return our attention to what for us is a vastly more important matter than debating what coaching is – what coaching delivers. This is our theme for the next chapter.

Summary

There may be no universal definition of what 'coaching' is; however, most commentators agree on common characteristics. In particular, coaching is intended to be transformative for the individual who is being coached, causing them to reflect, and to find fresh insight and inspiration; in short, coaching aims to help people become their best.

Confusion of meaning takes a further turn when we speak of coaching in the different contexts of a dedicated, one-to-one relationship, as an activity undertaken by a line manager and as a management style, amongst other variations. Views about what constitutes a 'coaching culture' are similarly varied. Opinions differ on whether or not a line manager can or should step into the role of a coach; however, few would argue that coaching is a highly valuable skill for managers to deploy in their everyday task of managing people.

Notes

1 'Clients for coaching': we use this term to refer to coachees, ie the individuals who are the subjects for coaching, who play an active part in the coaching process. Clients for coaching must both appreciate what coaching is about and how it may benefit them and be ready to commit themselves to playing their part to allow coaching a chance to succeed.

2 The question 'Can the boss be a coach?' was the focus for a lively debate hosted by the Association for Coaching in London on 11 September 2007.

3 The organizations cited are amongst the many case studies that are regularly featured in *Coaching at Work* magazine (see www.coaching-at-work.com).

4 The Johari Window model was developed in the 1950s as a means of mapping an individual's interpersonal awareness (see Luft and Ingham, 1955). The development of the 'conscious consciousness' model in recent thinking is often credited to Howell and Fleishman (Howell and Fleishman, 1982).

Why coaching?

What coaching aims to achieve for individuals and their organizations

For any organization or individual to spend any money on a new initiative, there must be an expectation that there will be a return from the expense of the venture that is worth having. Coaching investments concern not just 'What's In It For Me?' (WIIFM) but 'What's In It For My Organization?' (WIIFMO) too.

Predictions of what benefits or otherwise might result may well be speculative. Examples include investments in research and development activities that may or may not lead to a new product being discovered that will fly and money spent on new marketing campaigns that have no precedent to judge whether they are likely to be successful or not.

However, in each of these cases, past experience shows that these types of activity do usually yield positive outcomes, even if they result from just one out of a number of sales pitches, marketing campaigns or new product ideas that hits the mark. Very few would argue that proactively engaging in these activities is nothing short of crucial for most organizations, and especially those driven by commercial objectives.

We might reasonably ask whether the same could be said of coaching initiatives. After all, the time, money and human resource put into bringing coaching into organizations are often very substantial. Amongst other big-ticket costs, individuals are put through training programmes, coaches are hired and individuals are assigned to 'make coaching work'. Add to this the time that's taken in engaging coaches with coachees, time-out for coaching practitioners to further their professional development or spending time with supervisors, and of course, the time spent by both coach and coachee in coaching conversations, and it's not hard to see how coaching spend can quickly become a very significant element of anyone's learning and development budget.

Some may argue that there are good precedents for coaching's positive ROI[1] that can be pointed to, either isolated examples of how coaching has brought value when it has been offered on a limited basis within their own organization, or by referring to the many success stories touted in Human Resource journals, conferences and online forums.

It's certainly true that a number of convincing case studies do exist – amongst them those that feature in magazines such as *Coaching At Work* and *Choice: The magazine of professional coaching* and studies commissioned by professional HR bodies such as the CIPD (of which *The Case For Coaching* (Jarvis, 2006) is one good example).

However, there's more than just being able to point to a brief article that may emphasize the sell case for coaching. For example, giving examples of how coaching has been applied and what has been seen since may offer scant information about how much time and money has actually been spent to achieve this, or whether there've been as many disappointments as there have been positive outcomes from the initiative.

Reference might also be made to what the academics have to say, although consistent 'meta-studies' of the results of coaching within organizations are still in their infancy (at the time of writing, a global group of academics recently met to establish common parameters for coaching research[2]). The idea of such studies is to collect data about a range of the common underpinning factors that show why coaching is or isn't effective across a wide range of organizations, drawn from many different contributors.

Similar studies in other fields have revealed compelling explanations of the factors that have most influence in achieving success. For example, Hattie and Marzano are amongst those who've examined the 'effect sizes' of different teacher interventions and learning interventions in education (Hattie, 2009; Marzano, 1998). Such a database of coaching experiences could possibly allow all sorts of rich analysis and provide a basis for justifying investments; however, at present this simply doesn't exist at both the qualitative and quantitative levels needed for drawing reliable conclusions.

Another factor that has spurred many to believe that coaching is worth taking seriously is the experience of isolated examples of coaching that have achieved a breakthrough. A common example is when coaching has been used to help turn around the performance of a struggling individual when seemingly all other previous attempts to help them get back on course had failed.

However, with all of these possible indicators of coaching's strengths, one key question remains – how on earth will it work here?

What may be appropriate for a clinical trial manager working in a pharmaceutical company may be less appropriate for a trainee surveyor working in another company. Alternatively, the opportunity and encouragement to try out what's discussed in a coaching session in one company may not be on offer in other. Then coaching may be used for quite specific purposes in one business but a free rein might exist in another (even extending to allowing coaching to focus exclusively on personal over business objectives). The list of possible differences goes on. One thing is certain: that every organization's experience of coaching will be unique by virtue of the fact that every organization is unique. Simply put, coaching needs to fit the needs of the organization. We've seen this in every organization that we've consulted with, and believe that this distinction applies irrespective of the differing interpretations or blends of 'coaching' adopted.

What then does coaching typically deliver? Amongst those we've consulted with, the most common applications referred to were:

- inducting new staff ('First 100 Days' programmes and the like);
- integrating a newly acquired businesses into the parent organization;
- developing the talent of fast-tracked employees;
- supporting for a specific change in objective;
- performance-related coaching (for example, in a sales or contact centre environment);
- remedial coaching; and
- supporting leadership development.

We've certainly met a fair few disappointed HR, organizational development and training managers who privately reported that coaching hadn't delivered the results that they'd hoped for, even though they were able to point to a number of examples of coaching stories with happy endings too.

The ability to sustain an enthusiasm for coaching amongst the majority of managers who had been trained was apparent as a very common theme of concern. So too, relatively few of the organizations that we spoke to were able to confidently assess whether coaching had achieved a greater return on the investment that they'd put into implementing it, with many pointing to the difficulty of measuring the output of what's often seen as being a 'soft' intervention.[3] Convincing and meaningful evaluation is therefore critical when implementing coaching on any level other than a number of isolated coaching experiences. This is something that we'll give considerable attention to in later chapters.

The organizations with whom we've consulted point to a wide range of outcomes, amongst which is evidence of:

- better-motivated staff;
- more capable staff;
- more confident individuals;
- people who recognize and are better able to play to their strengths;
- happier individuals and teams;
- individuals who have a better appreciation and respect for others' points of view;
- completely changed attitudes and relationships;
- better organizational performance; and
- organizational culture shift.

In our experience, coaching can significantly lift an individual's motivation, even creating (as one of Jackie's former colleagues put it) 'a sudden outburst of morale'!

Notably, most of these require both a mindset and a behavioural change on the part of the coachee. Indeed, some have argued that these are invariably the main consequences of coaching (see, for example, Zeus and Skiffington, 2002).

CASE STUDY   Wagamama Australia: creating new mindsets

The launch of the restaurant chain Wagamama in Australia largely followed the template expected when the new national licensee began a process of replicating the successful model that had already been adopted in the UK and elsewhere.

However, as with many ambitious start-up companies, the business soon found itself being stretched to its limit when it attempted to grow too rapidly. Staff training and operational management came under severe pressure, and with a clutch of restaurants being launched at around the same time in cities as far apart as Perth and Brisbane, attention to good customer service was strongly endangered.

It was, then, an up-hill challenge that faced Mark Rowland when he took over the role of chief executive officer (CEO) of the company in 2006. Despite fresh shareholder funding, money was not being spent to fund growth and further injections of capital were required in the ensuing two years to keep the business afloat.

With a need to tightly control cash flow to avoid continuing along a course towards bankruptcy, an unsustainable operation and very limited budget for staff development, launching a coaching programme might have been furthest from the minds of most people.

However, Mark engaged coaching support (from the Sydney-based company Equilibro), a move that led to him radically changing his own thinking and sufficiently impressing others for his operational director, Troy Kelly, to want to commit to an intensive coach accreditation programme himself. What Mark describes as being a set of common 'psychological impediments' stood in the way of most people's performance, including his own.

Common impediments that detracted from individuals making constant customer-serving and cash-flow positive decisions included false assumptions about the principle of suggestive selling and a reluctance to view diners as guests. Supplementary training and mentoring had gone some way towards addressing such issues but hadn't changed attitudes – to have something pointed out as being wrong didn't engage the appreciation of and belief in a need to change that would empower and motivate individuals to work effectively with customers and each other.

Having recognized the change in personal perspective that could result from coaching, it seemed logical to assign it an important role in bringing about the change required. In particular, the top team, restaurant general managers and staff needed to quickly refocus their attention on service delivery.

Coaching was delivered on a one-to-one level for general managers (initially on a pilot basis) as well as playing a key role in facilitated team training events. Virtually all of the chain's 450 staff base responded positively to the intervention, including individuals from widely varying ethnic backgrounds and having differing language skills.

Changes that resulted included better accountability being accepted at a local level, more effective communication between individuals, restaurants and the management team, and a stronger willingness amongst managers and staff alike to give and receive non-judgemental feedback. At the same time, the meaning of 'good performance' became better understood, trust in each individual's ability to manage a task strengthened and a sense was engendered that everything the team works at is done with a positive intention.

With a rapid turnaround in mindsets being apparent, coaching quickly took on a very significant role in the company's people development effort – representing around 60 per cent of all effort put into this area. Feedback from staff through satisfaction surveys concerning the support given by managers was suddenly very positive, while mystery diner scores significantly improved during a relatively brief period, staff turnover fell and morale increased.

Profitability rose exponentially and, at the time of a visit by Wagamama's group CEO, the Australian operation had become the group's leading licence performer, comprising 14 restaurants and generating annual revenues of A$25 million.

Mark is convinced that the company's investment in coaching probably saved it from the brink of disaster – rather than scrimp on the level of coaching procured, highly experienced coaches were engaged during the company's critical transition in preference to more recently trained internal ones (the thinking being that strong coaching would produce the highest-quality results).

Looking back, Mark says that faced with a similar situation again (ie taking on a business that was possibly weeks away from collapsing), he would repeat the process, but with an even clearer purpose at the outset and a resolve to move forward more rapidly. As he observes: 'I can't think of anything better to get the culture you want.'

To come to a new way of thinking about things may involve a degree of learning, but normally, it critically depends on self-reflection, creating and testing out how and why things happen and why people think and act as they do. This may require suggestions to be introduced, such as a prompt to thinking about how another person might view a situation, but the crucial factor for instilling change is that an individual reaches their own conclusions.

Once a new perspective or belief has been established, it's usually a relatively simple step to find the motivation to change behaviour. In some cases, this may happen automatically. But in others, a conscious decision is needed for a person to start doing things differently, usually inspired by a belief that by so doing they'll achieve a particular goal that is motivating for them (whether this is of the 'push' or 'pull' type in nature – 'do this or else!' or 'do this and good things will surely come!').

Coaching is then fundamentally about changing people, and in a way that is beneficial both for themselves and for their team and organization. Here too, we find a common disconnect: coaching may well suit an individual, but the focus of what is being considered in a coaching conversation may not obviously be relevant for their organization. For some, this may not be a problem: they may say that if employees are getting something positive out of their coaching conversations, then that's as good a reason as any to allow such sessions to continue. Of course, individuals who feel that they're achieving more in their personal domain are likely in turn to translate some of that positivity into their work.

For others, this is too nebulous to justify considerable time and resource. For these, coaching has to serve a tangible business as well as individual objective. The need for what we call an 'agenda' for coaching, or a clear statement of how coaching is intended to benefit both individuals and the business, then becomes all the more important. We believe that all too many attempts to implement coaching have faltered because they've not been set in a clear business context. We'll therefore examine this notion in the next chapter in some detail.

By defining an agenda, the expected deliverables from coaching should become clear. These may be simply the direct outputs of coaching itself or be a consequence of such a change, possibly also resulting from the knock-on effects of other key differences (eg training and appropriate management).

Why coaching works

It will probably come as no surprise that we are firmly in the camp that believes that coaching is a worthwhile investment, at least when it is implemented effectively and applied to appropriate needs. An appreciation of what happens when someone is being coached is a good starting point for considering what coaching may have to offer.

We doubt that anyone yet has the full answer as to what happens within a person when they are being coached. The psychology has been well debated; however, we're only just at the beginning of appreciating what may be happening neurologically in response to a coaching dialogue, and it's fair to say that research into the neuroscience of coaching has a lower priority on the list of most scientists than many other fields of research.

Humans are remarkably complex beings, still evolving at seemingly quite a pace in terms of our neuro-development (McAuliffe, 2009). We may have discovered quite a lot about what makes us think and behave the way we do, how we store memories, make associations, form opinions, and the like – but we still know only a small part of the story.

Nevertheless, we might attempt to start answering the question 'How does coaching work?' by taking several different perspectives:

- the 'textbook' coaching experience;

- what selected individuals who've been coached have to say when reflecting on their experience;
- the cognitive-behavioural perspective;
- the neuro-biological perspective; and
- the learning perspective.

1 The 'textbook' coaching experience

This perspective considers the process of a 'pure' coaching dialogue. While simplifying a little, this usually includes:

- the potential value of coaching for helping an individual to address a particular need being identified;
- the expected outcomes of coaching as a help with the particular need being considered relative to other possible interventions;
- one or more attempts being found to identify a suitable coach to help (matching coach and coachee may involve meetings with several possible coaches before a relationship is committed);
- establishing confidence in the relationship, starting with a 'contract', considering such things as the confidentiality of what is discussed in coaching conversations and ensuring that each other's expectations are consistent;
- continuing to build the relationship and getting into the thick of coaching – typically this involves exploring in what is often a very probing way what the true nature of the theme presented for coaching is, piecing together different insights to build a clear appreciation of its underlying dynamics, attempting to decipher the perspectives of the different people who may be relevant to the issue and getting to the root of the true motivations, fears and beliefs of the coachee;
- working out a way forward: focusing on desired outcomes, considering options, identifying small steps that can be taken towards achieving bigger goals, creating, describing and moving towards living in a 'perfect' future;
- testing and encouraging motivation to see through the small steps; and
- reviewing progress and learnings in subsequent conversations, involving the process of self-discovery, future-driven activity and motivation, and recognizing when coaching has reached its useful end. At this point coach and coachee should agree to part company.

To be useful, there must be something that the coaching can 'get its teeth into' – in other words, a theme for discussion that an individual might find more difficult to make sense of on their own. Sometimes, all that's required for it to be useful is for coaching simply to help an individual achieve a better appreciation of a situation, but normally considering how a coachee could respond to this is also relevant. In this, the coach may need to challenge, encourage and otherwise help prompt an individual to move out of their comfort zone, to find their own motivation to commit to the activities that they set for themselves and to attempt new ways of doing things.

This coaching process also requires that coachees are ready to play their part in the dialogue, not only by being prepared to undertake actions that may push them out of their normal comfort zone, but also by being open in their self-analysis. This may often be to the point of disclosing anxieties, beliefs and facts about themselves that they may be loath to reveal even to a loved one and certainly do not want to publicize to their colleagues: coaching can be an emotionally challenging business! The ability for a coach to build a coachee's confidence is therefore an important ingredient for the success of their relationship and one that goes beyond just being able to speak the right words.

Since many individuals aren't ready to open up about their innermost thoughts with their own line manager, the textbook coaching process is normally restricted to the type of dedicated relationship between an individual and an independent coach (ie what we've referred to as a 'pure' type of coaching).

2 What selected individuals who've been coached have to say when reflecting on their experience

It's always very uplifting for us to witness the often-remarkable positive changes that individuals achieve through coaching. For a coach, it might be tempting to imagine that such transformations are in large part down to their own involvement, especially if other interventions have been attempted and not achieved similar breakthroughs before. However, this would be a mistake. While coaches have an important role to play, the individuals who experience real change must be able to dedicate themselves to deep self-reflection, at times grievous emotional processing, and take courage to break away from old ways of doing things. It is they who generally have most of the exhausting and difficult work to do, even if both a coach and a coachee bring their own contribution to what is ultimately achieved.

We could present quite a long list of anecdotes and comments fed back from coaches here (our work in evaluation has sometimes produced hundreds of such comments); however, we think that just a few selected examples should be sufficient to give a flavour of what individuals say has made the difference for them when being coached:

'After I've been coached, I feel buoyed up to go away and actually do things rather than brooding about why I can't do them.'

'Coaching gives me time to think, not just to let my mind roam, but really dig deep and find answers.'

'Coaching gives me the space for my inner self to come up with the solutions.'

'I don't think you should ask "why coach?" but "why not?"'

These may be just a few examples, but they illustrate commonly reported themes – finding inspiration, deep thinking, and an emotional or even a 'spiritual 'experience amongst them. In our experience, few other activities in which individuals engage in the workplace have such a powerful effect. Notably also, a number of those who've fed back to us had received very little coaching, most of it from an informal level of contact with a colleague or line manager.

3 The cognitive-behavioural perspective

Coaching can involve individuals exposing quite raw emotions, both to others and to themselves. For some, the opportunity to feel able to do this in a safe conversation with another person is a rare opportunity. Not only may the bond of trust that is established with a coach encourage an opportunity for an individual to allow themselves to be fully candid, but by also giving themselves the time for self-reflection, conscious realizations formed out of what may already exist in the subconscious seem to occur more regularly than when individuals are left coping with getting on with everyday tasks and decision making.

Some have suggested that we overwork the task-focused, logical, problem-solving left brain (meaning that the creative right brain is rarely given much opportunity to play its part), although this may be quite a simplified explanation for what's going on within our subconscious. Similarly, while some brain functions may largely be associated with either the left or right hemisphere, a 'left brain or right brain' depiction is normally generalized.[4] This is but one territory where psychologists may have a range of theories to offer to explain what is going on, but we'll leave such discussion for others.

One other dynamic at work during coaching that is worth mentioning is a cognitive-behavioural process. Simply put, this describes the way that our thinking affects the way we feel and respond to the world around us. By changing their thinking, an individual can change the way they behave and feel too (at least, this is the theory). Some of this may be conscious thinking that challenges us to act differently. For example, a hard-hitting anti-smoking campaign might spur someone on to really try to kick their nicotine habit – having deep emotions stirred and being reminded that they increase their chance of dying at a young age and so not seeing their grandchildren reach adulthood every time they reach for a cigarette might cause them to exert an extra effort to hold back.

Responses to the cognitive (thinking) are often somatic as well as behavioural. Not only are particular emotions triggered, but so too are physiological or body-related changes ignited – a 'hot flush', perspiration, shaking, chest ache or headache may be associated with fear or panic, for example, while an unfulfilled craving, dry throat or muscular tension might be experienced by the grandparent battling against lighting up another cigarette.

In coaching, the emotions and behaviours prompted by a challenge, flash of inspiration or realization of an opportunity may be at times uncomfortable, but sufficiently convincing to compel action. A more mundane switch in thinking can equally drive which way an individual chooses to behave.

For example, someone who is considering taking up an evening course to learn Italian might adopt one of two different ways of thinking: (1) 'I was hopeless at learning languages at college, so maybe I'll make a fool of myself and get left behind in the class' or (2) 'Maybe since I'm no longer at school and not facing an exam, I might actually enjoy learning a new language and – hey – I've nothing to lose if I do no more than to just pick up a few new words to impress my friends at the pizza parlour!' Option (1) might drive a feeling of despondency and apathy, while option (2) might produce optimism and excitement (Figure 2.1). The resulting behaviours may variously be to decide not to take up the course or to commit to it with gusto! Of course, a similar process may apply in workplace-based coaching.

Once the benefits of reaching a target and a way to achieve it become clear, a goal can truly become a determined point of focus that has meaning rather than some arbitrary point in the future. Similarly, having thought through alternatives (including the consequence of not taking a particular course and assessing the relative risks and benefits of each), taking and carrying through decisions should come more naturally for those who might otherwise have preferred to procrastinate.

What drives our thinking, ideas processing, decision making and action taking is something that cannot be reduced to simple theories. For us, what matters is recognizing that in coaching, people often respond very thoughtfully and express strong emotion, convincing us that not only are deep feelings very often at work, but that a person has determined to adopt a new approach or way of thinking and has convinced themselves that this decision is right for them at the time.

FIGURE 2.1 Cognitive-behavioural responses (two possible outcomes compared)

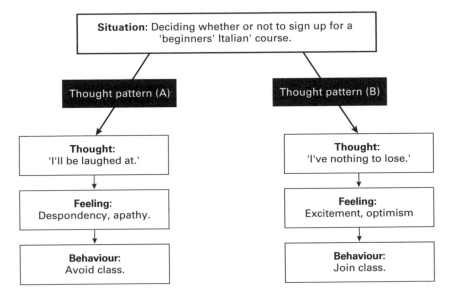

To witness this is not only to observe 'the penny dropping', but to see a person's physiology change. It is a magical, transformative moment that for the person concerned is likely to be long lasting, if not a permanent moment of change.

4 The neurobiological perspective

It would take a bold person to claim that they could explain exactly what goes on inside the brain when someone is being coached. However, we thought we'd have a try!

While recent discoveries in neuroscience are increasingly pointing towards a biological explanation for such things as what happens when we are asked a question, process a thought or come up with an idea, the truth is that when dealing with what one commentator has described as 'arguably the most complex organism in the natural world' (Zimmer, 2009), what we do know about what goes on inside the human brain can barely scratch the surface of what there is to be known.

Nevertheless, helped by the increasingly sophisticated technology available for research such as functional magnetic resonance imaging (fMRI) scanning,[5] some of what has been revealed seems to provide some of the bones of what is likely to be happening 'upstairs' before, during and after a coaching conversation.

Perhaps foremost amongst those exploring this field are the coaching specialists David Rock and Linda J Page. In their book *Coaching with the Brain in Mind* (Rock and Page, 2009), Rock and Page draw upon a broad base of thinking to identify themes emerging from neuroscience research that seem to be relevant for coaching practice.

Amongst the distinct elements of what they term a 'neuroscience platform', they point to the capacity of the brain to reconfigure itself to adopt new ways of thinking, creating neural maps as a way of interpreting the world around it as it does so. This *plasticity* or capacity of the brain to constantly reconfigure and grow offers the promise for anyone to change the way that they think, reinforce the significance of new insights and establish fresh beliefs about themselves. In turn, mindset changes should give individuals fresh confidence to try out new ways of working and build new skills. In other words, just the sort of changes that we mentioned in the last chapter that coaching sponsors might hope for.

Amongst other indications that physical changes in the brain have a part to play in explaining coaching's effectiveness, Rock and Page discuss the role of reward and pleasure ('the energy that arises any time that our brain sees things a different way and connects existing maps along new pathways is a very positive experience' (Rock and Page, 2009, p 264)) and point out the role of priming[6] in increasing individuals' awareness of things that might otherwise escape their attention. An owner of a new puppy who suddenly discovers that dog walkers are everywhere and the apparent sudden abundance of blue Toyota sport utility vehicles (SUVs) on the roads that becomes apparent to someone who's considering buying this very model are examples of this curious phenomenon.

So what does happen when a person is asked a question? The science writer Rita Carter summarizes at least a part of what is involved in the act of listening (Carter, 2009).

Carter explains that sound is registered in the auditory cortex about 150 milliseconds after words have been spoken. What is received is turned into electrical signals and is then sent out to the different parts of the brain for processing. A perception of the emotion conveyed in the tone of a speaker's voice is noted within the amygdala, and next each word is decoded in Wernicke's area, the anterior temporal lobe and inferior frontal cortex. Further levels of cognition are involved to add comprehension, notably the need to associate what's been decoded with what's held in memory, including general knowledge.

This complex activity, taking place some 400 to 550 milliseconds after words have been spoken, is a task for the brain's domain for higher cognitive processing, the frontal lobe. This miraculous sequence also requires comprehension of the meaning of what's being communicated non-verbally, for example, involving transmission and processing of information to and from the visual cortex and other systems of the brain responsible for sensory perception. Truly mind boggling!

If the art of listening involves an operation that's many thousands of times more complex than marshalling trains into the right platforms at King's Cross station, then we don't have to ponder for too long to appreciate what additional layers of complexity may be needed to cope with deeper levels of comprehension and thinking.

What happens when an individual is asked a question has a bearing on the way that patterns of neurons fire, connect and strengthen too. As Rock and Schwartz explain, 'focused attention plays a critical role in creating physical changes in the brain' (Rock and Schwartz, 2006). The crucial relevance of this for coaching is that, as Rock and Page put it, 'the questions you ask influence the result you see' (Rock and Page, 2009).

Quite apart from helping to focus attention, we think that coaching can play a useful role in distracting attention away from day-to-day worries too. Perhaps the mere opportunity of having time to think that coaching offers plays an important role in the creative process.

Not being rushed to come up with an answer not only allows the brain additional processing time, but by being more relaxed, stimuli that might otherwise not be noticed are given 'airtime', and from this, fresh insights often result. The effect is most obviously seen in the many examples of 'aha! moments' that have proved to be a turning point for many great inventors, artists and scientists. Often, crystal-clear realizations and wonderful discoveries have come when they might be least expected, when conscious attention was relaxed.

Sir Paul McCartney (for Yesterday), Otto Loewi (for conceiving an experiment to test whether chemicals had a role to play in nervous impulses) and Elias Howe (inventor of the sewing machine) are amongst those who have claimed that they've found inspiration in dreams. Even most of us mere mortals can testify to sudden memories of where we'd placed a lost key or found a forgotten name just pops into our head when we might least expect it.

Rock and Page also point to research by UCLA School of Medicine professor of psychiatry Daniel J Siegel (2007) that's revealed that the brain areas that deal with such things as intuition and self-insight are more strongly connected for individuals who regularly practise meditation as opposed to others.

It turns out that zoning out is much more common than most people realize (see Zimmer, 2009). It's during the periods of mind wandering or idling that new ideas are most likely to come to mind, perhaps because we've more time to entertain those stimuli that would otherwise pass us by.

A recent study at Southwest University in Chongqing, China used fMRI scanning to explore what happens when individuals experience a flash of insight when solving logogriph[7] problems (Qui *et al*, 2010). Analysis of the data collected pointed to specific brain regions involved in forming new associations and breaking set ways of thinking.

The surprising frequency of creative moments that occur when the conscious brain is idling might also be explained by the fact that the unconscious mind is fully capable of working things out for itself, without instruction from the conscious brain as is often assumed. As the Harvard psychologist Steven Pinker puts it in an article for *Time* magazine, 'the intuitive feeling we have that there's an executive "I" that sits in a control room of our brain, scanning the screens of the senses and pushing the buttons of the muscles, is an illusion' (Pinker, 2007).

That said, much of what goes on in the unconscious is directed by the brain's executive functions. For example, when we are asked a question focusing our attention on a particular topic, a command is issued for long-term memory stores to be searched and for relevant information to be brought back into consciousness.

In the neuroscience sense of the word, 'brainwaves'[8] are also at work in this process (see Thomson, 2010). Karl Diesseroth, associate professor of bioengineering at Stanford University in Palo Alto, California, explains that neurons are better able to transfer information if the brain is able to synchronize its response to a single stimulus (Diesseroth, 2010).

Brainwaves allow this synchronizing to occur, with waves forming and receding as huge clusters of neurons become excited together, then disengage and then become excited again. When the brain is being bombarded with all sorts of stimuli, such as the continual flow of questions and interruptions that feature in a high-pressured work environment, brainwaves oscillate at a higher frequency (the highest been classified as gamma waves) than when the brain is at rest.

The way that most people carry out mental arithmetic demonstrates another example of the need to have time to process thinking. Excepting a small minority, including some autistic savants,[9] most people need time to work out their answer.

Charles Witt Telford, a psychologist working at the University of North Dakota during the 1930s, was one of the first to suggest that the brain needs to have time to reset itself after each pulse of thought before it can be properly ready to process another (Telford, 1931). Telford's suspicions were initially aroused as he reflected on the way that a muscle needs time to recover from an electric shock before it can respond to another jolt.

When the recovery time between each set of neurons firing in the brain is very limited, processing of second and subsequent thought pulses is heavily slowed down. Research now suggests that the time needed for the brain to reset might be likened to the capacity of a computer router that is limited in the number of information transmissions that it can direct at any one time. In effect, not having enough time to process a thought properly leads to a build-up of neural 'bottlenecks' (Sigman and Dehaene, 2008).

Arguably, making time to think shouldn't require a regular commitment to coaching; however, in busy work environments, most of us are very poorly disciplined in practising this gentle art. But coaching offers more than just creating space: it puts most of its emphasis on individuals thinking for themselves.

A neuroscience perspective might also inform us that coaching prompts an individual to construct a narrative in their mind. In fact, it's suggested that around 70 per cent of our total verbal experience takes place in our heads (Robson, 2010) and that verbalizing has an important part to play in the process of thinking and forming perceptions. But in the case of shaping perception, it seems that it's not just language that plays a part, but the actual words that are used too.

Gary Lupyan, assistant professor of psychology at the University of Wisconsin at Madison, has demonstrated that naming an object evokes a much stronger response in people than when attention is drawn to the sound that an object makes (Lupyan, 2009), while a study at University College London has shown how our visual attention seems to be sensitive to simply hearing words that suggest directional movement (eg 'climb' and 'drip') (Meteyard et al, 2007).

Effective coaching, of course, relies heavily on the appropriate use of words, not just by coaches when framing questions and playing back what they've heard, but by coachees too in their articulation of responses.

We think that as an explanation of how coaching works, the neurobiology perspective is especially interesting since it goes some way towards demonstrating that physical changes in the brain lead people to form new mindsets, perceive fresh insights and take decisions. Relative to other branches of scientific enquiry, neuroscience is still very much a new kid on the block, but it's also surely a discipline that promises ever more surprising discoveries in the coming years.

It may be in the fullness of time that neuroscience provides us with sufficient evidence to suggest why some people may respond more positively to coaching than others, much in the way that differences in brain chemistry have already hinted at why some people may be more creative than others (King Humphrey, 2010). But we hope that the greater balance of evidence that's revealed will be sufficient to persuade those who remain cynical that coaching is underpinned by a science that's worth taking seriously.

One final thought before we move on to consider the next perspective, if a little tongue in cheek: it might be appealing to wish that what goes on up top could be explained in the way a simple cartoon strip used to amuse Clive as a child (Figure 2.2). In The Numskulls, a staple feature in *The Beano* children's comic, a group of hapless characters inhabited the brain of 'our man', each having responsibility for different departments such as the nose, the mouth and so on. These included 'Blinky', who hovered around the backs of the eyes with a bucket and brush ready to mop up falling tears, and 'Alf' and 'Fred', who used to balance on the tongue ready to shovel anything that came their way straight into their master's oesophagus! Explanations of the interior world of the brain offered for adults are a good deal more perplexing if sometimes just as fascinating!

5 The learning perspective

Coaching isn't always about learning, at least not in the sense of an individual amassing new information or developing new skills. Nevertheless, it usually does involve insights coming to the surface, with self-reflection usually leading to moments of self-discovery. We therefore think that it's instructive to consider some of the more common theories about how individuals learn in the context of attempting to understand why coaching works.

Perhaps the best-known learning model is the 'experiential learning' model developed by the philosopher David Kolb (Kolb, 1984), in turn rooted in the earlier thinking of the German-American social psychologist

FIGURE 2.2 The Numskulls © The Beano D.C. Thomson & Co., Ltd
"Looks like I'll need to put in another call to the reflection department."

Kurt Lewin. Lewin (1951) simplifies the change process into three stages – unfreezing current behaviour or thinking, making a change, then freezing (or letting new behaviours and thinking become the norm).

Kolb builds on this thinking, proposing that a learner cycles through four main stages (Figure 2.3):

1 Concrete Experience – engaging in a real and perhaps new experience.

2 Reflective Observation – reflecting on their experience, typically taking a number of different perspectives into account and breaking their experience down into different elements.

3 Abstract Conceptualization – generating theories about why things happen as they do, forming ideas about the rules of the game.

4 Active Experimentation – actively seeking out opportunities to apply their new theory. This may involve actively looking for feedback from others, deliberately planning actions, undertaking research or taking risks to try out a new skill.

The first and third of these stages concern acquiring knowledge – either tested or intuitive knowledge gained through Concrete Experience, or rationalized, cognitive knowledge developed through Conceptualizing.

By contrast, Reflective Observation and Active Experimentation are about transforming knowledge. The first concerns perceptions of experience and appreciating what has happened; the latter has a goal-oriented, active focus.

Of course, individuals perceive and process information in different ways and so in turn adopt different learning styles. Kolb's model caters for these differences, distinguishing those who perceive mainly through concrete experience and process mainly by reflecting from those who prefer abstract concepts (to perceive) and active experimentation to process information.

Translated to coaching, the model shows how a learner (or coachee) reflects on their experiences, conceptualizes possible explanations for what they observe and then plans future activities that take account of these.[10]

FIGURE 2.3 How people learn (a simplified model, after Kolb, 1984)

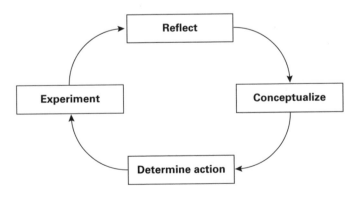

This three-step process is normally cyclical. In other words, further reflecting and more advanced conceptualizing usually follow as a coachee gains increasing experience.

Our preceding discussion doesn't pretend to offer a full explanation of why coaching is such a powerful force for changing beliefs and behaviour, although we hope that these different perspectives may shed some light on this matter. There is, of course, another effective way to appreciate what happens when being coached: to seek out a star coach for yourself!

Coaching vs other transformative interventions?

Even if it is not too difficult to accept that coaching can be a good thing, it's reasonable to ask whether it's always the 'right' thing. What's more, even if it is appropriate for meeting a particular need, we might reasonably ask whether it's preferable to some other intervention that might be used to help support an individual facing a particular situation. After all, as we said at the beginning of this chapter, any investment of time and money has an opportunity cost associated with it, attracting a likelihood of achieving a greater or lesser return from what is put into it over other options. We'll examine the first of these questions in the next section, but for now, we'll focus on the second of these ponderables – the opportunity cost of coaching.

In Chapter 1, we considered a possible way of categorizing what we introduced as the 'helping skills' according to the extent to which an individual has the knowledge or personal resources to find answers to their own questions and the extent to which any 'helper' gives answers or asks questions. Coaching usually falls quite strongly into the quadrant in which questions are being asked of someone who does have the wherewithal to find answers for themselves. As one of the coaching definitions we referred to earlier puts it, coaching helps individuals to 'unlock their potential'. This contrasts sharply with some other interventions, for example consultancy, where the expertise of the helper is what distinguishes it from just being about listening, analysing and reporting (although with some of the consultants that we've met, the old adage about 'borrowing a (client's) watch and then telling them the time' has at times seemed to be very apt!).

Coaching isn't alone in its use of questioning nor its assumption that an individual being helped has the ability to answer these questions. Neither do all interpretations of coaching always emphasize asking questions (although for those who prefer a pure definition, this alternative take might be controversial).

For example, Clive recounts a workshop he attended that aimed to take a group of assorted folks off the streets and turn them into singers, albeit the willing cohort exhibited wildly varying musical backgrounds (in Clive's case, not extending much beyond first-grade recorder and the first five pages of 'Tune A Day for the Guitar'). The workshop was led by a singing coach – Billy Bragg's former singing coach, no less – who spent much of her time demonstrating breathing techniques, how to shape the mouth so as to be able to emit a well-tuned 'ooo!' and the like. Learning for the assembled masses was then based on observation, experimentation, comments from the coach (sometimes a word of encouragement, sometimes a refresher on what had been taught) and then more experimentation.

Similar notions of coaching are commonly encountered in a variety of fields in which new skill or talent development is concerned, not least in the sporting arena. Indeed, one of the pioneering studies that is often quoted in business coach training is the seminal work of Timothy Gallwey, *The Inner Game of Tennis* (Gallwey, 1997). A part of Gallwey's thesis is that role modelling can play an important part in improving the performance of a sports person (or for that matter, anyone). A tennis player who closely observes a master at work on court and who seeks to emulate them not in a mechanical way but just by 'doing' or mirroring what they see can find that they connect with what they have learned from observing. By contrast, consciously thinking through a series of process steps while playing a serve will usually become too mechanical and also take too long to be of any use!

So what should we make of such interpretations of coaching? Should Clive's singing coach market herself under a different title – 'vocal accentuation consultant', perhaps? We don't have a strong view on this idea. But what is noticeable is that both in Gallwey's observation and in the techniques used by the singing coach, deep reflection on what's seen or described is involved, from which an individual should gain the insight and inspiration to attempt to put into practice what they observe. In other words, a large measure of inner analysis and self-found answers is involved.

Arguably, this alternative adoption of the label 'coach' is about unlocking potential, but what some here describe as coaching may be seen as 'role modelling' or more generally just 'training' by others. And as we described in Chapter 1, 'mentoring' often involves straddling the line between asking questions and giving answers, and can be a very powerful means of helping individuals to change and grow. Group facilitation, 360° feedback, action learning sets and transformational training are amongst other interventions that can produce a similar effect. While many of these may overlap to some extent and coaching inevitably gets brought into the mix too, in our view it's certainly not the case that either pure coaching or coaching as a management style has a monopoly on unlocking a person's potential.

If this were so, then we might reasonably ask why coaching should be used in particular circumstances. When committing to new coaching contracts between individuals and launching expensive training programmes for managers, this is a question that becomes particularly pertinent.

The question here, of course, is not so much whether coaching is potentially useful but whether it seems to be preferable over other investments in the portfolio of helping skills that could be made. Part of this requires a judgement on the likely impacts of pursuing one initiative over another. This is a task for evaluation.

Is coaching always appropriate?

From our foregoing discussion, it should be clear that there's more than one way to help an individual move from 'A to B' and to do so in a way that helps them find their own way forward. Whichever label we might choose to describe an intervention, it's a moot point whether the process of causing an individual to reflect, find insight and motivation is always 'coaching' in one form or other.

One person's view of when coaching steps over the line and becomes mentoring, for example, may differ from others'. Even in 'pure' coaching conversations, it's rare for a coach never to offer a thought that might help seed a coachee's thinking, or to unwittingly transfer subliminal messages. This doesn't mean that they necessarily may influence or lead a coachee's thinking, but rather help to encourage a person to consider a perspective for themselves that they might not otherwise have given any thought to.

The question of whether coaching is always appropriate as a means of helping individuals find their way forward can therefore only be answered by reference to whichever definition of coaching is preferred by the questioner. Coaching ventures can involve taking a leap of faith. But much as Forrest Gump explained that life is like finding some good chocolates in a box amongst an assortment that may not all be to your liking, so anyone who takes a leap of faith is likely to discover that it turns up some really positive surprises.

Where a serious investment of time (if dedicated coaching or something else) is being considered, then coaching is unlikely to always be the best option for every individual in every circumstance. Not least, for coaching to succeed, a coachee must be ready to play their own part in a coaching relationship. As the Canadian communications specialist Fletcher Peacock puts it, it's necessary to have a 'client for coaching' (Peacock, 2007).

Where the support of a peer network may be more appropriate for some, for others the wisdom of a more senior colleague acting as a mentor may derive from a desire to seek out and exploit their own potential. In particular, it can't always be assumed that an individual has the ability 'within themselves' to find their own answers, a principle that sits at the heart of coaching. Sometimes, the benefit of others' wisdom and knowledge is necessary to fill gaps, as is clearly suggested by the Situational Leadership model that we encountered in Chapter 1. Examples include drawing on the knowledge of political structures of an experienced senior colleague, being instructed in how to operate a machine (without learning where not to stick a hand the hard way) and pointing out points that may be missed by someone who has a mental blockage, psychological disorder or autistic condition.

Why choose coaching?

If we conclude that coaching may be worthwhile but that it's not always guaranteed to give the highest return for the investment of time, resources and money put into it than might be achieved through some other people-helping approach, the question that we posed at the start of this chapter remains – why choose coaching?

One response to this question might be that even if it does absorb time and energy, coaching rarely does any harm (at least not normally, if it's guided by an appropriate ethical code and practised properly). This view is worth considering where 'pure' coaching or dedicated, contracted coaching relationships are concerned; however, it's much less relevant in the case of line managers' use of coaching. Here, the problem is often encouraging managers to coach, not worrying whether they're over-coaching! What's more, coaching as a management style isn't likely to require greater time to deploy over most other approaches, with the possible exception of those moments where strongly directive action is appropriate, such as where rapid decision making is needed when responding to an emergency.

Once it's a part of a skills repertoire, a manager may drop into a coaching style as readily as they know how to answer the telephone. And if the theory that coaching helps individuals to improve their performance and develop as people is correct, then there should ultimately be a long-lasting payoff from ad hoc coaching as individuals become better able to identify solutions to their problems, become more effective at influencing others and feel more confident in their own decision making. In other words, a manager's support burden should begin to reduce.

To know whether a deeper commitment of time to coaching is yielding positive returns calls for robust evaluation. Often, a leap of faith must be taken initially before any conclusions can be drawn, and any such assessment can benefit if comparisons can be made between situations where coaching has been used to address a particular need and those where other interventions have been applied in response to the same need.

Most organizations are often left facing a choice about where coaching is most likely to be effective, where the return from coaching hours invested will be highest. How a return is measured is, of course, a matter for individual judgement, as is the time period over which the impacts of coaching are expected to play out. But whichever yardstick we choose to measure coaching success, it makes sense to attempt to identify those areas where coaching is likely to have most impact. This brings us back to the notion of creating an agenda for coaching, something that we'll turn our attention to in the next chapter.

Summary

Coaching may not always be the most appropriate amongst the helping skills for meeting an individual's needs; however, 'coaching' in some form does feature in mentoring, facilitation and training and most other interventions that might be called upon.

The transformative power of what most people understand as 'coaching' is what is most significant for bringing about lasting mindset and behavioural change in individuals. When they concern matters of relevance for an organization or a team, such changes can have a dramatic effect, with significant results for both an individual and a business.

Coaching encourages individuals to reflect, open themselves up to new ideas and find insight from within themselves, as well as building up the emotional resolve to set about making changes for the better. These may be elements shared with some other interventions, however coaching makes a virtue of them.

Notes

1 'ROI': return on investment.

2 The 'Measure for Measure' conference was held in London in November, 2009. A commentary on this event is provided by Garvey (2010).

3 'Soft skill': an interpersonal skill that involves more than mechanical competency. Development of soft skills may involve a mix of observation, practice and intuition. Examples include 'leadership' and 'personal influence'.

4 For a discussion of research in left brain/right brain differences and their need to work together, see Ornstein (1998).

5 'fMRI scanning': an imaging technique used to map neural activity evident when an individual is asked to perform particular tasks.

6 'Priming': the process of heightening attention to a topic of focus; for example, when an individual begins to wonder whether they should buy a new Honda SUV, their awareness of other Honda SUVs on the road is suddenly dramatically increased.

7 'Logograph': a word puzzle, especially an anagram.

8 'Brainwave': as used in neuroscience, the term relates to the difference in voltage in a changing pattern of clusters of neurons as the neurons are repeatedly excited and then lose their charge.

9 'Autistic savant': a person with an autistic condition who also displays a remarkable genius in some specific area, eg the ability to recite a musical score from memory after hearing a tune for the first time or carry out complex mathematical computations in a very short space of time. Savants need not be autistic, but typically have a development disorder.

10 The simplified stages in this learning model strongly overlap with the key elements in a popular model used in performance coaching, 'GROW' (and variations). In this mapping, 'Reflect' relates most closely to the 'Reality' step in the GROW model, 'Conceptualizing' compares with 'Options', while 'Agreeing' most closely aligns with 'Way Forward'.

An agenda for coaching

What we mean by an 'agenda' for coaching?

In the previous chapter we introduced the idea of an agenda for coaching as being a clear statement of how coaching is intended to benefit both individuals and the business of any organization. However, defining what such an agenda should be is not always a straightforward task: we sometimes liken this to nailing jelly to a wall!

Taken at a micro-level (or considering what it is intended to achieve for a particular individual), the purpose of the coaching may be defined quite simply in terms of how an individual should benefit from it and how this is expected to impact on the contribution that they make within their own team or wider organization.

However, at a macro-level, in which the contribution and role of coaching as it is being used overall are at issue, the notion of an agenda takes on a greater meaning. In this case, not only are the benefits for individuals and their impacts for the organization of relevance but so too is the question of whether coaching is being used to best advantage as a whole.

Arguably, a meta-level might also be considered, in which stakeholders who are external to an organization, such as clients, competitors and media companies, may observe an organization in a positive light because of the benefits seen to arise from its commitment to coaching.

How coaching can give best advantage is partly a question of how coaching is intended to be used – on a tactical or strategic basis, for example – but also concerns whether just allowing each individual and their manager to determine how to use coaching is more beneficial than identifying areas for which coaching should normally be made available. In some circumstances there may be a case for relaxing the condition that coaching should normally be directly aligned with a business need. For example, where coaching is provided to staff in call centre environments, simply allowing individuals time away from a very intense and conflict-charged environment could be beneficial.

The benefits resulting from giving a free rein for coaching may well be significant but be hard to aggregate in order to assess the value being returned to the organization as a whole. Similarly, coaching that is focused on specific needs may be more readily integrated with other initiatives designed to facilitate an envisaged change outcome: for example, highly focused training and action learning sets providing a platform for the coaching.

We've seen many situations where a combination of training and coaching has produced a powerful impact. For example, the UK motoring organization The AA used behavioural training with its contact centre staff to teach the principles of polite and effective call management, with individual coaching following on from classroom-based sessions. Here, the coaching allowed individuals to reflect and set actions relevant for their own call-handling experience. By being aware of the foundations provided by the training, coaches were able to refer to concepts taught and use a common language that was shared by all coachees.

We don't wish to suggest that there isn't a place for free-rein coaching, nor that this shouldn't necessarily deliver greater value over a more focused application. Our point is merely to illustrate that how the question of how coaching is used with an organization can quite quickly lead to a need to make decisions. In practice, of course, many organizations use coaching for specific purposes in some cases, but in others don't constrain its use.

The question 'What agenda for coaching?' features again when considering whether the type of coaching that we describe as free rein needs to tie in with what a manager or sponsor believes is useful. For example: should this allow coachees to explore matters that aren't immediately related to their work? Even where a total free rein is given, coaching usually needs to be justified as a business imperative rather than just as a 'nice to have': coaching should fit the specific needs of an organization rather than an organization fitting to the needs of coaching (as we've occasionally seen).

CASE STUDY
Power with the people: The Hewlett Packard Coaching Network

Being a small fish in a giant multinational of nearly a third of a million employees doesn't mean that you have to be a lone voice, but it helps if the company's culture encourages individuals to be innovative. The experience of the Hewlett Packard (HP) Coaching Network is a case in point, a member-led community of internal coaches within what IDC and Gartner rate as the world's number two global IT services company, being the first IT company ever to generate revenues of more than $100 billion.[1]

HP was an early adopter of coaching, promoting its use as a management discipline as early as the 1940s. Coaching has therefore become integrated into the company's management psyche. Its adoption has been further helped by the policy of encouraging individual contribution, flexibility and innovation that was written into what co-founders Bill Hewlett and David Packard defined as 'The HP Way', the management philosophy that underpinned the company's development.

The concept of the Network was born over a lunch in Fort Collins, Colorado in the late 1990s, when a small group of coaches came together to discuss whether there could be value in their comparing notes. Growing organically by word of mouth, what started as a small, localized forum has since grown to include members from around the world.

The Network's members include line managers, HR professionals and those with marketing and engineering backgrounds, amongst others. Few have coaching formally incorporated into their job titles, while those with a specific interest in HR/people development comprise around only 20–30 per cent of the total membership. Any HP employee who has an interest in coaching can join, including those who see coaching as a means of enhancing their coaching experience and those whose interest is primarily in how to gain the most from coaching in their daily work.

With the company having a presence in every time zone, the Network has adopted a variety of channels to enable knowledge sharing and learning. Monthly teleconferences are held, recognizing the importance of catering for those who prefer to engage in real-time dialogues. In addition, a quarterly newsletter, website knowledge base, blog and online discussion forum allow views, questions and answers to be shared, as well as providing useful ways for non-members to discover the Network. Topics debated vary, but an important focus is put on themes such as what coaching is bringing into the business and examining how coaching can be put in context with, but not detract from, the practicalities of fulfilling primary responsibilities.

Networking internationally has opened up opportunities for drawing on a wide base of experience, as well as highlighting the differing cultural differences of how coaching is defined and taken up. Those in Western cultures, for example, have often felt less constrained by a conformance to hierarchy when taking the initiative to apply coaching in their everyday roles.

The Network hasn't taken an introspective perspective. Notably, coaches have occasionally been able to provide coaching to support specific training and change programmes, offering a cost-effective solution to programme managers and creating an opportunity for one-to-one coaching support for programme participants that might not otherwise have been available to them.

Such mutually beneficial cooperation has been able to cater for the needs of coachees located anywhere in the world (both those who've participated in a specific programme and those who've sought out coaching for themselves), especially where coaching can be delivered freely by telephone.[2]

The HP initiative may not apply in other organizations, especially where cultures of tight control exist. Reflecting on its ability to grow organically, one of the Network's founders, Carl Dierschow, observes that the concept fits well with HP's culture of encouraging innovation from the grassroots.

A little over 70 years after being famously founded in a garage in Palo Alto, California, HP's success still owes much to the pioneering vision of its founders, both of whom had valued the mentoring support provided to them by their fellowship with a professor at Stanford, their alma mater. The coaching psyche that complements 'The HP Way' in turn owes more than a little to the passion and initiative of this self-started Network founded by a dedicated group of coaching aficionados.

We are grateful to current and past members of The HP Coaching Network for their help with this case study, and especially to Carl Dierschow, who is now a Small Fish Business coach working with owners of small businesses located in northern Colorado (www.smallfish.us).

Of course, coaching of any kind may generate wide-ranging discussion and uncover matters of personal interest that might not at first glance appear to be directly relevant to an individual's working role. These can nonetheless often be significant. For example, coaching might suggest that a need for being stretched or exposed to new and enriching activities may sometimes be found by pursuing a new hobby when an existing work role offers limited scope for manoeuvre. The result – a better-stimulated and happier employee – should clearly be a bonus for a business, irrespective of where the individual has obtained stimulation and satisfaction from.

But whether coaching sponsored by an organization explicitly focuses on personal (non-work-related) topics is very much a question of what type of agenda an organization chooses to adopt. It might reasonably be asked: 'Why worry about defining how coaching should be used?' After all, it can be argued that since coaching is meant to be strongly non-directional in its nature and since most useful goals that an individual might work towards can't always be established at the outset, any effort to impose thinking on how coaching should be used is anathema to the coaching creed!

This argument may well have some validity. However, it's also true that many organizations can't afford the luxury of just allowing individuals to choose to use coaching in any way they prefer. For all but the very richest organizations, any investment of time and money must be justified. This implies a need to be able to assess both whether the way in which coaching is being used is giving good value and also what coaching is intended to achieve before committing to it. With typically far greater demand for coaching than can be delivered, tough choices must inevitably be made.

What's more, some judgement must be made on the opportunity cost of any coaching dialogue – in other words, questioning whether the expected returns are likely to be greater than using the time, resources and money put into coaching in some other way. For some, this may be simply a matter of considering the value of using coaching on a case-by-case basis whenever a potential need arises. For others, decisions may be largely based around time and budget allocations for each person's training and development, involving trade-offs between time and money spent on coaching against (for example) classroom-based training.

In exceptional cases, where a luxury of time and money does exist, the opportunity to be coached on any topic, irrespective of its potential business relevance, may be seen as being an investment in an employee's benefit, in much the same way as allowing time and budget for a Christmas party or team meal. In this latter case, coaching may offer secondary benefits to the organization in terms of employee goodwill and motivation, enhancing its reputation as a good employer, and the like – and avoiding the kind of embarrassed conversations and misuse of the photocopier that are occasionally associated with company 'do's'!

But even for rich and advantaged organizations that don't need to sweat over whether to include coaching amongst their lists of staff benefits, some time at least does need to be spent focused on getting work done. No organization is exempt. Commercial firms obviously need to survive, generate profit, invest in product or service development and keep their shareholders satisfied. Public sector organizations are accountable for managing publicly funded activity prudently, while third sector organizations such as charities and NGOs must show that they are spending stakeholder contributions wisely, striking the right balance between attracting and developing the best people and fulfilling the fundamental purpose of their existence. Work-sponsored coaching is then no different from any other activity that must be judged to be worthwhile for an organization. After all, 'business is business'.

Coaching as an employee benefit?

In a bid to attract and retain talented individuals, organizations have become ever more innovative in the benefits they offer to employees. Mentoring, coaching and buddying feature strongly amongst the list of offerings used to distinguish company credentials, and this can undoubtedly add to a brand image of being a people-focused enterprise.

The opportunity to be coached and to use coaching for whatever purpose an employee wants might be seen as akin to offering free gym membership, preventive medical consultations and access to wellness specialists: creating a little personal space in an otherwise busy working diary, and intended to create happier and healthier employees.

Such offerings aren't just based on goodwill or the belief that positive things will flow from both individual and organization as a result either – as reasonable as having such views may be. Instead, the value of such initiatives is being borne out by a growing body of data that shows that companies with happier employees tend to perform better than their rivals (see, for example, the testimonies presented by Baker *et al*, 2006).

Coaching isn't the only bonus that might be included in an employee benefits package. Amongst the more interesting alternatives that we've heard about are: offering discount vouchers for purchasing a folding bike, cream cakes being provided 'on tap' alongside the coffee machine (a benefit that we thought was designed with the health of the organization's pension fund in mind rather than that of its employees!), and even having a cafeteria menu item named after them (cited by Weinstein, 1997)!

To a large extent, much of our preceding discussion relates to the type of dedicated coaching relationship in which regular sit-down conversations are held rather than to the more informal and typically much briefer coaching interventions used in everyday management. Since we've yet to encounter situations in which managers commonly overuse coaching, we think that this is unlikely to be a key concern when setting a coaching agenda. In this context, we'll therefore limit our attention to coaching of the more formal kind.

What business applications might be suitable for a coaching agenda?

What type of business applications might then be good candidates for coaching – the type of topics that might appear on a list of needs for which coaching is normally offered or at least is considered to be a good option? Such a list might serve to prioritize what could be considered the 'big hitters' for coaching, and so be offered as guidance for those who commit coaching contracts but who don't operate in the ideal world in which anything is fair game for coaching.

The following shows the more common applications seen in organizations that we've consulted with (Keddy and Johnson, 2006):

- managing talent;
- supporting a training and development initiative;
- supporting a new change initiative;
- free rein – for a manager and coachee to determine;
- instilling company values;
- supporting individuals transferring from a new business following an acquisition;
- maximizing individual or team performance – some selective (eg just for high flyers but not remedial for poor performers or vice versa);
- enhancing productivity;
- enhancing sales performance;
- encouraging exploration;
- inducting new staff (eg support during a 'First 100 Days' programme);
- competency development;
- motivating staff;
- supporting difficult conversations with staff;
- retaining staff; and
- introducing new ways of thinking/doing (eg in interacting with customers, adopting new technology or business processes).

Stated objectives for coaching include:

- grooming individuals for new roles;
- instilling improved self-belief and confidence (helping individuals to push-out from their comfort zones);
- up-skilling individuals to take on new tasks;
- addressing concerns about unpopular actions or knowing how to present unpopular ideas;
- being better able to influence peers;
- coping with bullies;
- crystallizing decision making;
- addressing (a manager's perception of their) limitations;
- moving on in a career;
- self-growth;
- dealing with a people problem;
- influencing another department;
- managing upwards; and
- preparing a coachee to change or supporting them following a recent change of role.

Our findings are consistent with studies by other organizations. For example, an extensive study commissioned for the seventh annual South African Coaching and Mentoring Conference noted that the applications used for coaching and mentoring include management development, building competency, succession planning, filling skills shortages, graduate development, employment equity learnerships and supporting professional development, amongst others (*National Mentoring and Coaching Benchmarking Study*, 2008). Most of these might be summarized as being focused on helping individuals:

- respond to change;
- make behavioural or mindset change; and
- develop competency.

These lists aren't, of course, exhaustive, but should help to illustrate the kind of topics that might find their way onto an organization's coaching agenda. They also illustrate how coaching can play a role in addressing a wide range of different needs.

Most of the items listed appear to address a 'How to…?', 'What should I do…?' or 'What do I need to do…?' question in the mind of the coachee. Of course, coaching can play a crucial role in helping individuals to find answers, but as we've mentioned already, doesn't offer an exclusive means for achieving this. Indeed, some organizations that had established a quite clear agenda for coaching – to help individuals' career progression – later had decided that a mentoring programme was more appropriate for their needs.

Surprisingly, few of the applications that our inquiries revealed relate to team objectives (for example, to encourage creativity in problem solving or for working through options for approaching a project task). This may reflect the scope of coaching training provided to managers or the way that coaches are often used, working on a one-to-one basis rather than engaged to work with teams.

Nevertheless, some anecdotal evidence suggests that this focus may be changing. We certainly hope that this is the case: coaching has as much potential to have impact when used in a team as on a one-to-one level, arguably more so in many situations. Our considerations throughout this book are therefore intended to relate to both team and individual coaching alike.

Perhaps interestingly as well, the coaching needs of executives didn't emerge as being noticeably different from other management or staff levels in the experience of most of the organizations that we spoke to. At this level, external coaches were usually employed to help their clients work through concerns about how to work with peers, build effective relationships with their teams and the like. A need for confidentiality rather than the specific application is what typically distinguishes executive from other uses of coaching. For executive clients too, options such as standard training programmes and mentoring are often less accessible or relevant.

A coaching agenda or list may be highly dynamic, expanding or contracting to include and exclude topics as organizational priorities change, new initiatives come and go, and different training and development activities are made available.

The choice of what to include on a list may be weighted by a number of criteria, including:

- change initiatives that require a revised way of working and which are pressing for the organization at present;
- observed impacts that have resulted from coaching offered to support particular needs in the past (both benefits that have compared well against previous expectations for the coaching and uses that haven't yielded a glowing performance);
- activities which primarily focus on achieving mindset and behavioural change – two main outcomes for most coaching;
- activities that need to put each individual's needs and circumstances in context with those of the organization; and
- activities that are best driven on a one-to-one rather than a team basis (although team coaching may also have its place on any organization's coaching agenda).

How each of these criteria is weighted is very much a matter of individual choice; however, we suggest that close attention should be paid to the relative benefits that coaching has previously delivered when comparing different applications. This isn't, of course, possible for newcomers to coaching, nor for organizations that haven't been able to monitor effectively the outcomes of previous coaching engagements (again highlighting the crucial importance of evaluation).

The number of items that might be included on a list of preferred coaching applications may be further restricted by the available budget and the anticipated demand for each of the themes listed, as well as for other more specific needs that can justify a strong case for coaching investment. We will consider the topic of demand forecasting in Chapter 10.

Defining an agenda that fits with an organization's needs, priorities and strategy

To summarize our discussion so far, we suggest that there are usually far more benefits to defining an agenda for coaching than there are negatives. Amongst these are:

- an ability to explain what coaching is being used for;
- forcing consideration of why coaching is likely to achieve better results for a particular need rather than other possible interventions to meet that need;
- limiting the potential for coaching to be misused (or at least, used in a direction-less way or for purposes which have little benefit for the business);
- enabling coaching to be more easily aligned with training and other forms of personal development intervention;
- potentially encouraging applications for team coaching as well as just using coaching on a one-to-one basis;
- providing an improved platform for undertaking meaningful evaluation; and
- sharing and applying organizational learning in a timely and consistent way (providing a confidential means of feeding back on emerging themes, and responding to issues such as bullying).

If we accept the benefit of setting an agenda, then the question next arises of how to approach this task. We've already referred to a number of variables that are likely to weigh into this process: using available information about how effectively coaching has contributed in particular areas in the past, forecasting demand for candidate applications and keeping in mind budgetary constraints.

These are each important considerations, but ones that might be described as being self-contained. In other words, these relate to the objective of a particular application but don't necessarily have to relate to priorities and objectives of the organization.

To take account of these, attention needs to be given to the organization's business planning process. A corporate or organizational strategy may potentially span several years and itself have been translated into a people management strategy.

Designing coaching to match strategic need

The value that coaching might offer for achieving strategic HR objectives may in turn be integrated with the objectives of specific change initiatives, training and development strategy and organizational development plans, amongst other areas. In addition to being hierarchically cascaded, the potential for coaching to support business needs must therefore also refer to lateral (project, department or functional) plans.

If they exist, organization and people management strategies should often be readily accessible to a leader of a coaching initiative. Published documents may include annual plans, three- or five-year vision statements and functional plans, amongst others. Balanced scorecards[3] and other means of defining key performance indices (KPIs) may also be used, often translating into more detailed targets for individual departments and teams.

Crucially, these plans should give insight into the key factors that are thought to underpin the organization's ability to achieve its aims successfully. A balanced scorecard, for example, should typically show the essential business drivers that are expected to impact on performance. A people management strategy should indicate the requirements for achieving these in terms of staff recruitment, retention and development.

Of course, we're moving into the terrain of HR strategy here, which many readers may well be familiar with. But in addition to the priorities and requirements that are explicitly defined, possible ways in which coaching may add value might be inferred.

For example, a change in business direction in response to the changing consumer market might require that staff move from a familiar procedure-driven way of working to a more flexible approach. Alternatively, a public sector organization that has decided to outsource some of its main functions may identify staff motivation as an area that may come under significant threat during uncertain periods of transition, and so coaching might be an intervention that could significantly help address this concern.

Becoming familiar with published material and consulting with others should potentially allow strong agenda candidates to be identified, but also make clear any other forms of people-help interventions that are currently planned – training, mentoring, team-building activities and the like. Taken together, there may be quite a long list of possible targets, although some may stand out as being more obvious applications for coaching than others.

In spite of the importance of liaison and the necessity of identifying whether others are amenable to using coaching, the decision about which candidates should form an agenda list may ultimately lie with the sponsor of coaching. To help make this selection, we suggest that a simple weighted scorecard approach might be used (see Figure 3.1), although this might not suit everyone.

FIGURE 3.1 Weighted scorecard – selected applications for coaching

Criteria		Score: Extent to which criterion is achieved by each candidate option (0–10, where 0 = 'Not at all', 10 = 'Completely satisfies')			
Description	Weight	Option 1	Option 2	Option 3	etc...
Fully aligns with strategic need	8	3	4	4	
Fully aligns with people management strategy	9	5	5	4	
Fully aligns with project, functional or operational need	8	5	4	5	
Complements or supplements existing L&D offerings	5	8	7	7	
Is appropriate for coaching (eg rather than counselling)	9	9	9	9	
Isn't obviously better satisfied by some other intervention†	7	8	8	7	
Allows discrete evaluation*	7	3	4	4	
TOTALS (score x weight)		307	309	301	
PRIORITIES (highest priority = highest weighted score)		2	1	3	

† eg Practical training may be more appropriate for developing a technical skill.

* ie Changes or impacts observed in evaluation can be confidently related to coaching rather than possibly a number of factors or interventions.

The beauty of using a scorecard approach is that it enables the relative merits of alternative options to be compared in one place, using quantitative measures that can help clarify thinking (albeit perhaps quite crude ones). The presentation of a scorecard as a simple 2 × 2 matrix in a spreadsheet allows any number of possible applications for coaching to be compared, while giving flexibility for adding as many factors to test each against as are thought necessary, and giving the option to apply a weighting for each factor. That said, it does of course make sense to keep the number of columns (or factors) to a manageable number.

Having decided upon the weights that should apply to each factor, each application may then be assessed in turn against the chosen criteria. A simple tick mark may be recorded in the relevant box of the matrix if the criterion (factor) is met, or, more likely in a spreadsheet, numbers may be used to indicate whether the criteria are satisfied or not – a simple 'one' or 'zero'.

Alternatively, each factor can be scored to indicate the extent to which the application is felt to match the criteria; for example, on a scale of 0 to 5, where 5 might mean 'totally matches', whereas a zero score might indicate a 'complete mismatch'.

As spreadsheet wizards and scorecard doyens will know, the purpose of using weightings takes account not only of how well each criterion is matched by a particular application but also adds to the significance of each criterion relative to each other. We suggest that weights might be applied on a 0 to 10 scale, with 10 representing the most important of the criteria (note that more than one criterion may be assigned the same weighting).

Hence in our example above (Figure 3.1), the weighting that we applied for 'Fully aligns with people management strategy' (9) indicates a view that this is a more critical consideration over whether coaching complements or supports existing learning and development offerings (which we've scored at only '5' in our example).

The last-but-one row in the spreadsheet shows a count of the product of the score and weighting for each criterion (ie the score × the weight) right from the column representing the application. Obviously, higher scores indicate what are more likely to be stronger candidates for coaching, whereas ones that register only single figures are likely to be prime targets for the chop.

Scorecard analysis isn't a perfect science, but it can be very useful to help clarify thinking. Of course, specific considerations beyond what can be described as general factors/criteria often need to be considered too, while the most that a methodical scoring exercise can achieve is a best guess based on what are often subjective judgements.

Partly for this reason, it may be necessary to run several alternative scenarios and compare the relative merits of these before making a decision; for example, considering the impacts when factor weightings are varied.

A starting agenda – for those who aren't ready or able to 'go strategic'

Tight linking-in of coaching priorities with the organization's or HR department's priorities may at first be too ambitious to contemplate for organizations that are just starting out with their coaching initiative or who've set a tactical rather than a strategic role for their coaching programme. Similarly, our assumption that knowledge about what is strategically important for the organization and how this has been translated into planning for managing people might not always apply. Indeed, not all organizations have plans of this kind and, even when they do, they don't always go to the trouble of communicating them within their management teams!

Sponsors of coaching may find themselves out on a limb, not only in terms of not easily being able to keep track of key business priorities, but also by not being in a position to influence others to embrace coaching. The ideal of liaising with training and development managers, organizational development directors, change project managers and others may not always be too easy to accomplish. Hence, there's a need to be realistic about what can be achieved, which may involve selecting just one or only a few target applications for coaching to showcase initially.

For this, decision making about how to develop an agenda may still be informed by an attempt to understand what the organization needs, even if less comprehensively than the approach we've just described. Attention might also be given to specific applications, including pilot experiments designed to prove the worth of coaching, or testing out its relative value by offering coaching to some individuals, distinguishing them from another group (a control group) who are working towards the same purpose.

In all cases, where decisions have been rationalized for prioritizing coaching applications, a basis exists for later evaluation. The expected outcomes of coaching will also have been thought through: if nothing else, the coaching that is committed will be with a sense of clear purpose. As we'll see later, being able to evaluate the impacts of coaching over time will ultimately allow better-informed decisions about suitable future applications as more intelligence is gained.

What if no agenda is set?

The value of determining an agenda for coaching became clear to us during our consultations with a wide range of organizations some years ago. From more than 40 organizations, only those who'd defined a clear purpose for coaching were able to say confidently that coaching had delivered a positive return for them. Others believed that their investment had been worthwhile, but this perception was based on good feeling rather than an ability to point to more than just a few examples of how coaching had made a difference.

Admittedly, this finding was biased by the fact that very few of the organizations with whom we consulted had an established approach for evaluating the impact of coaching and so were unable to generalize benefits from the specific case studies and examples that they were aware of. However, we were left with more than a sneaky feeling that a lack of a clear focus for how coaching should be applied was a major factor for the disappointments of those organizations who said that they'd not achieved as much as they'd hoped from their coaching experiments and who were unsure which direction their programmes should take next. For these, the opportunity cost of continuing coaching without a clear point of focus was impossible to discern. What's more, these tended to be amongst the vast majority of organizations with whom we spoke who did not enjoy the luxury of near-endless budgets for investing in what after all can be an expensive venture.

Is a coaching agenda always necessary?

Throughout this chapter, we've set out our case for organizations to consider how coaching should be applied rather than leaving this to the whim of managers and coachees (or, we believe usually unwisely, to coaches). You might then be excused for thinking that we would advocate that all coaching should fit in with a particular agenda. We don't believe that this is always the case. Indeed, many of the organizations that we've worked with had not had strong thoughts about the role coaching should play, but could nonetheless point to a good mix of success stories that had resulted from taking a free-rein approach.

Patently, free-rein coaching can deliver positive results, and especially if both coachees and their sponsors have a good understanding of what coaching is meant to achieve and can therefore set clear expectations before committing to coaching relationships. However, as we mentioned earlier, where this appreciation doesn't exist and where the value of coaching has not been assessed on a case-by-case basis, the benefits can end up becoming a very hit-or-miss affair.

Summary

A coaching agenda describes the types of personal and business objectives that coaching might typically be used to address. While not restricting other specific applications from receiving coaching attention, an agenda provides direction for the way in which coaching is generally used within an organization, avoiding the alternative unsatisfactory situation in which coaching investments are made without a clear reference to business need.

The need for defining preferred uses for coaching is especially relevant when the anticipated demand for coaching of any kind, including coaching for non-work-related objectives, is greater than can be satisfied. By ensuring that both business and individual needs are met, a coaching agenda provides a strong platform for evaluating the impact of coaching and for assessing when coaching is more likely to deliver results than other interventions.

Notes

1 Sources: http://www8.hp.com/us/en/hpinfo/facts.html (accessed June 2010); Scannell, E (2007) 'The Race to $100 Billion', redmondmag.com, 05/17/2007, http://redmondmag.com/articles/2007/05/17/the-race-to-100-billion.aspx, accessed June 2010.

2 We've often found that telephone or other forms of remote coaching can be very effective, while also saving travel time for both coach and coachee and enabling coach/coachee matching across distance and between organizations.

3 'Balanced scorecard': a technique for setting, organizing and monitoring progress towards achieving the key objectives of an organization.

Options and consequences

Introduction

You might recall Clive's account of his encounter with a loud and self-assured organizational development chief from Chapter 1. Sadly, this big cheese's version of what it means to have a coaching culture isn't uncommon.

For many people whom we've seen addressing conferences, whether organizational insiders or consultants enlisted to 'bring in coaching', the mere task of training a group of managers in the basics of coaching or having selected a panel of coaches whose résumés can be offered to their executive teams represents a giant leap towards becoming a coaching-oriented organization. For some, undoubtedly this may well be the case.

For many too, 'implementing coaching' is an objective in its own right – a one-off, bolt-on activity, rather than a means to an end. While the powerful effects of coaching might be universally accepted and so justify a leap of faith to invest, more than a few of the organizations we spoke to hadn't really stopped to consider how they might recognize real benefit. To properly add value, coaching must be implemented for a purpose, rather than just seeming to be a good idea or following suit because competitor organizations are shouting about the wonderful success of their own coaching ventures. But strange though it seems to us, this is precisely the reason why some organizations had embarked on coaching programmes (see also the findings of the South African *National Mentoring and Coaching Benchmarking Study*, 2008).

To be coached is a privilege that normally benefits anyone who commits to the role as a coachee seriously, but it isn't a right. Neither can it be guaranteed that the benefits that an individual may take from coaching will translate into positive benefits for their organization. Attractive though it may be to consider a working world in which the only conversations that managers want to engage in are coaching conversations with their teams or where 'one-to-ones' with a professional coach are happening all the time, this isn't all that organizations need to be successful.

For any business, priority attention must be given to serving its primary purpose for being, be that acting in the service of the general public, producing goods, delivering a service or generating a profit. To facilitate this, mixed styles of management are almost always required, while any time taken out to focus on an individual – a training programme, personal development planning meeting or coaching conversation – must be justified by the return this gives to the organization.

Of course for some, access to coaching may well be seen as a benefit in the same vein as receiving cover under a company medical insurance plan or enjoying increasing holiday entitlement based on seniority, but for most organizations, this isn't a sufficiently compelling reason for implementing coaching. As we mentioned in the previous chapter, the relevance of coaching must invariably be tied to a business agenda.

For an HR manager, organizational development director or training professional charged with 'bringing coaching in', this presents an obvious challenge: what should the agenda for coaching be? In this chapter, we'll endeavour to answer this question, considering a variety of factors that may have a bearing on the way a coaching initiative is focused. We'll consider a framework for deciding the potential role for coaching in an organization, taking account of the nature of an organization's business and the current state of any coaching forays that have been attempted before. We'll also sound a reality check on what coaching programme leaders may be able to influence and consider how coaching needs to be integrated within a wider strategy for people and organizational development.

Where should coaching fit in?

When gathered in a quiet room with a small group of people and a flip chart, it might be a relatively easy task to list a number of areas where coaching might potentially bring benefit for an organization. Some of these may address broad people-development needs such as talent development and performance management, whereas others may be concerned with quite specific business needs, for example to help change the way that customer service representatives deal with the general public.

Many of the items included in the list of coaching applications that we developed when consulting with others might be included on such a list (see Chapter 3). Possible opportunities for using coaching in teams, with suppliers and customers, and in just about any other relationship for that matter might be brought into the mix. Thoughts might be quite quickly formed about the likely relevance of encouraging coaching as a management style, either with selected individuals or with managers across the board.

CASE STUDY
Mission-critical change on a shoestring: ABC Life Literacy (Canada) Ltd

Serious benefits from coaching needn't be reserved just for large organizations. Indeed, for companies that are often resource-strapped, coaching may offer an almost unique solution when critical business change is needed.

ABC Life Literacy (Canada) Ltd, a small not-for-profit organization of just eight staff, is a case in point. ABC sources literacy programmes for a network of regional organizations that are responsible for their delivery, having a role to influence the community and its stakeholder partners, but without using a 'tell' style.

A newly appointed president (Margaret Eaton) recognized early on that meeting her objectives to move individuals from old ways of working to becoming effective in managing relationships with stakeholders, and especially in developing and influencing relationships with partner organizations, called for a change in the language of performance. This needed more than a strategic change and new blood to bring about.

The new president recognized that coaching could play a crucial role in effectively managing relationships with partner organizations, having been trained in Solutions Focused coaching and having witnessed its transformative capability at first hand. Consequently, she was quick to adopt Solutions Focused coaching into her strategic planning, further recognizing its ability to leverage diversity, benefiting different people by using coaching in different ways.

The business faced a familiar problem: staff didn't recognize why change was needed and were reluctant to embrace it. Eaton's approach was progressive, initially using coaching strategically and later more generally, recognizing that individuals need to be self-directed and capable of using coaching to reframe situations in the moment to move from a perceived problem to working with a possibility.

The solutions-focused approach created movement virtually immediately, with staff engaging with colleagues more readily and being better able to recognize what was already being done well already and what could be improved in future. Encouraging staff to carry out a series of micro-reviews as a part their day-to-day work proved to be especially helpful in facilitating this change.

Solutions Focused coaching was closely aligned with the objectives of the organization, not only by being adopted in strategic planning, but also as a foundation for communicating and working towards objectives. Over time it has helped individuals absorb a new language and way of operating almost unconsciously. It has had a powerful effect both within and outside the organization.

The organization has been able to recognize significant opportunities when compared with previous years. For example, when contracting with suppliers and sponsors, future perfect and positive thinking have been used to envisage a partner's perspective of the company's proposals, improving understanding and strengthening negotiations. Unsurprisingly, more is now achieved in less time than before.

Coaching has helped to break down the unintended silos. Team members have become especially turned on to the opportunities that Solutions Focused dialogues can bring about:

better engaging with each other and better influencing and working with partners (with their diverse mix of approaches and perspectives).

A real passion for coaching exists in the organization, although a remaining challenge is to ensure that what now exists stays 'within the bricks', for example being sustained should Margaret move on. Coaching has become instituted in a natural and normal way, with the Solutions Focused model having served as an effective enabler for implementing coaching quickly. Because it was attached to core business strategy, coaching has produced a systemic change within ABC, with both the use of and objectives for coaching being aligned with very specific, measurable organizational goals.

Margaret credits the company's achievements to its strategic approach, but also comments that it was important to ensure that coaching didn't become the 'hero', but rather served as a powerful tool for managing change. She also observes that she gained confidence from knowing that she had a strong team supporting her.

Coaching interventions may be simple but their impact and potential to save time and energy is clear. Changing habits and mindsets can have a far-reaching effect, leading not only to increased productivity but to improved cooperation between people and fostering an appetite for drawing on inner knowledge and collective strength. However, an ideal is to change as little as possible and to move to a new state as quickly as possible – as a popular solution-focused mantra puts it, identifying that what currently works well should be built upon, while stopping doing what isn't working.

We are grateful to Margaret Eden for this case study, and also to her coaching partner, Alan Kay, for sharing his experiences (Alan is the author of the excellent overview of solution-focused principles, *Fry the Monkeys, Create a Solution* (Kay, 2010). He can be contacted at The Glasgow Group, Toronto, Ontario, www.glasgrp.com).

Such an exercise would be a useful starting point; however, consultation with others and a reference to an organization's priorities is needed to ensure that others concur with the view of one or a few 'board-blasters'.

Consultation on possible alternatives to coaching should help give shape to a wish list, both by identifying preferences and priorities, and by indicating some items that might be best left off the list of initial coaching targets. However, to qualify preferred candidates, an attempt must also be made to consider how coaching is expected to help make a difference. For example, in encouraging talent development, coaching might be seen as being more likely to encourage individuals to examine their own strengths and identify ways in which these can be exploited. Used within the context of career planning, coaching may help an individual to connect with what really drives them, working through a range of possible alternative career directions to test how well each of these may satisfy their drive.

For each of these, alternatives might serve the same purpose: a canny mentor may point out what they see as being the strengths of a mentee; a career adviser may suggest the relative merits of pursuing one particular path over another; and so on. But here the question is why one approach rather than another might be preferred. We'll consider how to answer this question and so justify a business case for coaching in Chapter 9.

Producing a well-rationalized wish list is all well and good; however, the prospect of coaching hitting its intended targets necessarily also depends upon the readiness of others to embrace it. There's little point trying to push forward a wide-scale coaching programme to change the way that sales people operate, for example, if both sales managers and sales people aren't on board and ready to play their part. Similarly, coaching initiatives are unlikely to deliver the benefits that might be hoped from them if they are introduced independently from other people-management initiatives. Neither will portraying coaching as having remedial overtones be likely to invite enthusiastic take-up by would-be coachees.

Nevertheless, the process of identifying good candidates for coaching helps when it comes to tackling the issue of where coaching fits in at a strategic level. Here, the question is about whether the organization should (and is ready to) adopt coaching as an explicit means for achieving a strategic objective, although the transition to a desired position may not necessarily be sensibly carried out in a single step.

Several commentators have attempted to distinguish the way in which coaching might be adopted within an organization. We advocate a framework developed by the UK-based coaching and organization development specialist Coaching Focus (www.coaching-focus.com), which recognizes four levels and accommodates considerable flexibility for positioning coaching according to an organization's specific situation and need.

The four levels that the framework distinguishes are described in the box below.

Level 1: Tactical

At this stage:

- an organization shows little or no commitment to developing a coaching culture;

- no coaching strategy or plan is in evidence;

- while some coaching may happen, it is inconsistent in both frequency and quality;

- little or no support or guidance exists for coaches, line managers and coachees;

- where coaching occurs, outputs are not captured or managed;

- any coaching provided is uncoordinated and typically the result of specific needs (such as severe performance problems with a few individuals or to support those fast-tracked for promotion).

Level 2: Operational

At this stage:

- systems and processes are in place to support coaches and there are discrete HR systems such as succession planning and appraisal but the links between these and the coaching process are at best tenuous;

- coaching outputs and impacts are captured and managed using questionnaires and isolated case studies at a local level, if at all;

- most coaches are trained to a recognized level, but this is usually accomplished through an individual's own initiative and budget;

- coaches may receive supervision, but not consistently;

- there is a broad understanding throughout the organization of coaching and the potential benefits it provides, but commitment to and resource provision for it is sporadic.

Level 3: Strategic

At the strategic level:

- coaching activity is aligned to key business drivers and integrated with a wide portfolio of HR systems and at a mechanical level these work;

- an infrastructure to support coaching activity is in place with clear processes and policies;

- resources, support and guidance for coaches, coachees, supervisors and line managers are available;

- coaching is widely used by managers in team meetings;

- there has been considerable effort expended to educate managers and employees in the value and benefits of coaching;

- top management has accepted the need to demonstrate good practice and most of all set an example by coaching others;

- coaching is automatically used when it is relevant and is evident in a wide range of situations.

Level 4: Coaching culture

At this most advanced level:

- coaching is part of the organization's business strategy and is used to drive business performance;

- there is extensive resource, support and guidance for coaches, coachees and line managers;

- a high level of understanding and engagement for coaching is present throughout the organization;

- people at all levels are engaged in coaching, both formal and informal and with colleagues both within the same function and across functions and levels;

- top management demonstrates good practice and sets an example by coaching others;

- coaching is evaluated at all levels on a regular basis and is used to inform HR strategy.

The Coaching Focus model: the four levels

The four levels are flexible: for any one organization, a target implementation may mix aspects of (say) levels 2 and 4.

The Coaching Focus model doesn't assume that it will invariably be the case that an organization will wish to step up through each of the four levels; to achieve a version of 'level 1' may be all that's relevant for some. The model also doesn't assume that coaching should inevitably be a relevant part of the people management strategy for every part of a business. Rather, it forces the relevance of coaching to be questioned, and recognizes that a range of alternative interventions may be appropriate for delivering particular aspects of an organizational development strategy or to meet the needs of different tasks and functions of a business.

Similarly, the descriptive labels attributed to each level aren't intended to be definitive: what is seen as a 'coaching culture' by one organization may be viewed entirely differently by another.

The framework was designed to be used when auditing the state of an organization's current use of coaching, as well as providing insights to those businesses that have yet to adopt coaching but who aspire to do so. In both cases, a wide range of questions is presented to help organizations assess what they may need to focus on in order to achieve a more efficient and effective use of their resources to meet their coaching objectives.

These detailed questions (or criteria) are summarized under nine headings or 'indicators':

1 Coaching Strategy

2 Business Alignment

3 Infrastructure – Processes / Systems / Policies

4 Resources

5 Capability

6 Engagement

7 Quality Assurance

8 CPD and Supervision (for Coaches and Supervisors)

9 Evaluation (at organization, business and individual levels).

Note: The full framework adds a list of close to 200 criteria or items of evidence that are sought to assess the level achieved by each of these (more detailed information about this diagnostic tool can be found via the companion website for this book, www.managingcoachingatwork.com).

As an example of how the criteria would apply, to be assessed as level 1 ('tactical') against the Coaching Strategy indicator, a check against the criterion 'Coaching is being provided in line with a defined strategy' would indicate that currently no coaching plan exists for the organization and that coaching happens (if at all) without reference to any strategy or plan and coaching can be quickly ended. However, to qualify at level 2 ('operational') for this same criterion, available evidence must show that the organization has recognized the value of establishing a coaching strategy (although there may be little understanding of what that means or what will be involved), coaching by managers can be found in isolated pockets, a facility exists for individuals to be independently coached (using either internal or external coaches, or a mix of both) and heads of department are most likely to lead or be accountable for coaching initiatives affecting their area.

Taking a further example, evidence sought to qualify at 'level 2' ('operational') for the Resources criterion 'external and internal coaches available' includes: external coaches may be available on request, though their availability cannot be guaranteed and the most appropriate sourcing arrangement for providing coaches has been considered. Recognition at level 4 ('coaching culture') for the same criterion would require that: the use of external and internal coaches is effectively managed, executive coaches are provided for individuals and for addressing key business issues, there is a ready pool of potential coaches and supervisors, and there is a strong base of suitable coaches, capable of operating at different levels.

In helping to determine a business agenda for coaching, we think that one of the most valuable aspects of the Coaching Focus model is that it causes anyone who uses it to consider whether their intended use of coaching is truly strategic or not, as well as to assess whether coaching is meant to touch everyone and all aspects of an organization's operations. The model forces attention to be put on the extent to which coaching objectives can be, should be and are related to business objectives, and at an individual, team and organizational level. What's more, it also draws attention to how these contribute to broader people-management and organizational development goals. Finally, the model helps clarify the options available both for anyone starting out upon a coaching programme or who wants to move their existing programme forward, making clear the implications in terms of effort, infrastructure and stakeholder engagement that are likely to be needed to achieve this.

What type of coaching is needed?

Reference to a 'coaching implementation' may of course mean different things even within the same organization. A very high level of rigour might be demanded for implementing a programme to groom a cadre of in-house coaches, who might initially be able to support the coaching needs of only a small number of people.

In contrast, a programme that aims to train all of an organization's managers and encourage the use of coaching in every staff development meeting may not demand such a high standard of coaching proficiency to be achieved but involve a comprehensive roll-out to a large base of individuals. An initiative to recruit external coaches may similarly involve careful execution, while introducing coaching as a discretionary skill for managers to use at will may be less exacting.

As may be seen, we've returned to using a variety of definitions for 'coaching', and any number of these may be relevant within a single organization – in other words, more than one coaching implementation may be relevant for any company. In turn, the choice of which type of coaching implementation is appropriate determines the criteria in a framework such as the Coaching Focus model that should be satisfied – in other words, the type of support infrastructure, quality assurance process, nature and depth of training that will be needed.

How should implementation be approached?

Up until now, our assumption has been that coaching implementation is invariably an 'outside-in' process – in other words, a view is first taken that coaching may have a valuable part to play in the life of an organization and a decision is taken to invest in it; however, the choice of which type of coaching mix and the level at which coaching is applied are determined through a process of brainstorming, consultation and the appetite/capability to implement the elements needed to support a particular level of adoption. This is certainly a familiar scenario; however, it's not the only context for embarking on a coaching project.

We might distinguish a number of different approaches for implementing coaching as follows:

- a top-down strategic approach, in which coaching is seen as an essential means for delivering on one or more strategic objectives;
- a recipe influence, either on a cross-company level or more locally, in which the intention is to embed widespread coaching behaviours;

- a controlled roll-out approach, in which coaching is introduced progressively;

- a tactical approach, in which coaching is limited to addressing a specific operational or project need, or where coaching is combined with another initiative; and

- a guerrilla approach (or what we sometimes like to call 'the guerrilla in the midst' approach), in which attempts are made to promote the adoption of coaching through champions' evangelism or drawing attention to isolated success stories.

The top-down strategic approach

In some organizations, coaching isn't just embraced as a powerful enabler for achieving a people development need, but is seen as the main driver for delivering on the business's strategic objectives.

The experience of ABC Literacy Canada Ltd (see case study on pp 60–1) offers a good example of this. In this case, coaching was considered and chosen as a strategic option for delivering on a core business objective: the drive to employ coaching originated at board level rather than being a delivery option contemplated in a people management strategy or added to the portfolio of training and development options that others could choose from.

This is the level that we should perhaps be speaking about when we talk of using coaching strategically, but of course the term is often used more loosely. But for coaching to be recognized as a potential option for delivering on one or more corporate strategic objectives, those who are involved in formulating corporate strategy must be fully bought into recognizing its potentially powerful role and they must have a thorough appreciation of how coaching is expected to work its magic for meeting the crucial objectives that they have set.

CASE STUDY   A manager's crusade: Toray Medical Division

Even managers who've already achieved success can harness coaching to their advantage, especially when they take the need for their own development seriously and desire to do what's best for their team. The example of a sales branch manager who found himself climbing the corporate tree at a quicker pace than he'd previously anticipated is a case in point.

Masayuki Uenishi, while Tokyo branch manager in the Medical division of the giant pharma-chemicals company Toray Group, had already succeeded in doubling his department's sales performance within just two years before discovering coaching. Clearly doing something right, it might be thought that nothing more should be necessary to solidify Uenishi-san's reputation as a rising star.

However, his communication within the team was less effective than he realized, sometimes coming across as abrupt. When encouraged to give honest and anonymous feedback during an off-site team meeting (from which Uenishi-san had stepped aside), more than 80 per cent of staff said that they were occasionally troubled by his communication style, even though they recognized that he felt genuine warmth towards them. Their perception came as a strong shock to Uenishi-san, but his resolve was saved by knowing that his team perceived that he felt 'love' towards them nevertheless.

So began Uenishi-san's coaching journey. Initially immersing himself in coaching books, he set about an exercise of learning how to be a more effective communicator. The difference that was apparent to others was virtually instantaneous.

Later, having achieved several promotions, Uenishi-san was asked by his successor as general manager for advice regarding how to become a better leader. Uenishi-san suggested reading materials that he had found useful, but subsequently saw that both he and his new report could benefit from a two-day workshop that promoted Solutions Focus coaching. The workshop proved to be a further watershed in Uenishi-san's self-discovery, causing him to recognize that formulating open questions was not a skill that came naturally to him.

In his new role as divisional director, Uenishi-san set about expanding the use of coaching across the division, taking its progressive implementation through three main stages:

1 Training for executives and managers in the division, combined with one-on-one coaching sessions with five of his own reports.

2 Specific applications of Solutions Focused coaching.

3 Development of coaching management, including integration with manager assessment.

During the first stage, executives and later all managers participated in a coaching seminar (initially facilitated by a coaching company, with Uenishi-san taking on this role himself in later course runs).

A thorough review of the division's operations pointed out various areas where Uenishi-san believed coaching could be effective. In particular, he saw that coaching could help maximize both the quality and the quantity of the communication within the division. Consequently, during a second stage of implementation, meetings adopted a group coaching approach, Solutions Focused approaches were brought into discussions and even sales seminars took on a coaching emphasis.

The improvements in communication that had resulted from coaching had a chain effect. The tangible impacts included:

- Senior managers started receiving feedback from subordinates.

- Junior managers committed to keeping in daily contact with their staff.

- Greater self-knowledge and knowledge of others created a liveliness in the workplace.

- Senior managers started to have mid- and long-range sales goals, as well as adopting time-range development objectives for staff too.

- Appropriate communication types were identified for use in different circumstances and became widely applied in workplaces, in sales scenarios and even by some managers in domestic settings.

In further developing the achievements from the second stage, all senior and junior managers were subjected to leadership assessment at the beginning of each business year, from which what Uenishi-san termed 'coaching management' was established. Group coaching was adopted in all sales meetings across the division, with some meetings also incorporating training in techniques such as scaling (the opportunity to allow all managers to take time out for lengthier training was limited).

Solution-focused question structures (eg asking 'What's working?') and scaling proved to be especially powerful in changing the way individuals communicated, and were emphasized in the third stage of the coaching implementation as being what should be normal elements in everyday conversation. Further powerful impacts resulted during this third stage of coaching adoption:

- Managers recognized their role in supporting subordinates' personal development, valuing the small steps that they had taken and avoiding negative appraisal, resulting in improved team morale.

- Managers became more proactive in building stronger relationships with agents.

- Divisional and headquarters departments that had previously had some distance between them in appreciating each other's needs, ways of working and language became far better at communicating, understanding and cooperating with each other (helped by programmes including strength finding, World Café[1] and Random Access Card[2]).

- Controlling and 'tell' styles of management became complemented with supporting and dialogue styles.

- Coaching changed the way people felt – relationships became more satisfying and less intense than before. This had a recognized effect on productivity.

Following a one-day coaching workshop that focused on communication types, value systems and group coaching, the atmosphere in the division's headquarters was changed overnight. One executive who sat next to Uenishi-san in the post-workshop party wept because he was so overwhelmed by the power of positive communication and the acceptance of others. The workshop remained a popular topic of conversation long after the event.

Uenishi-san's position undoubtedly enabled him to influence those in his charge and to bring about a wide-scale use of Solutions Focused coaching across a large part of the division, but this required a leader who was ready to listen and to try something new, as well as recognizing that training alone wasn't sufficient to effect a major cultural change – support must be lived and ongoing. As Uenishi-san puts it, 'coaching should be seen as a means to an end – a method for achieving a business need – rather than an end in itself'.

Managers were expected to try coaching, but executives who first took part in coaching training were invited to drop out of the workshop if they didn't feel they were gaining value. None did, including several former sceptics.

We are grateful to Masayuki Uenishi-san for contributing generous time to this case study, and also to coaching specialist Yasuteru Aoki-san of Solution Focus Consulting Inc. Japan (www.solutionfocus.jp) for his advice and translation.

Recipe influence

Coaching may play a vital role in the context of what Johnson, Scholes and Whittington call a 'cultural recipe' (Johnson *et al*, 2007[3]). In this case, the goal to encourage widespread ad hoc coaching conversations (when these are relevant) may have a dramatic influence on the way in which colleagues interact with each other.

This is exactly what happened within ABC Literacy Canada Ltd, as well as in many of the other case study examples included in this book. Where coaching plays a prominent role in shaping a recipe, we might be allowed to talk honestly about the adoption of a coaching culture.

In the case of Toray Medical Division, coaching was initially adopted as a manager's response to better engage staff in sharing ideas and communicating effectively. Role-modelling and overt senior manager endorsement of coaching encouraged its widespread adoption amongst the lower ranks to a point at which it became almost universally accepted as being an appropriate way of managing in many circumstances and one that could be brought into play as second nature too. Perhaps this might be considered to be the point at which a true coaching culture could be said to have taken root.

The Toray Medical example also shows that a recipe influence can start at a relatively local, self-contained level – in this case, within a single branch of a large multinational corporation. A number of factors combined to enable a localized enthusiasm for coaching to spread much more widely, not least due to the increasing influence of the manager who had first advocated its use. However, the experience of others need not follow the same pattern: we firmly believe that it can be hard to keep the lid on a good thing!

The recipe approach to implementation is useful both when coaching is being used to drive forward a strategic objective and when coaching has been acknowledged as a valuable skill for managers and others to make a part of their interpersonal repertoire, but to use at their discretion.

Typically, it's the encouragement of coaching as a management style that recipe change seeks to influence – one to use in informal conversations as well as in more formal contexts such as personal development planning meetings. Initiatives that aim to encourage a commitment to what we've previously described as 'pure' coaching are usually best facilitated using a top-down or roll-out approach.

Controlled roll-out

Here attention is given to observing what works in an initial, limited introduction of coaching, and then applying this learning in a further, progressive expansion of the programme. The approach is most likely to be relevant when implementing an in-house coaching capability, or when a top-down initiative requires widespread training and engagement of managers as coaches.

The purpose of controlling the pace of roll-out isn't just to enable learning to be taken on board and acted upon as a programme progresses, but also to avoid the sudden heavy demands that might be placed on newly trained coaches and supporting infrastructure for a coaching service at a time when it is still being developed. A steadily controlled pace of roll-out also allows early coaching success stories to be championed, and may mean that the individuals who are initially groomed as coaches can later play a role in supporting others who pass through the same programme. In contrast, rushing through a 'big bang'[4] implementation can be catastrophic, putting excessive demands on those who attempt to match potential coaches and coachees and stretching the capacity to adequately support, develop and supervise coaches to the limit. See Figure 4.1.

A controlled roll-out approach may be most appropriate in larger organizations (in the case of very small operations, the issues concerning capacity that we've just described don't usually apply).

Controlling the pace of implementation brings with it the dilemma of needing to create sufficient awareness of the programme in order to attract strong advocates and suitable candidates to be groomed as coaches, while not opening the floodgates for a rush of requests for coaching. Many unsolicited requests may be inappropriate since awareness of the purpose that coaching is intended for may yet not have been made widely known (rather, managers may see coaching as an opportunity to delegate a part of their responsibility for developing or managing people).

This was a challenge that faced Jackie when she led the introduction of an in-house coach programme for the London Metropolitan Police Service. A defining moment for her was when she was asked in a meeting "Where do you intend to start?"

Her response was to separate communication of the programme's launch from the availability of a service for delivering coaching and to target a group of die-hard, macho, task-focused trouble shooters. Her thinking was that if she could win over a difficult audience like this, then she'd have all the evidence that should be needed to convert other cynics. Initially this involved advertising for potential coaches, making clear the commitment and criteria for selection that were expected, as well as obtaining agreement from the line managers of candidate coaches to support the significant dedication of their time that would be involved.

The recruitment of coachees was initially restricted to a limited communication campaign, focusing on a number of police districts and a few headquarters functions, ensuring a reasonable representation of the Force's diverse workforce. Coachees who would act as clients for the coaches who were still completing their training were carefully selected, being aware of the project they were taking part in and also being ready to provide constructive feedback for their coaches. Even before engaging this initial pilot cohort of what were hoped to be sympathetic coachees, the novice coaches had already received significant training and personal coaching and had gained practical experience of coaching through co-coaching each other (as well as with training facilitators, actors and others who had been engaged to act as 'safe' guinea pigs). Wider advertisement of the availability of the coaching service followed only after the initial cohort of coaches had completed a six-month development

FIGURE 4.1 (a) Controlled roll-out (b) 'Big bang' roll-out

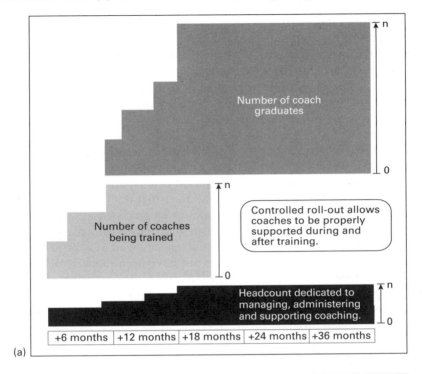

Number of coach graduates

Number of coaches being trained

Controlled roll-out allows coaches to be properly supported during and after training.

Headcount dedicated to managing, administering and supporting coaching.

| +6 months | +12 months | +18 months | +24 months | +36 months |

(a)

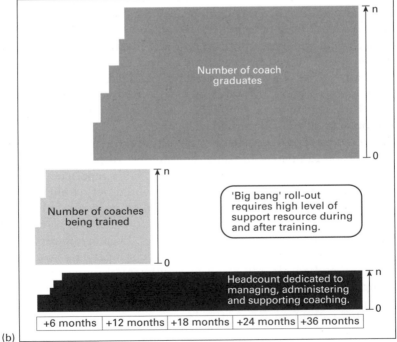

Number of coach graduates

Number of coaches being trained

'Big bang' roll-out requires high level of support resource during and after training.

Headcount dedicated to managing, administering and supporting coaching.

| +6 months | +12 months | +18 months | +24 months | +36 months |

(b)

programme, and continued to be restricted, as Jackie remained mindful of the still limited capacity that the team would have to meet the demands of an organization of nearly 60,000 people.

This carefully paced approach and limited budget allowed the Force to judge the support that would be necessary for coaches passing through training, as well as to establish a more meaningful forecast of the likely demand for coaching once a full service was launched than was possible at the outset. At the same time, coaches who graduated from the first programme were available to help support those passing through its second and later iterations. In turn, graduates from these formed an increasingly larger pool of qualified coaches able to support a faster induction of others.

Still, in such a large organization, the increasing pace could not continue exponentially without quickly reaching a capacity limit. Rather, the capacity to train and support coaches as well as ensuring consistent quality in coaching delivery and being able to administer coach and coachee matching needed to be catered for. Similarly, it continued to be important to ensure that adequate numbers of suitable candidates to be coached in a guinea-pig capacity could be accommodated, while gradually opening up access to the established coaching service.

Each of the implementation approaches that we've described so far involves careful project management; however, the controlled roll-out approach perhaps most obviously conforms to the type of sequential plan that most project managers will be familiar with, complete with definite milestones, sequenced stages, and task schedules.

Tactical implementation

Another common approach to implementation is what we term as 'tactical', although we use this term in a slightly different way from the way it's used in the Coaching Focus model. By tactical, we here mean a use of coaching for a very specific purpose, including time-limited initiatives. Examples might include coaching that is combined with a training programme or business change project, or where coaching is used only to support specific business applications such as developing future leaders.

One of the appeals of tactical implementation is that coaching is introduced as an integral part of training or some other project, then becoming seen as being complementary to other interventions rather than as an alternative to them as may otherwise often be the case. When coaching is introduced as a part of such a package, we believe that there can be a greater readiness for newcomers to give coaching a try – much in the same way that a participant in a training programme might be more open to taking part in psychometric testing, syndicate exercises, role-plays and the like, but might be less enthusiastic were these offered as optional extras in their own right.

Tactical coaching is set in a clear context – what the training programme or other initiative aims to achieve – and because it's usually tightly time bound, can be more readily committed to than open-ended coaching relationships.

The opportunity for individuals to experience being coached without feeling pressure to commit to an ongoing engagement can serve to sell the potential value of coaching to newcomers more powerfully than an aggressive communication campaign. We've often seen senior managers return from a leadership programme that included perhaps just one or two hours of dedicated coaching, fully switched on to what for them has been a very inspiring experience and wanting to explore further, both to receive further coaching for themselves and to consider how coaching might be extended to benefit others.

Indeed, in his coaching and training evaluation work, Clive has encountered many who've claimed that it was an unexpected and limited exposure to coaching that had turned former sceptics into advocates for coaching. As one former wing commander in the UK Royal Air Force who'd become the chief executive of a charity organization once remarked: 'I never thought I'd be one of those people who would have any time for this coaching thing, but I have to confess, after just half an hour, I was really hooked.' With stories like this proving the value of experiencing the role of the coachee, promoting coaching by offering opportunities to be coached can become something of a 'soft sell' exercise!

The tactical approach may be used to introduce most of the different types of coaching as we've described, although it is more commonly used for providing a taster of pure coaching.

The guerrilla approach

A variation on the tactical approach is what we like to term the 'guerrilla' strategy, despite its possibly sinister overtones, none of which are intended in our use of the term! This approach aims to establish strongholds of coaching that may serve as advertisements for others. The individuals or groups that act as champions may be small in number, although sufficiently well spread throughout the organization or a part of it to be visible to others and so able to spread their influence (Figure 4.2).

The idea with a guerrilla strategy is that as coaching begins to be taken up by others with whom early champions have regular contact (often neighbours in the organizational chart), coaching strongholds grow in size and ultimately connect with others where coaching has become entrenched. But unlike in a war game, the guerrillas in this exercise are enthusiasts for coaching whose biggest selling card is the success that coaching delivers for themselves and their teams – achievements that are sufficiently apparent to impress others.

In following a guerrilla approach, the task of a coaching lead or project manager is not only to support and facilitate training for champions, but to be effective in enlisting individuals who are likely to be become strong advocates when starting implementation and become a virtually supporting team.

Coaching leads may be able to set an example for others when their role also involves managing people. Furthermore, even without the existence of a coaching programme, champions may be self-taught (the Toray Medical case study provides a good example of this).

FIGURE 4.2 Guerrilla influence

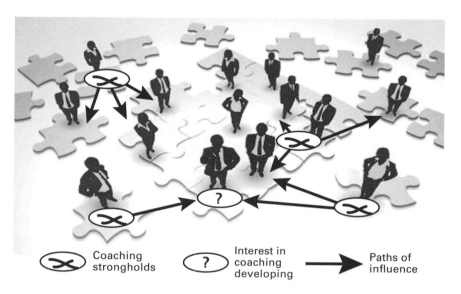

⊗ Coaching strongholds	? Interest in coaching developing	➜ Paths of influence	

The prudence of piloting and perils of a 'big bang'

Where tactical and guerrilla approaches are concerned, small pilot projects or forays into coaching may be used as a means for testing the appetite for coaching. The same may be said of the controlled roll-out approach, although, by definition, this invariably involves applying learnings from a pilot project or early experience of implementation.

You may notice that we've omitted a 'big bang' approach to implementation from our list, or one in which widespread introduction of coaching is attempted in a very short space of time. While such an approach may form an important part of a top-down or recipe approach, in this context we use the term 'big bang' to refer to an implementation that isn't directly related to business strategy – in other words, one that puts coaching implementation as a sufficient end in itself to be pursued.

We've deliberately excluded this option because we believe that it is rarely likely to achieve the benefits that each of the other approaches can deliver, and because we don't believe that an objective to just 'implement coaching' without a clear business context is wise.

Implementation consequences: what each approach implies

Each of these approaches may be appropriate in different circumstances; however, there are also implications for implementation that are attached to each. Table 4.1 summarizes what we believe are the more significant of these.

TABLE 4.1 Comparison of implementation approaches

Approach	Typical uses	Benefits	Implementation requirements
Top-down	Delivery of strategic objectives	Coaching is mandated or at least prioritized Coaching is visibly seen as being endorsed by the organization's leaders and likely to have active sponsorship Clear contribution expected of coaching is laid down	Effective evaluation and tracking of coaching performance is critical Implementation likely to be integrated with other interventions In larger organizations, coordinated implementation, suitable training and support infrastructure are essential
Recipe	Improve staff engagement Encourage managers' discretionary adoption of coaching	Introduces coaching as a desired practice Adoption is likely to be sustained over time Forces consideration of the role coaching may play in the organization's people development and cultural mix May be influenced by one or just a few individuals Typically supports a 'light touch' approach to effecting change	Integration with wider HR policy Role-modelling by key influencers likely to be essential Training and support capable of meeting the needs of all managers needs to be available

Controlled roll-out	Early learnings can be applied to benefit later roll-out Control group comparisons of alternative approaches to implementation can be compared Likely demand for coaching can be forecast and planned for Necessary support for developing coaches can be anticipated and planned for Consistency in coaching delivery can be moderated	High level of training and CPD for coaches Provision for coach supervision Central coordination of roll-out Requires comprehensive evaluation and feedback mechanisms High level of supporting infrastructure for coaches
Tactical	Coaching can be trialled by both coachees and the organization without needing a wide-scale commitment Coaching usually aligned with a clear organization development or business objective Coachees likely to feel unpressured in forming their own view of coaching rather than having an initiative imposed upon them	Dependent on choice of coach sourcing options/type of coaching deployed, though may often be more limited than for other options Limited ongoing CPD and support infrastructure required for training

Approach	Typical uses	Benefits	Implementation requirements
Guerrilla	Promotion of coaching by 'lone voices' who may lack the authority to sponsor a wide-scale initiative	Requires limited integration with other initiatives Can be embarked upon without a clear business agenda for coaching (providing champions can identify how they will achieve benefit within their own areas of influence) Reliance on others who take up coaching voluntarily after recognizing the benefits they should gain means that coaching is likely to be adopted enthusiastically and sustained over time	Training, support and networking for targeted coaching champions

As can be seen, similar considerations about the time, resource and infrastructure that each of these approaches implies apply as for those relating to the factors in the Coaching Focus model regarding the choice of implementation level to be targeted.

Changing strategy

Once a particular implementation approach has begun, it usually makes sense to stay committed to it. However, possible good reasons to change course shouldn't be overlooked when they do arise. Organizational priorities may change, management structures are often subject to revision and other initiatives come and go. What's more, as experience is gained with evaluating coaching, the strongest candidate applications that are likely to benefit from coaching should more easily be identified (for example, better returns may arise from encouraging ad hoc use of coaching rather than investing in an expensive external coach programme).

There's also always the possibility of unexpected glitches and barriers that might prompt a mid-way rethink on implementation strategy. What began as a top-down initiative, for example, may lose sponsor support if other priorities capture the board's attention. Without a current strategic mandate, a recipe or roll-out approach may become more relevant for sustaining a coaching initiative, providing, of course, that the business case for coaching remains valid.

A change in approach may also be called for when available resources for supporting a coaching initiative are changed, and notably when budgets come under pressure. In such circumstances, it may become necessary to curtail a programme of training for all in favour of following a tactical or guerrilla approach.

One further reason for considering a change of course is when alternative implementation approaches have been attempted in parallel, perhaps deliberately to allow comparisons to be made between one group that has been subjected to one approach and another group subjected to a different approach. All things being equal, a direct comparison should allow an informed decision to be made on which single approach should be adopted for wider roll-out.

Further influences affecting the choice of implementation approach

For each of the five approaches (with the exception of the recipe approach), a mix of different coaching types may be appropriate; however, those shown in Table 4.2 are most likely to be relevant according to each approach.

TABLE 4.2 Typical coaching mixes and implementation approach.

Approach	Typical coaching mix
Top-down	Ad hoc coaching Line-manager-led coaching Project team coaching Coaching aligned with specific training or communication programme(s)
Recipe	Ad hoc coaching Line-manager-led coaching Team coaching
Controlled roll-out	In-house coaching
Tactical	External coaching In-house coaching Line-manager-led coaching Project team coaching
Guerrilla	Ad hoc coaching Team coaching Line-manager-led coaching

Making the right choice of implementation approach at an early stage is important. While there may be some overlap between the different approaches, particularly where a recipe influence is needed to support other approaches, agreeing an appropriate strategy for implementing coaching requires that one approach is given prominence.

As we mentioned in the preceding discussion, a decision on which approach to adopt many fall naturally out of the originating context for introducing coaching (in the case of the top-down strategic approach) or otherwise be guided by the objective for introducing coaching and the appetite and available resources for supporting an implementation.

Combined with these, the capability of a coaching sponsor or project leader to influence others may have a strong bearing on deciding which strategy is most likely to succeed. We'll turn our attention to this important factor next.

Personal influence

Those charged with 'making coaching happen' aren't always gifted with the authority needed to ensure that others will commit to the venture with the gusto that is needed. Similarly, sponsors may be a lone voice amongst their peers, even if they command a position of power in the organization's hierarchy. What's more, sponsors may be committed to a coaching project in name only and when approving funding, rather than being true evangelists who actively campaign for the project's cause.

Unsurprisingly, sponsors typically have many, changing priorities that demand their attention. Coaching may be just one of a number of initiatives that are being pursued at any time, caught up with political manoeuvring and often competing with other projects for attention and resources. Given the freedom to choose between these, any stakeholder that a coaching project leader wishes to engage may be persuaded to commit their time and active participation based on what they perceive to be most valuable for themselves or their team. As we've said before, to ensure that engagement with coaching is taken seriously, a strong effort is usually required to sell the benefits, and especially during the earlier stages of implementation. To be taken seriously, others must believe that coaching will make a positive difference. As one HR commentator put it: 'Value addition = Place at the table' (Shekar, 2010).

Competing initiatives that appear to offer greater immediate benefit and are evidently more fully endorsed by a top management team or which simply appear to be 'sexier' than others are more likely to engage interest amongst the stakeholders that a coaching project manager might want to appeal to. The pull to embrace one of a number of initiatives on offer is likely to be stronger where direct and usually immediate benefit can be seen by the individuals to whom the initiative appeals, while the influence of what others perceive is also likely to have a strong influencing effect.

Of course, a coaching project leader's task will be generally easier if coaching has become accepted as one of the initiatives that is seen as career enhancing by a body of opinion leaders or influencers, or when it is being implemented as a top-down edict or mechanism for delivering on a strategic objective. Coaching may also be easier for others to embrace when it complements other initiatives that have already been accepted as a 'way to go'.

The point here is that irrespective of how much potential an initiative offers, it can't simply be assumed that others will readily embrace it simply because a good sales case can be presented for it, nor indeed should opinions be swayed simply because – from an objective point of view – it is the right thing for an organization to be doing. As we all know, many organizations provide the perfect stage for playing out career-driven politics, demonstrations of competitiveness and even blatant narcissism.

Personal influence isn't just a matter of the accepted right to instruct, reward and discipline others that comes with a particular position, but also the extent to which a person can articulate and sell an idea, engage with others and make themselves heard. Unsurprisingly then, strong skills in influencing and effective communication are valuable attributes for any coaching project leader to possess. When combined with strong emotional intelligence about the environment in which they are working, dogged determination and genuine passion can quickly attract others to a particular cause.

Collective influence

Group dynamic usually plays an important part in what individuals do and say, and invariably it is the prevailing or most powerful set of beliefs and behaviours that wins the day. This phenomenon is what's sometimes described as being a 'dominant discourse', or as Bob Garvey, professor at Sheffield Hallam's Centre for Individual and Organizational Development, puts it: 'Language is the engine of culture. Within any setting it is backed up by behaviour and organizational structures. The dominant discourse creates a narrative, which then creates and informs human action' (Garvey, 2010). The point is that dominant discourses can be hard to challenge, even when they're based on false perceptions.

In the absence of strong senior manager sponsorship, prevailing opinions about people development initiatives are especially likely to be swayed by group influence. In such circumstances, promoting coaching can be all the more difficult when the dominant perception is that coaching is a soft skill that doesn't sit well with a preference for 'strong management'. An organization's recipe mix may then become all the more important for a coaching programme leader to seek to influence.

When choosing which implementation approach to adopt, a sponsor or project leader therefore needs to take account of their own ability to influence others. Individuals who carry the flag for coaching need to be honest about the level of their own personal influence and the extent to which they feel comfortable in challenging themselves to expend effort on this, even to the point of potentially isolating themselves from the power-brokers in their organization. This said, to succeed with a project from an initial base of limited support may be seen as being an attractive challenge for some, and one that can result in rapid career progression.

From our consultations, it seems that many of the people who've championed the introduction of coaching within their organizations started out on their campaigns as lone voices. At least half of these had set about implementation with minimal budgets and resources (some close to bankruptcy), and others without having the real, active support of a senior sponsor.

The good news is that the majority of these succeeded not only in establishing a strong and lasting role for coaching, but in raising their own profiles and level of respect given by peers too.

Impacts of existing culture

A recipe influence that requires a radical change in ways of thinking and behaving cannot easily be achieved single-handedly, unless the individual who seeks to change the recipe mix also oversees the people management policies of the organization or is otherwise able to exert a significant influence on these.

Organizations that have long-established, rank-focused and directive management cultures may be especially hard to convert to a coaching mentality through a simple recipe change. Here, a quite prolonged stirring of the ingredients may be needed by someone who has a strong hand to resist the resistance to change that is likely to be encountered.

But even strong performance-driven cultures in which soft approaches to management are alien can be sufficiently challenged to allow coaching a chance to succeed. For example, in some organizations it has first been necessary for senior managers to demonstrate that it was acceptable for anyone to admit to a weakness before coaching could be accepted by lower-ranking managers as being an appropriate management style.

Not untypically in such organizations, emphasis is put on individual performance, to the extent that staff can expect to be put through a performance management process at the year's end if they don't achieve the expected grade. In such environments, coaching might easily be seen as being an activity for softies, not a serious focus of energy for outcome-focused, would-be high achievers whose total attention is given over to making good on their numbers. Of course, where views such as these prevail, it can come as quite a shock to discover that perception isn't always reality!

Summary

In this chapter, we've seen that various choices are available when considering how to approach coaching implementation. The type of coaching that is targeted, the readiness of others to engage with a coaching initiative and the influence of both sponsor and project leader assigned to see through the implementation all play their part.

So too, the influence of dominant groups is likely to be a crucial determinant of success, alongside the extent to which coaching can be aligned with outcomes that are seen to be beneficial for the individuals whose support is needed to make the programme work.

We described a way for considering the implementation requirements implied when setting different levels of ambition for coaching, based on a range of indicators and criteria incorporated in the Coaching Focus Model. Finally, we returned to consider the role of the coaching project leader and in particular the attitudes and attributes that are most likely to enable them to succeed in what can at times be a lonely task.

Having compared the various implementation options available and determined a business agenda for coaching, we can now turn our attention to the task of implementation in earnest. This will be our focus for the next part of this book.

Notes

1 'World Café': an approach for hosting debate that encourages individuals to develop their thinking based on what they've previously discussed and by promoting a mixing of ideas. The method is promoted via a global networking community, the World Café Community of Practice. See www.theworldcafe.com.

2   'Random Access Card': an approach in which a coach asks questions by randomly drawing these from a pack of question cards.

3   'Cultural recipe': the mix of regulatory controls and informal beliefs, behaviours and language that define a modus operandi for individuals' interactions with each other within an organization. The concept was originated by Johnson, Scholes and Whittington (2007).

4   'Big bang implementation': a rapid roll-out of a new initiative designed to affect the greatest number of people in the shortest period of time.

PART TWO
Implementation

Preparation

First steps

Planning any new initiative should never be taken lightly, although of course the extent to which detailed preparation is necessary will vary according to the complexity and scale of what is being implemented as well as the degree to which the existing status quo or current management mindset is being challenged.

Where coaching is concerned, a project that aims to influence an organization's cultural recipe – in other words, to bring about a wide-scale change in attitudes at all management levels and across the staff base – is likely to be more challenging than (say) implementing a limited coaching service that will be largely sourced by external coaches.

Similarly, a programme to develop an in-house coaching capability that can support high levels of demand for coaching is likely to require greater attention than a simple campaign of workshops aimed at raising awareness of the possible benefits of incorporating coaching into managers' skill repertoires. Consequently in this chapter, as we begin to consider the practicality of implementing coaching, not everything that we suggest will apply in equal measure to every implementation.

When preparing to launch a coaching programme, a paradox that is often encountered is that not everything can be properly prepared before some experience of implementation has first been gained. An obvious example is where a programme roll-out is informed by what is learned from a pilot project. We'll encounter a range of similar examples in this chapter, and this challenge is the reason why we often favour a rolling-wave approach to planning implementation, an approach that we'll describe in a short while.

However, there are a number of common activities that usually form a part of any coaching project's preparation phase, depending on the type of coaching being introduced, the implementation approach being adopted and the level of coaching implementation aspired to. The relative priority that's likely to be relevant for these is summarized in Table 5.1 (note: in the table, 'level' refers to the system used in the Coaching Focus Model introduced in Chapter 4).

TABLE 5.1 Preparing for implementation

Preparatory consideration/activity	Most appropriate for:		
	Type of coaching	Implementation approach	Aspiration
Needs analysis	All types	All approaches	Any level
Sourcing external support	Programmes involving accredited training Sourcing external coaches (eg for executive coaching)	Controlled roll-out Tactical implementation	Levels 2–4
Coach recruitment	In-house coach programmes Sourcing external coaches	Recipe influence Controlled roll-out Tactical implementation (eg executive coaching) Guerrilla	Levels 2–3
Integration with other programmes and change initiatives	Programmes aligned with a business agenda Programmes designed to equip managers as coaches or with everyday coaching skill	Top-down strategic Controlled roll-out Tactical	Levels 1–3
Stakeholder engagement	All types	All approaches	Any level
Accreditation	In-house coach programmes Coaching training that is integrated with wider manager or leadership development programmes Sourcing external coaches	Top-down strategic Controlled roll-out Tactical	Levels 2–4

We'll consider each of these considerations and activities in the following pages.

Needs analysis – and why many managers prefer not to coach

Managers can develop entrenched habits and so be reluctant to try out new approaches. Even when a major new initiative has gained a head of steam or is being heralded by an influential leader, some can find it hard to really set aside familiar ways of working and join the 'love train' (even though they may have no difficulty in paying lip service when declaring their support). Many of the case studies we feature included a number of individuals who chose to let themselves fall by the wayside or who did not take to coaching, and this might be reasonably expected of any major initiative.

A coaching programme leader therefore needs to look beyond what individuals say they will do and recognize that many will be less enthusiastic about embracing coaching quite as openly as they might claim. Of course, evidence gained through evaluation may later show whether coaching has been taken up with gusto or otherwise; however, such information will normally only be available some months after an implementation programme has begun and not at the critical stage when individuals are being trained.

In our discussions with organizations whose 'manager coach' programmes had faltered, it was often the case that an opportunity had been lost in the period following on from individuals' training – in other words, when managers were left to their own devices and weren't supported, many went back to following their old habits. It is vital to nurture and support coaches, especially at the onset.

It's fair to say that a few with whom we spoke had been nervous about putting coaching into practice. In some cases, this hesitation hadn't been helped by the type of training they'd received, such as assuming that managers would invariably coach staff in dedicated, one-to-one conversations, rather than in brief unexpected encounters on the fly.

Consolidating what is learned during a training programme usually involves a mix of belief in the value of what is taught, confidence and persistence to gain practice with new or unfamiliar skills, and having an incentive to do so. To jump from just appreciating how to coach to making coaching an unconscious habit usually involves not only repeated practice but also a strong base of personal experience to prove that coaching has delivered on what was hoped for. This is the jump that Donald Kirkpatrick refers to in his well-known method for evaluating training, the four-level model (Kirkpatrick, 2006).

For a manager, the successes seen at first hand as a result of their attempts at coaching may need to be quite significant to persuade them that it's worth their while to make time to coach (at least this is likely to be the case where regular, dedicated coaching conversations are concerned). A more ad hoc use of coaching may be easier to justify, typically taking little or no extra time to apply than other styles of conversation with which a manager may be more familiar.

Ad hoc coaching is much less challenging to try, not just because attention may be given to framing (perhaps) just a single question in a particular way, but also because this can be achieved without needing to label a dialogue with a team member as being a coaching conversation. In short, not only is less time involved, but the risk of appearing to be out of control in a conversation is far lower than might be the case in a pre-planned coaching session.

Feeling comfortable with long-established ways of communicating or managing and fearing a loss of a perceived balance of power in their relationships with subordinates, as well as just having preferred styles, are amongst other reasons why managers may be reticent to embrace coaching with open arms. For some, and despite the best efforts of trainers, colleagues and coaching champions to persuade them otherwise, coaching may remain seen as being essentially a soft activity, one to be reserved only for those occasions when the luxury of time allows the freedom to do anything other than the normal day job.

Given that it's a primary responsibility of staff managers to focus on the performance and development of the people who work in their teams, this may be a surprising perspective. However, in our observation at least, this isn't a view that appears to be uncommon. Rather, for most managers, attention to getting the job done is paramount, and when they've previously been successful in achieving this, there may be little incentive to start changing the ways of managing people that have served them well in the past.

Quite apart from this common objection, we can't assume either that all managers do take their responsibility for the professional growth of their people as seriously as others might believe they should. Not only is managing people seen as a necessary evil by some, but it also presents an opportunity for playing out a personal need for power and control. Genuine narcissists are at large within many organizations, and many have found their way into the management ranks (see *Bully or Strong Manager?*, a survey that we commissioned for the International Conflict Management Forum (ICMF, 2010)).

Even without the contribution of the narcissist, the priority that many managers give to gaining political advantage over their peers, lobbying or kowtowing to powerful lobbyists, and serving their own career interests above all others are often far more prominent in Western cultures than is the motivation to uphold the interests of their teams. It's fair to say, though, that a greater emphasis on the group is more commonly found in many Eastern cultures.

If we assume that the most receptive audience for coaching is likely to be a group of people who bring bucket-loads of empathy and have boundless concern for the good of others, then the profile of many managers we've just described – with bullies, taskmasters and diehards amongst their number –

isn't likely to be a promising starting point for grooming coaches. Neither are many managers likely to take up coaching with a vengeance just because an HR manager or training facilitator suggests that this is a good idea.

Admittedly we've exaggerated the picture of the management team seen in many organizations, but the fact remains: many managers aren't naturally predisposed to coach. A coaching project leader therefore not only needs to sell the benefits of coaching, but also anticipate and counter objections and encourage individuals who fear that coaching may weaken their influence as managers. This means ensuring that the training that managers receive is supportive, appropriate and meaningful, giving delegates the confidence to coach and the techniques to coach in the moment, rather than just focusing on the type of coaching that takes place in dedicated meetings behind closed doors.

Principles for implementation and programme design

When the time comes to begin programme implementation, the objectives and intended scope of the programme should already have been thought through and a decision should have been taken regarding the implementation approach that will be followed. This chosen approach will largely drive the activity plan, as well as inform the attention that might need to be given priority – such as how to engage stakeholders and choosing whether or not to seek accreditation for coaches and coach training, both matters that we will consider later in this chapter.

The main work packages that are likely to be needed for each of the five implementation approaches described in Chapter 4 are shown in Figure 5.1.

Both when planning implementation and in designing a coaching programme's content, care needs to be taken ensure that the programme's objectives can be properly satisfied. For this, we recommend referring to the following set of guiding principles:

- Coaching is developed to suit the needs of the organization, not to fit the needs of coaching.
- Coaching is presented as a means to an end, not as an end in its own right.
- The intended meaning of coaching is well defined.
- The sensitivities that individuals may have towards embracing coaching are recognized and catered for (for example, the reluctance that managers may have towards adopting a coaching style are appreciated and addressed).
- Coaching is never forced upon anyone, nor seen as being the only or an automatically preferred intervention for every circumstance.

FIGURE 5.1 Implementation work packages

Top-down strategic	Recipe influence	Controlled roll-out	Tactical	Guerilla
Needs analysis	Needs analysis	As for top-down strategic	Needs analysis	Needs analysis
Audit (including identifying existing coaching skill)	Audit		Stakeholder engagement and communication	Audit
Stakeholder engagement and communication	Stakeholder engagement and communication		Integration with other initiatives	Recipe influences
Integration with other initiatives	Integration with other initiatives		Recipe influences	Sourcing options
Recipe influences	Recipe influences		Sourcing options	Procurement
Sourcing options	Recruitment		Role definitions	Recruitment
Role definitions	Training design		Procurement	Support team infrastructure
Procurement	Training development		Recruitment	Foundation training
Recruitment	IT support system requirements		Process definition	Advocate support
Training design	Support team infrastructure		Support team infrastructure	Evaluation
Training development	Foundation training		Piloting and refinement	
Process definition	Evaluation		Foundation training	
IT support system requirements			Evaluation	
Support team infrastructure				
Piloting and refinement				
Foundation training				
Advanced training/other CPD activities				
Evaluation				

- The benefits of coaching should be pitched and sold to middle-ranking as well as more senior managers.
- To appreciate the powerful effect of coaching, individuals who will act as coaches must experience coaching for themselves.
- Coaching should not be presented as a separate, bolt-on activity to other management or people development practices.
- Coaching training shouldn't put emphasis on a single coaching model.

- Training should be relevant to need (eg equipping managers to know when it may be appropriate to use a coaching style in informal conversations, and having the techniques to coach effectively in such situations).

- Training should be designed to encourage delegates to commit to trying out what they learn, as well as incentivizing reflective practice and post-course networking amongst delegates.

- Newly trained coaches must build experience before they may graduate into an in-house coach pool, which may require co-coaching with other recent trainees, buddying with other coaches (possibly from partner organizations) or coaching and accepting feedback from more experienced coaches.

- Coaches must be supervised.

- An adequate infrastructure must be in place to support coaches following their training.

- The effectiveness and sustainability of coaching should be regularly evaluated, and lessons learnt should be communicated to others who may benefit from insights gained and acted upon.

This list is not exhaustive and will vary according to the type of coaching that is being introduced. For example, micro-tools for ad hoc coaching may need far greater emphasis when introducing coaching as a management style than might be the case when a programme aims to build in-house coaches' competency.

The task of identifying guiding principles of this kind helps to highlight activities, course content or prerequisites for successful implementation that might otherwise be overlooked. This process also helps to identify tactics for implementation, or methods used to ensure that a coaching project has the best chance of success.

Planning for implementation

The activities shown in Table 5.1 (see p 88) offer our suggested starting point for planning implementation, although, to an extent, the task of planning can be informed by activities undertaken during implementation. Learnings from pilot projects, the implications of deciding to seek accreditation for a coaching programme, and the feedback received when attempting to engage with project stakeholders are amongst possible variables of this kind.

Participants in a coaching programme and their coachees may offer suggestions on how they feel implementation might best proceed. In some cases, quite small requests might be made; for example, we've encountered suggestions made in the middle of a training course when a number of options are available for covering a particular topic – unplanned, live demonstrations being a particular favourite amongst many delegates. We've also found that encouraging input from individuals before they come to a training programme can help inform training design, as well as increasing trainees' motivation to participate in a course that they feel they've been consulted on. We like to suggest that another advantage of pre-consulting on training preferences is that this avoids the need to take time out during a break-in session at the start of a training course to ask delegates to spell out what they hope to achieve from the programme, when many won't have given this more than a moment's thought before the question is asked!

A rolling-wave planning approach provides what we think is a suitable compromise for keeping control while allowing flexibility to move away from earlier plans when appropriate. This involves high-level planning of future phases of work, showing the timeframes, budget thresholds and overall resource loadings that are expected for each, as well as any critical dependencies on other projects and key reporting milestones, while detailing task and resource requirements for the current phase of work. For example, a rolling-wave plan for introducing coaching into managers' skill sets in its initial stage might appear as shown in Figure 5.2.

Sourcing external support

Budget constraints or personal choice may preclude the option of engaging consultants for supporting an implementation from outside the organization. Not uncommonly, even in large-scale implementations, any external support may be limited to just calling upon training facilitators.

Training may be the most obvious candidate for external sourcing if the programme is expected to run infrequently and so doesn't easily justify significant in-house development effort, or when it's decided to pilot a particular type of training before creating an internal course. Training provided for what may be a relatively small number of in-house coaches may often fall into this category, especially since the scope of training required is likely to be significantly greater than might be provided in manager training, optionally also aiming to deliver coaches who can be accredited at a recognized professional level.

Engaging a supplier who is able to provide a well-proven course taught by trainers who have strong coaching experience can bring undoubted clear benefits, especially if similar training and experience are currently unavailable in-house.

However, as we mention repeatedly, coach development can't be restricted to training alone. Ongoing support, coaching proficiency moderation and opportunities for continuing practice are necessary to build coaches' competency. To achieve this requires continuity and a project manager who is visibly committed to the task. Invariably, this role is usually best undertaken by someone who is an employee of the organization rather than a person parachuted in to kick-start a major project.

FIGURE 5.2 'Rolling-wave' project plan

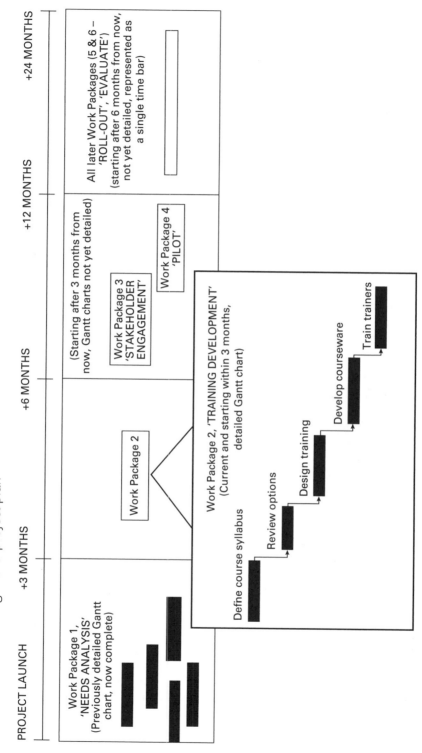

This isn't to deny that there can be a valuable role for external support beyond providing training. As Jackie likes to put it, someone who has 'been there, done that and bought the T-shirt!' can bring valuable insight and experience and credibility that may help a programme to roll out quickly. This doesn't mean to suggest that what's applied in one organization should automatically be relevant for another, but being aware of the type of pitfalls that may be encountered and being able to recognize approaches that have proved to be especially effective for achieving particular ends.

Consultants may bring ideas, ready-made templates and be able to take on a lot of the practical tasks involved in implementation, although they may lack an understanding of an organization's political structures, informal and formal regulatory mechanisms and not have established relationships with key stakeholders. Through being detached from organizational politics and relationships, they can usually more readily ask the 'beginner's mind' and tough questions that an internal project leader might be less inclined toward, feeling less concerned about possibly risking damage to their reputation with the organization's powerbrokers (well, perhaps).

Clearly, the scope of an external consultant's assignment will need to be well defined, and may also need to be complemented with help from internal specialists (such as IT technicians who may need to play a role in implementing intranet pages to support coaches.

Coach recruitment

Where a programme is focused on building an in-house coach resource pool, special care should be taken to recruit suitable candidates to be trained as coaches. An often-overlooked necessity too is that a ready group of individuals who want to be coached will be available as clients for new coaches, each coming with a proper appreciation of how coaching is intended to help their specific needs and ready to play their part in the process.

The need to select individuals who can not only demonstrate strong attributes for coaching but who are also likely to become advocates for it later are all the more acute during the recruitment of early programme cohorts. The same can be said when recruiting external coaches, and we've seen quite elaborate processes put in place to select panels of executive coaches (in one case, a process that took more than three years, which we believe is not a good example to follow!). However, where in-houses coaches are concerned, many commit to the role voluntarily, in addition to their 'day job'. It's therefore all the more important that those who are inducted into a coaching cohort are made of the right stuff.

When she took on the role to establish an in-house coach practice for London's Metropolitan Police Service, Jackie adopted a recruitment approach that was no less rigorous than most external recruitment campaigns.

Role profiles were defined, line managers were consulted with and had to consent that candidates would be released for training and for coaching, application forms were sorted through and dozens of interviews were conducted. Coaching competencies were the interview marker, taken from the European Mentoring and Coaching Council's definition. A carefully worded intranet advertisement and application briefing that made clear the attributes and personal level of commitment sought from would-be coaches helped with the initial qualification of applicants. Even so, significantly more applications were received than time allowed for interviews.

In addition to looking for evidence of interviewees' likely suitability to act as coaches, one of Jackie's primary concerns was to explore each applicant's motivation for wanting to take on the role. Those whose interest was largely driven by a desire to acquire another skill or seeing an opportunity to take on a secondary role to their normal responsibilities were questioned more deeply than others. Simple role-play scenarios were also included during the selection process, for example asking candidates to consider ethical challenges that they might encounter in the coaching relationship and to describe how they might respond to these. Interviewers/ assessors for later programme candidates were drawn from the original coaching cohort, again carried out on a voluntary basis.

The intention of this exercise was to assess whether candidates' core values were likely to be compatible with the ethical code for coaching that had been drafted, rather than to evaluate any coaching competency. Indeed, attitude, commitment and personal values were weighted far more highly than any demonstration of coaching skill, which wasn't assumed and of course which the programme was intended to develop. One senior manager jokingly said that their recruitment experience was harder than when they were put through their paces by a promotion panel!

A significant effort was required to carry through this recruitment campaign, and the exercise was repeated several times as further cohorts were engaged for subsequent runs of the programme. Some unsuccessful candidates even appealed against not being accepted into early cohorts, in which case a robust audit trail helped to show that the decision making was fair.

Recruitment involves a necessary lead-time between advertising for potential candidates and their short-listing and selection: it's a task that cannot be rushed. Role profiles that would be unlikely to change, a purposeful and rationalized code of ethics, and a process for selecting and communicating with both successful and unsuccessful candidates and their line managers all usually need to be put in place before recruitment can begin.

The activities that will follow recruitment need to be determined well in advance. Expected time frames for training and other development activities need to be defined and agreed with programme participants and their managers, while training activity should ideally be initiated soon after recruitment, allowing a momentum in interest to be maintained.

The exercise that Jackie undertook to engage well-motivated and suitable candidates paid dividends in very little time, allowing the programme to proceed without the lack of continuity, cancelled places on training modules and half-hearted commitments that might otherwise have resulted. We strongly believe that preparation of this kind is essential.

We've included a number of templates in Appendix A and on the book's companion website (www.managingcoachingatwork.com) that might be used in a similar recruitment campaign, including a possible advertisement for coach candidates, a sample coach role profile and checklist of possible candidate selection criteria.

In some ways, establishing a pool of external coaches in a coaching practice is more straightforward than building an in-house capability. Coaches shouldn't need to be trained, their practice credentials can be readily assessed and attested, and competing priorities with other activities should be less of an issue for them than might be the case for internal coaches (provided, of course, that coaching contracts can be pre-planned and accommodated alongside other client commitments).

In recruiting external suppliers, we believe that essential checks are to assess whether potential coaches are likely to be well matched to the range of personalities and the contexts for coaching that they might expect to face, as well as determining their motivation for wanting to work with the organization.

A coach's specialism or experience of working with particular client needs may also be relevant. For example, when coaching women to feel empowered in their careers, one prominent New York City-based executive coach, Dr Stacey Radin, told us that she draws on insights gained through her research and work with more than 150 women leaders across the United States who'd succeeded in scaling the corporate ladders of their organizations. Such insight has been critical in helping to highlight the factors that many of Radin's clients choose to focus on.

We also believe that focus should be given to selecting individual coaches rather than supplier companies. This view is echoed by Maxine Dolan, previously head of leadership development at the supermarket giant Tesco, who told the 2008 CIPD Coaching at Work Conference that she'd 'rather have a small group of people who really trust[ed] us and work[ed] with us' (Hall, 2009).

The relevance of professional accreditation also needs to be considered (see below). In addition, both observed demonstration of practice and testimony offered by other client referees should help enable each candidate's coaching competency to be assessed. In the same way that the core values of in-house candidates may be explored to ensure that they are compatible with the organization's ethical code, those of external candidates might be elicited using role-play scenarios.

We suggest that, at a minimum, to qualify as a member of a coach panel or pool any candidate must be able to point to a record of continuous professional development that includes practically oriented training, be actively committed to receiving supervision, and have completed a minimum of 100 hours of coaching.

Globally, coaching remains an unregulated profession, although some countries are making moves towards correcting this. In the UK, for example, the creation of a national register of coaches has been mooted, while several leading coaching accreditation bodies have taken steps of their own to qualify the credentials of coaches listed in their own registers (see, for example, the International Coaching Register, maintained by the International Coaching Register (2010)).

A lack of regulation means that it's possible for anyone to enter into coaching practice, even without appropriate training.[1] Some have done so, justifying their suitability on the business experience that they have gained, eg by having operated at a board level within other organizations. Others have confused the practice of coaching with that of mentoring or psychotherapy (for which they may well be qualified to practise), while others may simply see that setting themselves up as a high-fee-earning coach is a wonderful business opportunity for any budding entrepreneur. That said, we have met excellent coaches who haven't received extensive training, but whose actual coaching experience (or 'flying hours', as we like to call it) has been important. Some might call the last of these types charlatans, but we'll leave this thought to your own judgement! However, we do believe that rarely in corporate procurement is the maxim 'Buyer beware!' more appropriate than when engaging external consultants.

The importance of the training received by external coaches having had a strongly practical emphasis cannot be overemphasized: it remains the case that some advanced-level coaching qualifications emphasize academic rigour in research and studying theory as opposed to practical application and experience.

One Masters-level programme in coaching that a former client of ours had undertaken included less than 10 hours' coaching in its entire syllabus! Unsurprisingly, one unfortunate graduate of this programme who came to us was panicking after having been quickly shown the door by their first executive client. In our view, a beautifully written dissertation pondering the use of psychological models in coaching could never substitute for the value of sitting in a room with another person and actually practising coaching. Maybe we're just old-fashioned that way!

The attributes sought in an external coach shouldn't be any different from those sought in an internal one. Indeed, more or less identical role profiles might be used for each (the difference being that in the case of the external coach, a high level of coaching competency should be in evidence, while their suitability and experience for coaching at different levels of seniority within an organization may also be an important qualifying factor).

As with building an in-house coaching capability, it makes sense to engage only as many external coaches as are expected to be in demand or at least just a small number more. The profile of coaches available in a coaching pool should give flexibility for matching requests for different needs and from different personalities, ideally allowing coachee clients the option to select from a number of possible coaches who are presented to them in initial 'chemistry' meetings.

At the same time, a pool shouldn't be so large that assignment opportunities for coaches are few and far between: coaches' motivation to commit to a genuine interest in the client–supplier relationship may suffer otherwise. Advice offered by procurement specialists may differ; however, we generally believe that retainer or call-off contracts are less desirable than fixed contracts, with the latter generally encouraging closer engagement in interest and commitment.

Where a strong engagement exists, it's not unusual for external coaches to give some time freely to help take part in supporting occasional activities such as in-house coach review days or playing a part in 'coaching circles'.[2] However, this shouldn't be assumed. Similarly, coaches who feel that they have a close relationship with their client are more likely to be accommodating of sudden demands or be more ready to operate beyond the basic expectations of their contracts when they are able to do so. For this reason too, we believe that organizations shouldn't prejudice engaging with lone-operator coaches in preference to negotiating a single contract with a preferred supplier: the most important task for procurement is to engage good coaches, not to sew up punishing contracts with suppliers.

Possible selection criteria for external coach candidates are included as a checklist that may be downloaded from the website supporting this book, www.managingcoachingatwork.com.

Integration with other programmes and change initiatives

As we've seen, coaching is rarely introduced in isolation from other programmes, but rather is very often integral to a broader initiative rather than one in its own right.

A mix of activities may be relevant for achieving a particular end, including training in processes, techniques or ways of working, communication programmes, reward systems and personal development planning. These in turn may be complemented by a range of techniques designed to help individuals raise their self-awareness, for example 180°/360° feedback surveys, psychiatric indicators and leadership inventories.

Any programme that is intended to bring about a lasting transformational change in the way individuals think and operate may benefit from combining a number of these different methods, not only to cater for different learning preferences, but also to encourage consideration of different perspectives.

For some too, feedback or other concrete suggestions offered as material to reflect upon may be needed to help an individual realize how others perceive them. Without having access to such information, many may struggle to see beyond their own narrow perspective of themselves, however much they may believe that they can take an objective view.

As we mentioned before, coaching is only useful in helping individuals find answers as far as their capacity to soul-search allows. Those who struggle to empathize with others may find that the inspiration they can draw from coaching may be limited; those in power are as vulnerable as anyone in this regard, even succumbing to a psychological disorder that the doctor and former British Foreign Secretary David Owen has labelled 'hubris syndrome' (Owen, 2009).[3]

Delusion is not the only reason for misinterpretation or blockage in coaching; the inability to distinguish what we know and what we don't is a limitation faced by coachees and coaches alike. In the language of Charles Handy, commenting on Luft and Ingham's Johari Window construct (Luft and Ingham, 1955), it is in the cognitive realm in which we are unable to see how others observe us and the remote 'room' where neither we nor others are able to grapple with what the subconscious knows that our understanding is most likely to be lacking (Handy, 2000).

Arguably, one of the principal benefits of coaching is that it helps to unlock what is in the subconscious. But revealing insight requires an inner knowledge to be present in the first place, as well as knowledge that's based on reality.

The implication of all of this is that when planning how coaching should be introduced, it's often important to consider whether other interventions may be likely to enhance an individual's ability to find answers and change their ways of thinking and acting. Taking a business agenda for coaching, this involves an honest assessment of which interventions (alongside or even instead of coaching) might make a difference, and which of these are already on offer or planned.

We believe that this is an early point at which many coaching projects come unstuck: coaching project leaders, just like project managers of other initiatives, may evangelize about their own concerns to the point of being blind to the potential that something else might be able to offer. In short, many may easily sleepwalk into introducing coaching in a silo. Preparation (involving consultation with others) should prevent against this fatal error occurring.

The need to integrate coaching with other initiatives of course depends on the particular business contexts for which coaching is being introduced. For example, a response to meeting an objective to improve sales performance might be to both coach and train salespeople in how better to handle clients' objections, build perceptions of value in what they are selling and develop their confidence to close deals. Conversely, where coaching is being introduced to help newcomers settle into an organization, mentoring and training might be used in parallel with coaching to help fill in knowledge on company processes and systems.

Stakeholder engagement

Perhaps of all the tasks involved in coaching implementation, stakeholder engagement is usually the most challenging but also one of the most critical. Even for those who are able to pull strings, there can be a world of difference between what individuals say they will do and what actually happens in practice.

The purpose of engagement is therefore not just to make others aware of why a new programme is starting, the part that they are expected to play within it and the benefits they may gain from taking part, but also to excite, inspire and motivate their active support and/or involvement. Given its importance, this is a task that needs to be taken seriously. We suggest that engagement should start with a consideration of who the stakeholders of the initiative are, what their interests and perspectives may be, and what part it's hoped they will play in the project.

Coaches, coachees, manager coaches, coach supervisors and coaching project sponsors are amongst obvious stakeholders, but the influence and interests of others too need to be catered for. Amongst these are the line managers of individuals who are intended to receive coaching or act as coaches, project leaders and sponsors of related initiatives, and those responsible for organizational development and people management strategy. In addition, individuals who may take on responsibility for elements of the project will need to be consulted with. These may include IT technicians who will develop supporting websites and computer systems, procurement specialists who may draft contracts with external suppliers and training managers who may commission or design training.

To help with the process of identifying stakeholders and their perspectives, a simple mapping technique might be used, as shown in Figure 5.3.

Once stakeholders are identified, thought can then be directed to how they may be engaged, either collectively or as individuals (in some cases, the latter may always be necessary, and is advisable where an important influencer or interested party is concerned).

It makes sense at this point to plan project communications and consider how best to appeal to stakeholders' interests. A communications plan might take the form of a mini project plan, identifying the key objectives for engagement and communication at different stages in the implementation. This may be translated into simple and impactful messages, choosing the media and methods for relaying the messages and finally confirming that they have been received. Taking account of the importance of not overloading others with information and (where possible and appropriate) integrating with communications concerning other initiatives, a plan might be extended to show the level of importance that particular stakeholders are likely to attach to different messages. As an example, Table 5.2 shows an extract of a plan to engage stakeholders in a managers' basic coaching skill training programme.

FIGURE 5.3 Stakeholder perspectives

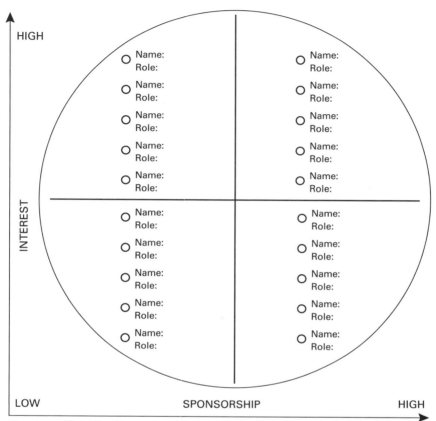

Use the grid to identify stakeholders according to the importance of keeping them engaged in sponsoring coaching and their level of direct interest in the outcomes of specific coaching applications. Colour coding may be used to identify each person or group marker (O), eg to distinguish active participants from those who have a direct interest in the outcomes of coaching, the perspectives taken by each, etc. The choice of coding used is discretionary.

A copy of this template together with a worked example may be downloaded from www.managingcoachingatwork.com

Note that this example includes a range of messages that are designed to raise awareness, others that aim to sell benefits, and others which are simply updating on progress, giving or receiving feedback. To be effective, communication needs to be two-way, allowing the perceptions of stakeholders to play back what they've understood from a message and offering a coaching project leader an opportunity to act on their feedback.

Information that is played back should highlight any objections that stakeholders may present against engaging in a project, although an effort can be made to anticipate these ahead of embarking on communications planning. Amongst the more common objections that we've encountered are those shown in Table 5.3.

TABLE 5.2 Communications plan (extract)

Project stage	Key message(s)	Audience	Channel(s)
Pre-engagement	Engage sponsor to appear in recorded video	Project sponsor	
Initial engagement	Confirm alignment of project to business agenda Engage support for trialling the project/allowing managers and coachees time for participation Obtain agreement to endorse a cascaded e-mail for line managers	Heads of department	E-mail, followed (1 week+) by pre-scheduled brief meetings. Note: Consider splitting communications (one for each message)
Follow-up to initial engagement	Explain the purpose and intended benefits for coaching training	Line managers (of managers to be trained), managers to be trained Engage support for trialling the project/ allowing managers and coachees time for participation	E-mail cascaded by heads of department, followed by lunch-break briefing workshops (1 week+) Sponsor's video recording (accessed via the intranet)

Mid-project: 6-monthly after initial roll-out	Progress: early successes and testimonies	Heads of department, line managers, programme participants	E-mail and intranet news page
Launch of training	Confirmation of training schedule	Managers participating in training and their line managers	E-mail
Launch of first evaluation study	Announce plan for evaluation. Obtain commitment for a sample of individuals to participate	Line managers of trained managers, trained managers, coachees	E-mail, followed by telephone calls if required to encourage participation (1 week+)

TABLE 5.3 Objections for not coaching and possible counter-responses

Objection	Possible response
'I don't have enough time to commit to coaching' or 'I've got a day job to do!'	'After a little initial investment, coaching can often save time/pay dividends later [giving examples]' 'Very little time will be involved, especially since coaching should fit in with the staff meetings you have now'
'I don't see the value of coaching'	'That's what many others said before giving coaching a try and discovering the benefits' 'Will you give me just 10 minutes to try to convince you otherwise?' 'There's a lot of evidence to suggest that coaching does make a difference (eg competitor benchmarks)' Note: This objection may be raised because of an inaccurate or too limited understanding of what coaching is. A simple explanation to fill this knowledge gap and explain why coaching is often so powerful might be offered in such cases
'I know how to manage my people' or 'The way I manage my staff has worked all right up until now'	'Are you open to at least giving something else a try?' 'Do you want more time for yourself to be able to just get on with the job?' 'I don't doubt that, but you may be pleasantly surprised by what coaching has to offer, just as others [performing a similar role] have said they've come to see the benefits' Note: Always respectfully acknowledge push-backs of this kind and steer clear of assuming that coaching will invariably improve on management practices that are being followed currently. Other approaches may well work best for some management needs
'Coaching's not my style [not for me/us]'	'You're not alone, but even if it never becomes your preferred style, how do you feel about the possible benefits that can come from giving coaching a try?'
'I've heard that this coaching thing is flavour of the month amongst you HR [Training] guys'	'It's certainly popular, but it's been around for quite some time now, and has stayed the course because many people have found that it works' 'We're not trying to force anything on anyone – we wouldn't dare! – but are offering this as we've seen that many others find it has been very powerful in helping them achieve their goals'

'I prefer a mentoring approach'	'Mentoring is usually best when a mentor's knowledge and experience relate to the topic being considered, whereas coaching aims to help individuals think, learn and decide for themselves… Are there situations when a coaching approach might also be useful for you?'
'Don't try to sell me on all this "pink, soft and fluffy" nonsense!'	'Would you give coaching a look if you knew that it could help you hit the numbers [free up more time for you/get more out of your staff]?'
'I like to keep a distance with my staff – let them know who's the boss' and 'Haven't you heard that familiarity breeds contempt?'	'What might persuade you to try something different?' Note: An objection of this kind might reveal an underlying fear that by using coaching, a manager's sense of security provided by their perceived power relationship with their staff may be undermined. A gentle challenge backed up by reassurance may be appropriate in such circumstances, eg: 'Are you concerned that some of your staff might question your management ability? That's not uncommon, but most managers I've spoken to who've taken the plunge have discovered the opposite…'
'What's the difference between coaching and mentoring?'	'Coaching puts emphasis on helping an individual reflect and act on what they already know; mentoring may introduce advice, reflections on personal experience and guidance of the mentor…'
'My job is to make sure that we only budget for things that have a clear business case. How much in real money is this thing going to cost and save us?'	'We can't be 100% precise on this at the moment, but there's a huge amount of evidence from others that shows what kind of payback we should expect [giving examples]. We'll put some very clear measures in place from the start to make sure that we stay on top of what returns we're getting…'
'Right now, we've got to cut budgets, drop our headcount and focus on the redundancy programme. Can't you see that now is not a good time for us to be seen ramping up a coaching programme?'	'Obviously we need to be careful with presentation and the way people could interpret this, but coaching is needed now more than ever – to help with outplacement of those who are leaving, to help those who are left to pick up new and busier workloads face up to their new responsibilities and for us to be effective in providing this support…'

Of course, the charisma and personal influence of a project leader can also be a considerable boon when it comes to engaging others. In commenting on Jackie's success as the leader of the London Metropolitan Police Service's in-house coach programme, Clive observed that 'she took to her charge with the enthusiasm that a rookie racing driver might display where first taking to the wheel of a \$multi-million car, an enthusiasm that was contagious, matched only by her perseverance and passion to ensure the success of all would-be coaches who came into her orbit. Gently relentless, she persevered in spite of sometimes saying that she felt she was trying to scale a mountain on roller skates!' Not everyone may be blessed with such strength of character, but for those who are, the task of promoting a coaching initiative should come as second nature.

Informal communication is obviously important too, although generally it relies on unplanned opportunities that can't be guaranteed to happen. With this in mind, it can help to be ready with a 'lift test' explanation of what the project aims to achieve or summarizing the current progress (different lift tests may be applicable when speaking with different people or at different stages in the project). As you may be aware, the idea of a 'lift test' is to condense a critical statement into just one or two sentences – a brief comment that might be offered when posed a question by a colleague during a chance encounter in a brief elevator journey.

Informal communication can play an important part in building relationships, but so too can showing interest in the priorities of others and being ready to play a part in the initiatives that they are responsible for when appropriate.

Writing in *Personnel Journal*, Peggy Stuart suggests that there are other ways for leaders of HR initiatives to endear themselves to the movers and shakers in their organizations, including getting the buy-in of individuals who work for the people you most want to engage with and using external consultants to put in context what's been achieved compared with competitor organizations (Stuart, 1993).

In addition, the potential for using online social networking tools to raise interest shouldn't be underestimated. Many of those targeted by communications campaigns may be active users of social networking sites and, as communications specialists Kathryn Yates and Kathy Kibbe put it, '[this] means the conversation about change starts as soon as the change happens – sometimes very publicly... however, there are ways to use social media internally and externally to the organization's advantage to find out what people in the organization are really thinking and what they really want to know before they commit to the change' (Yates and Kibbe, 2010).

CASE STUDY
The view from both sides: an HR VP takes coaching to a new audience

Marilena Beuses wasn't alone amongst fellow HR executives in the early 1990s in being bugged by a perennial concern – how best to nurture and retain talented staff? Then an HR vice president (VP) with Citibank, it was with enthusiasm that she started to listen to the new claims that coaching wasn't just for those whose lives were tied to the sports fields, but that it had a role to play in developing leaders too. However, her first exposure to coaching, at a conference in Vancouver that had more of a 'New Age' flavour to it, left her wondering whether such claims were premature.

She persevered with a coaching trial nonetheless, and her faith quickly paid off. Coaching conversations brought about a marked change in individuals' readiness to talk openly about matters that they had previously feared they shouldn't come forward with, for example feeling able to challenge the ideas of people in authority with respect and adopting emotionally intelligent approaches to their own development rather than pursuing a 'push–push' approach of passion mixed with impulsiveness. In Marilena's view, coaching produced many examples of rapid potential realization and gave ambitious 'leaders in the making' a clear perspective of the options available to them and a timeline for best positioning themselves to achieve their objectives.

MBA graduates were amongst those that were especially prone to jumping regularly between employers, often with high expectations of achieving rapid promotion. Entrepreneurial opportunities presented by the dot-com boom were a further incentive for those working in the IT sector to consider looking outside and for whom strong mentoring, excellent management training and the advantages of working for a well-regarded multinational organization weren't in themselves sufficient reasons to remain loyal to any particular organization.

Marilena encountered the same challenge after leaving Citibank to take on a senior HR role with PepsiCo International. Here too, she found an organization that was committed to its new manager on-boarding programmes and embraced a culture of care and mentoring. The company recognized the benefits of absorbing coaching into its graduate support programme, applying this as a deliberate policy.

With a focus on the Latin American region, it was a natural step for Marilena to find that managers in the Hispanic world would become an important part of her client base when she transitioned into private practice in 2000. She returned to work for both Citibank and PepsiCo as an executive coach, and took on new clients within organizations such as Procter & Gamble, General Electric and Chevron, all of which had included coaching in their leadership development programmes and were actively committed to monitoring the outcomes of coaching using relevant measures that had meaning to them (eg a manager's ability to deliver more quickly and more effectively after being coached).

Marilena believes that the successes that such organizations have achieved from coaching can partly be attributed to the diligent approach each has taken in its executive coach recruitment, ensuring that appropriate coaches are engaged who can relate to their clients and the environments in which they operate. To relate effectively in this way requires not only a dialogue of understanding, but seeing clients as people who have leadership expectations placed upon them and whose decisions can affect the lives of many people. Coaches who've undertaken a similar role themselves and so faced similar challenges may often be better able to appreciate this perspective and be less distracted by their clients' titles or positions of authority.

Ways of working and the ethos prevailing in different industries and organizations have an important impact on the speed of take-up of coaching too. Often, executives themselves decide whether coaching is worth investing time in, and not all take to coaching as well as others: much depends on the individual.

Marilena makes the point that coaching isn't just about asking the right questions, but working with individuals to make sense of the contexts they work within. In this regard, she has adopted an approach that she terms 'systematic complexity' for understanding the nature of clients' operating environments, self-interests and inferences, seeing this as an essential foundation for later coaching.

Marilena observes that cultural differences can play their part too in how well coaching is adopted. Face-to-face coaching is the preferred modality in many Latin American countries, although domestic cultures vary significantly. Layers of complexity that impact on attitudes may arise from personal/family relationships, appreciating the changing dynamics of different economic markets, their histories and mindsets. In some countries, executives often feel reluctant to reveal their thoughts to a coach, feeling that this leaves them vulnerable to criticism. However, after taking time to work with a coach, many suddenly become evangelistic and actively promote coaching into other parts of their organizations, having come to realize that coaching is about achieving more in personal potential rather than becoming 'superhuman'.

The challenge of coaching across borders is made clear when considering a not untypical scenario in multinational organizations, when a (say) Mexican executive manages a largely Brazilian team and reports to the Russian head of division based in the London office of an American company, while being coached by a Colombian! Unsurprisingly, coaches whose experience is gained solely from a domestic base are often less effective at helping executives articulate the complexity of the cultural differences and barriers that they need to negotiate in multinational working.

While cross-border coaching undoubtedly raises a number of challenges, with appropriate people and understanding it is capable of proving its worth anywhere. The power of being able to talk frankly, reflect and learn is (it seems) a unifying force for positive change that can benefit company chiefs and staff everywhere.

Marilena Beuses is CEO of 4 Total Success, Inc., based in Florida USA (www.4totalsuccess.com). A frequent speaker and contributor to national press and TV, she works extensively with Hispanic-speaking clients working from Latin America, the United States and elsewhere.

Accreditation

Despite the lack of regulation of coaching practice, several professional bodies have established strict standards that their members are expected to meet, including minimum levels of training, required levels of coaching experience and commitments to professional development and supervision. To achieve an accredited status, a coach typically needs to demonstrate evidence that they can satisfy such criteria, including offering client testimonies and in some cases sample recordings of coaching conversations. Varying levels of accreditation may apply, typically depending on the level of experience and training that a coach can offer. Accrediting or certifying organizations include the International Coach Federation, Association for Coaching and the Worldwide Association of Business Coaches.

Similarly, coaching programmes may be accredited by an external body, either a professional coaching organization, a body able to provide a nationally recognized qualification (such as a National Vocational Qualification in the UK), or an association committed to developing high standards in leadership and management. Examples of such bodies include the Institute of Leadership and Management, the International Coaching Council and the European Mentoring and Coaching Council.

The option to seek accreditation for their in-house programme was chosen by Jackie and her colleague Anna O'Neil when introducing an in-house coach programme for the London Metropolitan Police Service. Setting the achievement of a high quality standard as a goal ensured that the programme's coverage and teaching approach were no less demanding than might be expected in the training of external coaches, while allowing the programme to be facilitated internally rather than relying on external support each time it was run.

Generally, when selecting external coaches, we suggest that it's wise to favour those who are accredited by an established professional body. Not only should this ensure that they have received appropriate training and bring adequate experience, but it might indicate their commitment to working with other coaches and keeping abreast of developments in their profession.

When sourcing training from an external supplier, there can be an advantage in preferring an accredited programme too, provided of course that the course content on offer is relevant for a programme's specific need. As with individual coaches, accredited training must satisfy stringent minimum requirements that usually include validating the qualifications of training facilitators and confirming the suitability of quality assurance processes applied during course content design and delivery.

Satisfactory completion of an accredited programme may provide a certificate for an individual that can be recognized as a mark of the level of training that they've received, either within their own organization or more generally. In some cases, this may contribute towards achieving a high-level qualification diploma or other qualification, or may open up the possibility of taking up membership of a professional body. The latter may be applicable where training for managers is concerned, potentially allowing coaching training to contribute towards achievement of a general manager qualification or professional membership.

In our view, incorporating some form of accreditation as a part of a coaching development programme is most relevant when the aim is to develop a cadre of in-house coaches, although credentialling need not rely on external bodies (most of which charge for the privilege of certificating each individual). For us, the real value of accreditation is that it sets a standard to be aspired to and provides a benchmark against which an individual's suitability to practise as a coach can be assessed.

The requirements that we recommend for accreditation include completing a minimum level of training, undertaking a recognized level of practical coaching, and mixing both observed and self-assessed coaching conversations. For example, in the case of Humberside Police Constabulary, a client of Jackie's, the following were defined as criteria for an in-house coach's accreditation:

- 30 hours of foundation training;
- 15 hours of coaching practice;
- completion of two review days and action learning coaching sets; and
- observation and approval of a candidate's readiness to coach by an experienced supervisor.

Accreditation won't be relevant for everyone, although it is an option to be considered during an early stage of implementation and one that can have a significant impact on the direction of a programme as well as on other preparatory activities.

Summary

Few would argue that time taken to create a firm foundation for launching a new venture usually represents time well spent. In the case of a coaching initiative, the steps that are taken to prepare for later activities are likely to be critical to the project's success.

The relative attention given to different areas during a coaching implementation's preparatory phase will vary depending on the nature of what is being implemented. Nonetheless, these are likely to include a mix of deciding how best to engage stakeholders, assessing the relative advantages and disadvantages of pursuing an accreditation process for coaches or a coaching programme and thinking through the approach for recruiting coaches.

The path that is taken in the later stages of implementation may need to be informed by other activities. For this reason, we suggest that planning should allow flexibility to adapt to what is learned and to take account of what coaches, coachees and others feed back to a project leader.

Notes

1 The idea that the coaching profession should be regulated is controversial. Many argue that requirements for coaches to register with or be certificated by a professional body will not in themselves guarantee good coaching practice, but rather that good coaches are retained by their clients and develop their competency through their own commitment to reflective practice, coaching experience and a receptiveness to feedback. Others point to the question of who regulates the self-styled regulators. Richard Boyatzis, Professor of Organizational Behaviour, Psychology and Cognitive Neuroscience at Case Western Reserve University, suggests that regulation can actually result in undesirable consequences, such as 'institutionaliz[ing] mediocrity' and 'creat[ing] forces that inhibit adaptation and change' (Boyatis, 2010).

2 The concept of a 'coaching circle' is described in Chapter 7.

3 'Hubris syndrome': a term coined by former British Foreign Secretary and doctor David Owen that describes the tendency of individuals in positions of power to become deluded by their sense of worthiness and destiny. Owen contends that this is a genuine medical disorder that frequently affects prominent politicians.

Action

Introduction

As we saw in Chapter 5, both the nature of tasks required in coaching implementation and the scope of work that each requires will vary according to a number of factors. Amongst these, the chosen approach for coaching (recipe change, high-level strategic, etc), the intended audience (limited and specific or a wide-scale, cross-organization roll-out) and preference for in-house or external sourcing of coaches (or a mix of each) will have a significant bearing. So too will the extent to which a coaching initiative is being driven by a wider people development strategy, the existence of any coaching practice at present (or previous attempts to test the water) and the readiness of the organization to accept coaching into its ways of working.

In this chapter, we'll look at the essential activities that are likely to apply irrespective of a coaching project's scope, although we'll point out those considerations that are more relevant for different types of implementation. We'll explore the practicalities of putting an implementation plan into action and consider the challenge of keeping vital stakeholder support alive. We'll also bring together a range of practical tips that we and a host of others have found helpful when bringing coaching initiatives to life.

First, let's consider the essential tasks. Amongst the work packages that we suggested might form part of a typical implementation plan in Chapter 5 (Figure 5.1), we considered the task of recruiting coaches and assessing needs, and we devote considerable attention to evaluation in later chapters. Hence here we'll restrict our focus to two main topics:

- developing coaches' and managers' coaching skills; and
- managing coaching.

Developing coaches and coaching skills for managers

Training

As a profession, coaching has come a long way since a groundswell of organizations first began to take it seriously in the 1990s, albeit some had recognized its power earlier even if they hadn't necessarily given the practice a name. Today, the experience, level of commitment to continuing professional development and working with a supervisor are widely considered to be important hallmarks for any coach who plies their trade professionally, while a knowledge of cognitive techniques is amongst the topics that are seen as valuable complementary knowledge for coaching. Many operating in the professional field are committed to coach support networks, are prolific readers on coaching topics (not to mention writers as well, in many cases) and actively participate in coaching associations and conferences.

It might then reasonably be thought that the prospect for developing a level of competency needed for coaching from amongst an organization's workforce might be doomed at the outset, given the excessive time and commitment of resources that this might entail. For those who are recruited into an in-house coaching pool, the commitment question may well hold some truth. Certainly, in-house coaches need to be thoroughly trained and be committed to ongoing personal development in much the same way as external coaches; however, it's our view that a high level of training, study or even experience isn't enough on its own. To produce a great coach calls for personal attributes such as humility and passion, as well as strong self-awareness and self-control. Highly effective coaches are committed to working in a co-active relationship with their clients, earnestly work through each situation their coachees are facing in partnership with a supervisor, are ready to learn and take constructive feedback from others on board and may have just a small fraction of the experience and education of some so-called 'masters'.

Coaching project leaders who have limited budgets and who are working with 'coaches under construction' who can offer only limited amounts of their time shouldn't therefore despair. Neither should there be necessary cause of concern where only a small group of managers support the idea of coaching – as we've suggested already, this is a prime condition for guerilla implementation to be seized upon.

Recruiting the right people, giving appropriate encouragement and making sure that maximum benefit is squeezed out of training hours are more important than arranging an impressive programme of staged training events. Even if this doesn't produce a group of 'great' coaches, it should equip a cadre of individuals who are more than capable and equipped to deliver excellent value for their internal clients.

Selecting the right people to be coaches may well be vitally important, but this shouldn't mean that everyone who is brought into the in-house coach fold needs to come with a perfectly formed set of personal attributes. Rather, a willingness to learn, to work at developing ways of thinking and interacting with people, backed by a genuine passion to be a positive agent of change for clients are amongst the qualities that are most likely to mark out strong candidates.

Experience and training can provide the skill to know how far to probe (to allow a coachee to access the information that they need to find understanding), to feel at ease using simple but powerful questions that are presented at the right time and in a way that speaks directly to the coachee, and cultivate the mindfulness[1] to tune into a situation that an individual is describing. The coaching 'master' in this sense is someone who is far more akin to a meditative, calm and receptive wise person than someone who is steeped in coaching qualifications.

If we can accept this principle as true, then training that helps individuals to develop empathy must be as important as teaching coaching models, lessons from psychology and coaching theory. We favour training that emphasizes self-reflection and experimentation that allows individuals to exhibit weaknesses and make mistakes, as well as training that focuses on the essentials of communicating and building rapport.

We believe that these priorities should also apply when training coaching as a management skill, ie coaching that is intended to be used in everyday conversation as well as in staff development reviews and the like. Such training may set a less ambitious objective than that proposed for an in-house coaches' programme, not least because most managers are unlikely to give the time needed to just coach, at least not in regular, pre-planned coaching sessions with each member of their team. Though perhaps because of this, and also due to the usually more complex relationship that exists between line managers and team members when compared with the relationship with an independent coach, the challenge for training managers is in at least one way greater than training others. This is all the more the case when a coaching initiative is intended to impact on all or a large part of an organization's management cohort and where an opportunity to select individuals who want to coach doesn't exist.

In the absence of being able to train an attitude of mind or being, helping managers to see and appreciate what coaching aims to achieve and how it may be of use to them, as well as giving them the confidence and a sufficient basis to start coaching, may be reasonable objectives for initial training. Invariably, this is likely to involve providing some basic frameworks for conversations, suggested question structures and the like to help get managers started: what we call 'micro-tools', using a term coined by the solutions-focus coach, Michael Hjerth (Hjerth, 2008).

We subscribe to the school of thought that believes that those who want to develop as professional coaches will find inspiration from a variety of sources, not just the traditional coaching literature and its common links to psychology.

Coaches who have open minds to learnings from any direction will not stagnate in their thinking nor become complacent about what they believe they know. David Rock and Linda J Page provide a comprehensive coverage of such underpinning themes in their book *Coaching with the Brain in Mind* (Rock and Page, 2009), including topics such as ontology, psychotherapy, and health practices amongst what they suggest are 'bedrocks' for coaching practice.

From our preceding discussion, we can now suggest possible training content both for a coaching programme that aims to upscale a group of in-house coaches and one that's meant to equip general managers with basic coaching skills.

Suggested scope of training for in-house coaches:

- the meaning of coaching – distinction from mentoring and other disciplines;
- the relevance and use of at least three coaching models (eg OSKAR,[2] TGROW,[3] CIGAR[4]);
- JaM ('Just a Minute'[5]) – for coaching on the move;
- an understanding of and application of coaching principles (eg using the 'Solution-focus' concept);
- level 1–3 listening;
- powerful questioning techniques;
- establishing and maintaining empathy;
- paraphrasing, summarizing and reframing;
- helping others to maximize their potential;
- basic concepts of interpersonal psychology (eg theory of mind[6], transactional analysis[7]);
- giving and receiving feedback;
- affirming coachee strengths and efforts;
- defining actions;
- principles of the 'inner game';
- familiarizing with coaching ethical codes;
- familiarizing with the coach supervision process;
- developing a signature presence[8];
- principles of a learning model/learning style concepts and their relationship to coaching;

- contracting for coaching;

- developing and ending a coaching relationship;

- handling challenging coaching scenarios.

Suggested scope of training for managers:

- defining coaching – as a discipline and as a style;

- why coaching works;

- uses of coaching (eg in situational leadership);

- what coaching achieves for individuals and teams;

- reflective practice;

- essential skills for coaching: level 1–3 listening, question structures, building rapport, paraphrasing, summarizing and reframing, giving and receiving feedback;

- alternative approaches for coaching (eg cognitive-behavioural coaching);

- coaching micro-tools for everyday applications;

- knowing when and how to challenge and adapt coaching models;

- coaching for performance (eg using the TGROW model);

- coaching teams: coaching vs facilitation, questions for teams;

- contracting.

Our suggested scope of training for supervisors is included in Chapter 10.

Keddy Consultants offers courseware supporting each of the training content described above. Further details may be found at the website, www.keddyconsultants.com.

We suggest that the content included in the lists above is the minimum that should be considered, although this shouldn't suggest a limit on the way that training is delivered or the time needed to deliver it.

In the case of both manager skill and in-house coach programmes, we've found that staggered training tends to be more effective than courses that are run at a single time, and especially if training can be combined with opportunities for practice and other inter-class activities. Indeed, in our conversations with organizations that had put managers through coaching training, a higher percentage of those whose initial training module had extended to only half a day reported a greater enthusiasm and take-up of coaching some months after the training than many that had committed to courses running over several days.

Training for coachees

Arguably, there may be value in offering some training for coachees, not to mention briefing workshops for their line managers. Coachees who come to coaching with an appreciation of what it aims to achieve and the part that they might expect to play should be better prepared to engage with the process, while their managers may also be more committed if they recognize what their staff might be doing in their coaching sessions!

Such training need only be brief, perhaps taking no more than one hour and possibly being provided via a self-taught e-learning package (we've also seen coachee 'briefing guides' being used). Coachee training might include the following content:

- What is coaching?
- How does coaching work?
- What is the role of the coach?
- What role should a coachee expect to play, and what type of commitments might they expect will be necessary?
- What potential challenges may coaching involve and how can these be faced (eg how to break free from a comfort zone)?

Training design

Training design obviously needs to address the objectives that are set for a particular course, not just in terms of which topics are to be covered by the programme, but also by employing learning approaches that will most engage trainees, help them appreciate the concepts that are taught and then focus on applying these. Crucially, any coaching training must involve an element of live role-play interaction (though this can be achieved without face-to-face contact if necessary). We also strongly recommend allowing sufficient time for self-reflection and for individuals to receive feedback from role-plays (as well as having opportunities to act as observers alongside playing the roles of coach and coachee).

The purpose of including such elements as these is to allow individuals to reflect honestly and thoughtfully on their own performance and learning needs, and to register which aspects of what has been taught they've found to be true when attempting to apply theory in practice. The sequence of exploring a new concept, experimenting with it and reflecting on the experience is not dissimilar to the TGROW model that is often taught in basic coaching training: when an experience confirms a concept to be useful, this then normally becomes a part of an individual's conceptual model of what they should apply. This traditional model of learning has been extensively explored by Kurt Lewin, David Kolb and others (see, for example, Lewin, 1948; Kolb, 1984).

Defining the objectives for training and thinking through a course's design strategy are obviously important before being able to assess whether to source training externally – whether bespoke or customized – or whether it may be preferable to develop new materials from scratch. What training is provided, how and when, and in which format are therefore matters that shouldn't be taken lightly. It may often be the case that training offered by well-established coaching suppliers won't be the best option for meeting an organization's particular needs.

Piloting training

Where a significant roll-out of a coaching programme is planned, it makes sense to pilot training and post-training support using a small group of willing volunteers. The ability to obtain honest and constructive feedback from participants of such a project is obviously important to allow any needed improvements to be made before the programme is more fully rolled out. We suggest that not only should proper time be dedicated for following up with early pilot participants as a part of their training or just following this, but also perhaps two to three months later to establish what they have found to be most useful or perceive was lacking in the training since they've returned to their normal duties and attempted to put what they learned into practice.

Continuing skill development

Training is, of course, only a part of what's required to help individuals develop. Support for learning doesn't need to be restricted to group-based classroom sessions or pre-scripted courseware material either. One of the many roles that coaching can play is helping individuals to learn, consolidate and apply learning to support training, but there are other complementary activities too that can substantially add to training on its own.

We've observed that the following can be especially useful for helping coaches' development:

- coaching circles;
- informal networking (eg triads);
- informal information networks;
- inter-organization knowledge sharing;
- participation in coaching associations;
- review days;
- co-coaching (with or without observation);
- self-coaching; and
- supervision.

We'll briefly consider each of these in the next chapter.

Many of these can be equally helpful for facilitating line manager learning, especially where they allow a manager to experiment with coaching in a supportive and non-judgemental environment or where they enable access to help when required.

Amongst the activities that may help managers feel safe to come forward with 'dumb questions' and potentially expose a weakness or two when practising coaching are:

- co-coaching with managers from other parts of the organization or possibly from other organizations;
- mentor support from a professional/in-house coach or learning and development specialist;
- buddy coaching;
- anonymous bulletin board systems that allow questions to be raised and answers to be given;
- coaching circles.

Back-up networks and points of contact for support may be offered as a selling point for some managers; the ability to talk freely with others about personal learnings or pose questions about a staff development topic may be rare. But networking is also important for another reason: it enables coaching skills to be practised.

Practice can be hard. Self-doubt can quickly set in when an individual perceives that they are making many mistakes, perhaps when attempting to act against their natural style to form 'good' coaching questions or when trying to exercise self-discipline to avoid their mind skipping on to another question while a coachee is still in mid-thought about the last question posed.

Despite the frustrations and disappointments that practice can sometimes entail, it's essential for individuals whose natural style is to tell and form quick conclusions based on what they hear. Only through practice can slipping into a coaching approach become less of a hard graft and more of a second nature; by applying themselves to practice, a manager actually trains their brain to rewire itself in much the same way that coaching often helps coachees to change their mindsets.[9]

CASE STUDY
Individual shall speak truth unto individual: coaching at the BBC

The BBC represents many things for many different people: for some, it's an immediately recognizable brand and one of the world's leading broadcasters and programme makers; for others, it's a curious self-governing and part-commercial institution that's also publicly accountable. For others too, it's a forerunner amongst technology companies.

With an operation spanning virtually every country on earth (the BBC broadcasts in more than 30 different languages) and an annual budget of more than $6 billion, the BBC's diverse operation has spawned a culture that is uniquely its own. In addition to its TV and radio channels, serving global to highly localized audiences, the corporation operates one of the world's largest websites, and combines a commercial arm whose programme-selling, DVD and publication enterprises generate more than $200 million per year and include major brands such as Lonely Planet travel publishing.

Furthermore, the BBC is a long-standing pioneer in developing and initiating new technologies: it was the first broadcaster in the world to transmit colour television in the late 1960s, one of the first to pioneer NICAM stereo broadcasting, and a major partner in the development of teletext, high-definition television, and digital and interactive media technologies such as the 'red button' and the BBC iPlayer.

Given its role as a technological pioneer and the need to engage the highest levels of talent in what is a fully creative industry, the BBC can rightly claim that its future success lies in the strength of its people. Possible regulatory and likely funding changes and a changing and increasingly competitive media landscape mean that the corporation faces strong management challenges; in its domestic television market, a complete transition to digital broadcasting should be completed within just two years.

In the history of workplace coaching, the BBC was an early adopter, and has since established one of the most admired internal coaching practices, a function that is totally dedicated to coaching.

A 'can do' culture was an important factor in giving coaching its early push. Greg Dyke, the then Director-General of the corporation, brought a personal style, ambition and belief in encouraging self-initiative and new ways of working that allowed coaching to flourish (although he wasn't directly involved in sponsoring its growth). After gaining the support of Brenda Stocking, who led the management development team, Liz Macann took on the mantle of creating an in-house practice dedicated to 'the art and science of facilitating the performance, learning and development of another... to raising individuals' awareness of who and what they are, with an acknowledgement that it is their responsibility to make the change and difference to their own situation and others, to come up with [their own] solutions'.

Macann believes that coaching took off in the BBC because, after a slow but steady start, it became an integral part of the extensive leadership development programme that ran in the early part of the past decade. To ensure best practice and professionalism, the Coaching Network is now run as if it were an independent coaching company and is part of the College of Leadership in the BBC Academy. The dedication and commitment of coaches is immediately apparent to observers, while those who've experienced the power of coaching and seen the results that transpire from it have produced a self-generating learning cycle that feeds on itself.

The practice invests heavily in coaches' professional development, drawing upon internal expertise and resources to fit with budget restrictions. A practice of 'learning, learning, learning' is insisted upon, as is a drive to ensure that coaches remain thoroughly 'tooled up' through supervision.

Goal setting is kept in step with organizational objectives, ensuring that the focus of coaching remains relevant for both the individuals who receive coaching and for the business: the vital organizational link is maintained. While business goals and coaching objectives may vary between organizations, Macann believes that these must be set to prevent coaching possibly degenerating into pleasant but non-value-adding conversations.

Alongside taking coach development seriously, a solid foundation combined with the active, supportive management of someone who really believes in coaching and is committed to driving it has enabled the BBC to grow its coaching impact during a period of rapid change. The carefully selected staff (recruited for their authentic intention, presence and demonstrable emotional intelligence) have become a respected network of coaches who are dedicated and passionate about what they do, operating without receiving financial reward and often within tight time constraints.

Afterword

Jackie can testify to this dedication, having consulted with Liz when forming plans to introduce the London Metropolitan Police Service's coaching programme. In Jackie's words: 'Liz Macann is a true inspiration, a non-precious mentor and a wonderful coach who always took the time to talk things through and share her learning.'

Note: the title we chose for this article owes more than a little inspiration to the BBC's guiding motto, adopted more than 90 years ago – 'National shall speak peace unto nation'.

Process definition

A need to support managers, nurture in-house coaches and supervisors, not to mention coachees themselves, implies the need for a process for administering such requirements. A process need not be long or complex – certainly no more so than for other business functions that processes are developed to describe – but should be clearly communicated and lived!

Typical content may include defining the responsibilities for delivering different aspects of the process, any information or other prerequisites for a part of the process work, as well as the outputs that they should deliver. We've included a process template covering the main scope of coaching management in Appendix A. This recognizes sub-processes for:

- coach–coachee matching;
- supervisor–coach matching;
- close-out of coaching relationships (timeliness and learnings capture);
- contracting;
- coach recruitment;
- coaching request handling;
- coachee reflection;
- supervisor development;
- coach management (IT system) support maintenance;
- information systems maintenance (eg intranet pages);

- provision for coach support;
- review of coaching training;
- distinction between private and organizational goals for coaching;[10]
- coach moderation;
- evaluation;
- organizational learnings (capture and response);
- changing business priorities review.

This list may be added to when required. For simpler coaching implementations (ie those that don't involve formal contracting between coach and coachee as required in pure coaching relationships), a process may be restricted to simply identifying the responsibilities/accountabilities of a coaching project leader and sponsor, describing how individuals can subscribe to training and what support they can expect once they've completed this.

Processes may also be put in place to define when and how evaluation should be conducted and to describe how lessons learnt from coaching can be fed back for the organization's wider benefit. We'll return to these considerations in later chapters.

We've often been surprised by the number of organizations that don't have a written process for their coaching function, although the absolute need for this may be less acute where coaching is being practised on a very limited basis or in small organizations in which all the participants in a coaching programme are known to each other and where regular verbal communication is maintained. However, in other circumstances, we believe that maintaining consistent quality in coaching and maximizing the efficiency and effectiveness of a coaching function will be difficult unless how information should flow and be processed has been clearly thought through or where responsibilities for administering coaching or how to make a request for coaching and the like aren't properly established.

Certainly, evidence of a clearly described process to ensure that training is delivered in a consistent way and that modules are kept up to date and reflect relevant delegate feedback will be needed for any programme that is put forward as a candidate for accreditation by an external body.

IT systems and other supporting infrastructure for coaching

Except where there is a high level of trust in the value of coaching or where others (such as department managers) take on the responsibility for monitoring coaching spend and time-sheet recording, maintaining data about coaching activity is normally an important task for those responsible for coaching management. As it's often said, reliable, timely and complete information is the lifeblood of any decision-making system. We believe that the needs of coaching management are no exception to this.

Without a record of numbers that have been coached, when and for how long, and the training hours that have been dedicated to coaching, it will be difficult to make objective judgements about whether particular coaching investments have been worthwhile, identify whether some coaches appear to require longer engagements in order to achieve similar objectives for their clients than others, continue to sell coaching to remaining sceptics and to be able to forecast future demand.

An effective information system also supports:

- better informing of decisions about coaching spend (eg future sourcing options and training);
- reporting on what has been delivered;
- forecasting demand for coaches and coaching applications;
- administering requests for coaching/identifying suitable matches;
- facilitating knowledge share, online bulletin board/forum question and answer, and supporting tools for coaches and managers.

Relatively simple spreadsheet or database applications should be able to handle most of these needs, although a good starting base of content may be needed to launch a knowledge/tools-share facility (perhaps as part of an intranet offering). Additional functionality may also be needed to handle more sophisticated functions such as bulletin board forums and for managing coaching requests.

Where only a limited implementation is concerned or when running a pilot project, basic home-grown systems may suffice. However, the systems required to support coaches following their initial training need to be quite robust from the outset. Similarly, once coaching training has been rolled out to a large number of managers and when a coaching service is made available across a large organization, the task of administering such needs will quickly become challenging without the support of suitable information systems. For example, request matching may soon evolve to require a small team of administrators rather than being handled by just one person alongside other tasks or even being completely automated. Other content may be built up over time (for example, the résumés of coaches who've been added to the coaching pool).

More sophisticated needs such as supporting different access needs for information for different users and protecting the privacy of information may call for specialist IT expertise. Alternatively, it may be prudent to invest in a proprietary software package that is capable of performing these tasks. The 'Mye-Coach' system is one example (www.mye-coach.com).

Mye-Coach also provides a comprehensive set of tools for coaches and managers. Other tool kits are available, including *Cameo* and a package developed by Clive, *people-assist*, which combines more than 250 tools and techniques (see our supporting website for more information, www.people-assist.info). Another Kogan Page title, *50 Top Tools for Coaches* (Jones and

Assessing requests for coaching

It may be tempting for managers who are aware of the existence of a coaching service to propose members of their team as possible coaching clients for all manner of developmental and remedial performance needs. Such individuals may undoubtedly often benefit from coaching; however, a normal task for a coaching manager is to weigh up the relative merits of different requests, and especially where demand exceeds the availability of coaching resource. At the same time, requests that are accepted without question could encourage laziness amongst some who make such proposals and, worse, result in some not taking their responsibility for staff management seriously.

Assessment should therefore seek to explore what type of effort has already been applied to help an individual meet the particular need for which coaching is being proposed, as well as ensuring that line managers are committed to playing their part in helping a coachee put into practice the actions that they determine from their coaching conversations.

Commitments to allow individuals time for coaching – not just for coaching sessions, but also for preparation and follow-up – must be agreed, and the consequence of individuals failing to participate in pre-agreed sessions should be properly understood. Crucially also, a clear purpose must exist for the coaching, although, as we've seen, this needn't involve having to define precise goals at the outset.

The expected benefit of coaching to help achieve its intended purpose should be clear, and ideally the reasons why coaching is considered to be preferable to other interventions should be explained. Finally, assessment needs to ensure that a critical prerequisite test for coaching to have a chance of succeeding can be met: whether or not the proposed coachee is a client for coaching (ie they understand what coaching aims to achieve and are committed to play their part in the coaching process).

All in all, responding to these various questions calls for a business case to be made every time a request for coaching is made. The agreements and commitments shouldn't be made half-heartedly, especially when an organization's capacity to offer coaching is strictly limited. Consequently it makes sense to standardize a process for coaching requests and to obtain the signatures of both coachees and their line managers to confirm their commitments. We suggest a possible template for this purpose in Appendix A; however, this may be usefully supplemented with verbal communication.

Matching

The process of matching coaches with coachees isn't an exact science, and it may not always be able to achieve perfect matches either. The depth of experience that a coach brings may be an important factor where an individual's needs appear to be particularly challenging, while a coach's field of knowledge may be relevant in some cases. For example, it may be helpful for coaches working with clients in professional fields such as banking to be able to understand the business language that is commonly used by their clients.

In the fashion of any good dating agency, coaches can help explain what they believe they can offer a coachee in a simple biography, helping to take attention away from their role, rank or position to what led them to become a coach. Experience aside, matching should aim to connect coachees with coaches whom they feel comfortable working with (and vice versa), and with someone they can trust. Typically this will be someone who is independent of their line management and with whom they don't have regular contact otherwise.

Only a coachee and coach can assess whether they feel good chemistry, and consequently the best that a coaching service manager can usually do is to propose one or a number of possible matches based on what they know about the styles and personalities of the coach and any preferences of the coachee. For example, if a coachee is known to be shy or nervous, a coach who has a calm and non-energetic manner may be appropriate. Conversely, a coachee who is fired up to get moving on working towards their objective may be better suited to a coach who naturally operates at a similar pace. However, it's for a coach to tune into a coachee's preferred style and to mirror and match this as appropriate.

We suggest that 'chemistry meetings' are always allowed for when practical, allowing each party an opportunity to get to know the other and judge whether they feel comfortable working together. These meetings may also be used for setting the scene for the coaching that may follow, including boundary setting and addressing other contracting topics. Irrespective of whether an option to meet with several potential coaches is available (and usually this may prove too expensive for many organizations), a coach should be aware that if a coachee chooses not to engage with them, this need not reflect on their competency: it's far more important for everyone concerned that relationships start on a good footing.

It may not always be possible to make ideal matches, but this shouldn't prevent a coaching relationship from being productive. Much will depend on the attitude of both coach and coachee. For example, Clive recently encountered a situation in which an individual who was well known to a coachee for whom she acted as coach subsequently became the individual's project manager (not as a result of the coaching). The coaching relationship was able to continue as before because both parties had strong respect both for each other and for the strict boundaries of their coaching relationship relative to their other working relationships. The coachee remarked that the manager acted as almost a different person when performing their normal management role, while reference was never made to anything discussed in coaching conversations outside their dedicated sessions.

As a secondary objective, matching might also aim to smooth the utilization of coaches: in other words, to attempt to avoid overburdening some coaches with requests while denying others opportunities to coach. Coaches may often prefer to work with a coach who brings significant coaching experience; however, encouragement should also be given to individuals to work with new coaches who need to cut their teeth through live practice. If lacking experience, novice coaches should be committed to offering their best and be especially sensitive to coachee feedback. We've rarely heard of coachees reporting that they were disappointed with a coaching engagement because they'd felt that their coach lacked experience, although where business-critical coaching is required, experience may be an important factor (as in the case of Wagamama Australia – see the case study on pp 26–27).

Coaching engagements may last for only a brief period, even for just one or a few conversations. Usually, this is because coaching has achieved its purpose. However, occasionally a suggested ending of a coaching dialogue may be warranted if it becomes apparent that another coach may be best suited to working with a coachee at the point they have reached.

The onus is on both coach and coachee to determine when it's appropriate to bring their relationship to a close, and this should be kept under regular review. Reviews of the progress of coaching engagements by a coach undertaken with a supervisor can also help ensure that relationships aren't continued beyond their natural endpoint. In practice, we've found that coach and coachee typically know when it's sensible to bring their engagement to a close, and sometimes this happens in a moment. It's also a mark of a professional coach to say when they feel that the relationship has achieved its purpose. Coaches and coachees who prefer to prolong an engagement – perhaps because this offers a coachee a respite from other work – can quickly erode the investment-benefit return of their engagement, although deliberate heel-dragging can be difficult to spot.

Additionally, both to help maximize what is achieved in coaching sessions and to keep fresh the question of whether continuing with their coaching engagement is appropriate, we suggest that coachees are encouraged to document their reflections on coaching conversations and to set down what they would like to achieve from their next session. A template reflection form is included in Appendix A for this purpose.

Helpdesk support

New coaches and recently trained managers often encounter coaching situations in which they feel a need for some guidance or opportunity to sound out their thinking. Supervision can provide the perfect opportunity for this, as can coaching support networks and development activities such as coaching circles. However, at other times, it's helpful if coaches or managers can have a point of contact that they can turn to. A dedicated e-mail address or phone contact with a coaching project manager might be offered, even if queries are then referred on to another coach. Similarly, bulletin board forums that might only normally be used for knowledge sharing can help fill the gap, assuming of course that there are sufficient numbers of experienced coaches using the service who can respond to any queries posed.

We suggest that some committed provision for support should be made, not in the sense of a person or small team permanently manning a 24-hour 'hotline' (complete with multi-option telephone keypad numbers for callers to press and assurances that their call 'is important to us' for those who are left on hold), but providing a channel for questions to be raised and answered within a reasonably short period of time. An intranet-based service might suffice for this purpose. Coaching managers may find that they need to operate the service themselves, although we suggest that this prospect shouldn't need to present a considerably higher workload, especially if the intended use of the service has been properly explained.

Practical tips and insights to assist and pitfalls to avoid in implementation

Both from our own experience and through consulting with others, we've observed that there are a number of practical tips and common pitfalls that regularly feature in the course of implementation. In Tables 6.1 and 6.2 we summarize those that have most frequently been pointed out to us, drawing on interviews conducted with more than 70 organizations. Discretion is preferable over interpreting these as hard-and-fast rules; however, we suggest that the collective experiences of a wide base of organizations may at least provide food for thought.

Summary

Moving from planning implementation activities to actually undertaking them requires strong project leadership and organizational support. Initially, a coaching project leader's focus is likely to emphasize selling the benefits of coaching, recruiting suitable candidates for initial training and actively engaging with stakeholders. Once a coaching service has been established or manager training has been rolled out, attention may shift to managing the day-to-day needs of those who coach or who use coaching services.

Common pitfalls can be avoided and benefits gained by understanding what other organizations learned had helped their coaching implementations run smoothly (Jackie asked two questions when conducting her research to gather evidence for her 'inside job' – 'What has really worked?' and 'What one thing would you do differently if you could go back?'). The continuing support of sponsors shouldn't be taken for granted, and even highly experienced coaches can benefit from committed support.

While it may ultimately be possible to reduce many of the needs of coaching management to business-as-usual processes, any coaching investment needs to continue to be nurtured. Without ongoing attention, the benefits that may have been recognized earlier may not be sustained. In the next chapter, we'll turn our attention to consider how to confront this unavoidable challenge.

TABLE 6.1 Implementation tips

Simple micro-tools can be very valuable to encourage managers to coach initially, even when these may occasionally break some of the principles of 'pure' coaching.
Ensure that the meaning of 'coaching' is clearly defined for the contexts in which it is to be used, eg distinguishing between coaching and mentoring and between dedicated coaching engagements and coaching as a management style.
Where possible, engage individuals amongst early programme recruits who are likely to be open to the training and become potential advocates for coaching to others.
When recruiting for an in-house coach programme, take time to select individuals who demonstrate the right personal attributes and passion to grow as coaches rather than choosing candidates based on their past coaching experience or organizational rank.
Encourage coach and coachee chemistry meetings, allowing both parties to assess whether they are likely to be well matched.
Even where the opportunity to receive coaching is offered to all, each coaching engagement should be justified in business terms and each potential coachee should be a suitable client for coaching.
Be sure that managers, coaches, supervisors and coachees understand the time commitment that coaching involves.
If coaching training for managers is to be mandated, ensure that the reasons for the training are clearly explained (avoid presenting a programme as something that is being imposed on managers).
Ensure that in-house coaches are properly supported and have access to a supervisor.
Ensure that provision is made for in-house coaches' ongoing professional development.
Be realistic about the ambitions of a coaching programme, especially if embarking on a coaching initiative for the first time or when a substantial culture change would be necessary to achieve the expected outcomes.
Pilot training initially if possible and relevant (eg this may not apply in small organizations) and refine what is rolled out if necessary, based on feedback from individuals who've participated in the pilot project.
If coaching isn't being implemented within a particular business context, be sure that there is a valid demand for what is being proposed (eg coaching training or provision of coaching services).
Ensure that training is appropriate for need, eg equip managers to coach on the fly before they engage in 'pure' coaching relationships if using coaching in their everyday management is where they're most likely to see benefit.

Sell the benefits of coaching with sympathy for the needs of the target audience.

Consult with the target audience for coaching before training design/sourcing (consult with a sample of all stakeholder groups, not just coaches and coachees).

Make training role-plays meaningful for the business contexts that trainees operate within.

Plan to be proactive in encouraging managers to coach following their training, not assuming that they will automatically take on ownership for this.

Solicit and respond to feedback: organizations that are aware of the types of issues coaches face and invite feedback from them were amongst those that report the most success with their coaching programmes. These had also typically acted to help address the specific questions and concerns which were raised, eg via informal counselling for coaches.

Involve top team members if possible in initial training. Encourage individuals of different ranks to mix within coach cohorts (coaching frequently crosses normal management lines).

Teach in-house coaches relevant psychological concepts as a part of their continuing training (this is seen as a useful aid for supporting behavioural and development change).

Involve and consult staffing unions (where relevant), by demonstrating the benefits to staff, which may encourage them to become staunch allies for driving coaching forward.

TABLE 6.2 Potential implementation pitfalls

Don't restrict evaluation to just the occasional surveys or assume that positive survey ratings alone suggest that all is necessarily fine.

Don't set too ambitious targets for initial coach/manager training.

The use of coaching models can be overemphasized in training, particularly if a primary focus is put on just one model such as TGROW.

Opportunities are likely to be missed if coaching isn't implemented with reference to other initiatives and where ongoing liaison with the leaders of these initiatives isn't maintained (eg with those responsible for HR projects, business change projects, learning and development activities).

The investment benefits from a coaching engagement can quickly be eroded if both a coach and coachee aren't able or willing to say when their relationship should end.

Don't present the general concept of coaching as a challenging discipline that is best left to professionals, or one that carries mystique.

Don't teach managers 'to suck eggs' in a classroom scenario, even though many may lack polished questioning and listening skills. Present such training as a refresher and offer back-up aids that can be referred to privately.

Coaching initiatives may deliver only partially against their planned objectives if they aren't tied to the initiatives whose objectives they seek to address (eg complementing PDP programmes, competency frameworks and other training).

Notes

1 'Mindfulness': a state of being aware of the 'here and now', involving deep, focused attention. Observations of what is sensed or perceived are noted but not judged.

2 OSKAR (Outcome, Scaling, Know-how and Resources, Affirm and action, Review): a Solution Focused coaching model, developed by Jackson and McKergow (Jackson and McKergow, 2006).

3 TGROW (Topic, Goals, Reality, Options, Way Forward): a popular model, mainly used in performance coaching. Variation of a model developed by Whitmore (Whitmore, 2009).

4 CIGAR (Current Reality, Ideal Outcome, Gaps, Action, Review): a coaching model adopted from TGROW, often used in management consultancy (see Lee, 2003).

5 'JaM (Just a Minute)': A simple dialogue structure developed by Jackie that is relevant to use when unexpectedly encountering the hard-to-resist interruption 'Do you have a minute?'

6 'Theory of mind': the ability to theorize about what someone else is thinking without their needing to express their thoughts explicitly.

7 'Transactional analysis': an exploration of the differing ego states that individuals play out in conversations and the effects that they have on the course of dialogues and relationships. The concept was originated by Eric Berne. See Berne, E (1996) *Games People Play: The basic handbook of transactional analysis*, Ballantine Books, New York.

8 The concept of 'signature presence', developed by Mary Beth O'Neill (O'Neill, 2000) refers to a coach's ability to combine strong coaching competency with a style and personality that are authentic and uniquely their own.

9 The capacity of the brain to reconfigure itself in response to external stimuli (the principle of neuroplasticity) is extensively discussed by Daniel Siegel (1999). In particular, Siegel references the way in which neural pathways strengthen in response to particular stimuli, for example to form a memory, then being more likely to 're-fire' in the same way when encountering similar stimuli in future.

10 To insist that any coaching paid for by an organization must only ever address explicitly identified organizational goals may prove too restrictive in a coach-and-coachee dialogue. Not only may issues brought by an individual about their life outside work, their thoughts, values or feelings be relevant for what matters to the organization (as well as being necessary for a coachee to appreciate what makes them 'whole' in the way they react to particular situations), but a private goal may be a key to addressing an organizational one. For example, the route for addressing an organizational goal that concerns a manager's perception that a coachee 'never delivers on time' might only be revealed by appreciating a coachee's private goal to address 'working effectively with a manager who's constantly changing their mind'.

Sustaining and developing coaching

Introduction – what next?

Once the last of the planned in-house coach cohorts or front-line managers has graduated from their training events, a coaching project leader might be justified in cracking open a bottle of their favourite wine or otherwise marking the occasion with a little celebration. This, after all, is undoubtedly a significant milestone!

However, it would be foolhardy to believe that the hard work of making coaching stick can stop here. Indeed, the period following training is a critical time as individuals endeavour to put their new-found skills into practice, sometimes with difficulty, and often finding the temptation to revert to familiar ways of working too strong to resist.

In this chapter, we'll consider what can be done to avoid all the good work of preparing and seeing through a coaching programme to its operational stage from becoming undone. For coaching to become an unconscious competence, or in other words to become a second-nature skill that is deeply ingrained in general management practice, sustaining an interest in coaching is an imperative.

Some types of implementation may require less energetic attention than others. For example, a guerrilla approach should produce coaching advocates who should need little motivation to sustain their interest even when other matters compete for their attention.

However, in all cases, for coaching to be sustained let alone to be developed and extended to meet new business needs, it's essential that those responsible for sponsoring and overseeing a coaching initiative don't take their eyes off the ball, or feel that they can divert their energies to some other initiative, now that the coaching project has reached a point at which it might be seen that their task has been completed.

Quite apart from continuing to motivate individuals to embrace coaching in their everyday practice, the systems, processes and activities for operating coaching that we've already mentioned need to be nurtured, supported and maintained, while provision also needs to be made for training and integrating new staff into the coaching frame. Supporting the coaching team is critical at this stage. So too, where both 'pure' coaching and 'manager as coach' implementations have been pursued, separate attention will need to be given to developing the coaching practice of the coaches/managers covered by each.

Why coaching often goes off the rails

When we originally consulted with a range of organizations who'd invested heavily in coaching some years ago, we were astonished to discover how many of those to whom we spoke believed that their programmes had delivered less than they had hoped for. Some years after introducing coaching, a majority of those with whom we consulted were raising concerns about how to sustain an interest in coaching. In quite a few cases, increasingly frustrated HR and training managers were wondering how to revitalize what had become very patchy pictures of coaching commitment. Even amongst those who considered that engagement with coaching had endured over time, questions were often raised about how possible backsliding could be minimized.

Most significantly, a fall-off in interest in coaching was most prevalent amongst managers who'd been put through a 'manager as coach' programme, rather than amongst in-house coaches. That said, we did speak to several organizations who reported that their in-house practices had not evolved in quite the way that had been hoped.

Perhaps surprisingly, when we originally consulted with a large number of organizations who'd implemented coaching programmes some years ago, we found that those who reported the most obvious success had not set their initial ambitions too high, rather giving quite basic training to line managers encouraging further personal development. Those who'd taken all managers through a two- or three-day coaching programme often reported that the incidence of coaching conversations that would be apparent to an observer touring the company premises had radically fallen off two or three years after the training: the hoped-for take-on of a 'coaching culture' had failed to materialize. In this chapter we'll therefore focus on the key question of how to sustain coaching as a management discipline, although many of the principles apply equally to in-house coaching programmes as well as to other types of implementation.

Coaching can go off-piste for a wide variety of reasons, including:

- Coaching implementation is seen as a one-off event rather than an ongoing activity.
- Inappropriate training is provided (eg managers may be taught how to coach when in the context of a normal coaching relationship, but not how to coach in very brief, unexpected conversations with their staff).
- Early perceived 'failure' when trying to apply coaching skill discourages further attempts.
- Insufficient numbers of people come forward to request coaching, meaning that new coaches gain little or no practical experience in the period following their training (which is vital for consolidating skill).
- Everyday management and responses to changing priorities 'get in the way' of coaching.
- Coach selection is overlooked (in some cases, being delayed over several years).
- Managers feel uncomfortable coaching their staff (eg due to their perceived loss of relationship power).
- Coaches/managers fear taking the first steps in coaching in case they fall flat on their faces – and so put off trying.
- Coaches/managers feel uncomfortable admitting to a need for training or support in what they perceive as being a basic skill (eg questioning), or are reluctant to raise what they believe may be seen as a 'dumb question'.
- Senior manager support weakens or becomes diverted to other things (eg when a top team resolve that all efforts must be put into what they regard as core activities, perceived desirable support for activities such as coaching may be played down).
- Coaching isn't sold as an opportunity but is seen as an additional encumbrance by busy managers.
- The coaching implementation model that has been pursued isn't appropriate for organizational need (eg managers are expected to operate coaching practices within their teams when both coach and coachee feel uncomfortable with the concept).
- The meaning and purpose of 'coaching' are misunderstood and so not properly applied.
- The organization's cultural recipe remains unchanged when the prevailing culture isn't conducive to coaching being widely accepted.
- Insufficient resource is committed to supporting coaches and managing the operational needs of coaching.
- No one individual is clearly identified as having responsibility for overseeing the organization's coaching initiative.
- Coaching isn't integrated with business need.

- Coaching isn't integrated with HR, learning and development or key change initiatives.

- Promotion is overlooked.

- Important stakeholders are overlooked and so not engaged (eg staff unions, occupational health specialists, other functional managers).

- Coaches have few or no opportunities for continuing practice, knowledge sharing and receiving feedback (eg through buddy coaching and review days).

Notably, a number of these refer to situations in which individuals want to apply their coaching skills but become discouraged or encounter barriers when they attempt to do so. For example, Clive worked with an organization whose managers wanted to have coaching conversations with their staff but who were regularly prevented from doing so by their own line managers (who perceived that other activities took a higher priority). The organization concerned was subject to tough public sector targets and frequently changing demands imposed from on high.

In other cases, expectations of what coaching should deliver in the short term are set too high. Some who backslide simply aren't prepared to allow coaching an opportunity to have effect. For others who'd previously been sceptical about the value of coaching training, any evidence that their earlier view was being borne out in practice may be sufficient to convince them that coaching should not warrant any further investment of their time. This is an attitude that psychologists call having a 'confirmation bias'.

A recent study to explore the factors that encourage line managers to make a coaching style a normal part of their management suggests that demographic factors such as a manager's age or gender and the work or task environment that they operate within have little bearing on their take-up of coaching. Rather, the research, undertaken by Portsmouth University and commissioned by CIPD, corresponds with our finding that a manager's self-confidence plays a crucial role. So too, the range and type of support available to managers to develop and practise coaching skill stands out as being especially important, and effectively managed team relationships also feature as a powerful influence (Anderson *et al*, 2009).

Low confidence was underscored by characteristics such as a perceived lack of skill to coach. Perhaps unsurprisingly, a lack of time was also considered to be a significant constraint by managers who otherwise claimed that they wanted to coach.

Interestingly, a factor analysis[1] of the study data revealed a distinct clustering of factors into two groups, which the research study's authors term primary and mature coaching characteristics (Anderson *et al*, 2009, p 17).

The former includes a manager's focus for developing people and their effectiveness at giving feedback and in committing to goal-setting activities. Mature characteristics include effective team participation in decision making and problem solving, highlighting the study's general finding that organizations that encouraged participative styles of management tended to be those that were most likely to embrace coaching into their cultures. Given that very often a combination of such factors may impose upon the healthy life of a coaching initiative, the risk of confirmation bias amongst cynics is particularly high.

Of course, just as there are cynics, there should almost always be enthusiasts for coaching who will stay the course come what may. But these aren't the groups that should attract the most attention from a coaching project leader. For the project leader, the most vulnerable group includes those who fall between the cynics and the advocates – in other words, everyone else. In many cases, this group will form a majority of those that the scope of the programme embraces.

So what can be done to bolster the confidence of novice coaches and limit the prospect of a coaching initiative from losing momentum?

Based on the experiences of organizations whose coaching programmes not only survived the critical post-training honeymoon period but continued to grow and thrive, as well as from observations from those who were disappointed in the outcome of their own initiatives, we believe that a combination of the following is likely to be needed:

- continuing sponsor engagement and *active* senior manager support;
- continued promotion of support services for new coaches/managers, including tips, techniques and knowledge that are likely to be directly relevant and useful in addressing day-to-day coaching and staff development needs;
- sustaining the enthusiasm that may have formed during training, including continuing delegate networks;
- maintaining early-warning alerts of possible backsliding and intervening when necessary;
- supporting the continued development of coach/'manager as coach' skill, not just by providing additional training, but by engaging with training delegates to understand what will most help them;
- providing training and appropriate support for newcomers to the organization, sufficient to enable them to become familiar with how the coaching service operates and (when appropriate) to receive training and other support necessary for building coaching skills to the level expected in their role;
- proactively seeking opportunities for individuals to practise coaching, and especially to identify opportunities for novice coaches;
- continuing to promote the benefits of coaching and publicizing success stories (subject to the agreement of those involved);
- ensuring that the systems, processes and other infrastructure needed to support coaching practice work are developed in line with changing needs (eg the ability to match requests for coaches in an in-house practice needs to be kept in step with changing demand).

We'll consider each of these below.

In each of these, while often playing the role of a facilitator, a coaching project leader needs to be proactive in seeking new opportunities for further developing the reach and business impact of coaching. This isn't to say that the responsibility for putting coaching into practice or for developing coaching skill shouldn't lie with coaches/manager themselves (and in some cases, with their own line managers too). However, project leaders who assume that all will take on this responsibility without an occasional need for a nudge from outside shouldn't be surprised when backsliding occurs.

Of course, even the best efforts of a coaching project leader can't guarantee success. Organizations are complex entities with widely varying cultures, belief sets and ways of working. What works in one organization may not work in another. To help determine what mix of interventions may help sustain and grow a coaching initiative, as well as to inform a revitalizing or relaunching of a programme, those charged with the responsibility of supporting coaching need to know their own organization and be aware of the factors that have contributed to individuals backsliding in their coaching practice. As with many things that we've mentioned, this information can be revealed through robust evaluation of individuals' coaching experience. This is a topic that we'll return to in later chapters.

Continuing sponsor engagement and active senior manager support

Engaging the ongoing interest and involvement of managers and coaches is one thing, but maintaining business sponsorship is crucial too. Not least, budgets for training and coach resources need to be sustained, commitments to allowing individuals time to coach or be coached need to be seen as continuing to be worthwhile, and the real contribution that coaching makes needs regular high-profile acknowledgement.

Coaching project leaders can play a full role in gaining the attention of and influencing their top teams and critical sponsors by being proactive and even evangelical. This will invariably involve networking within their own organization as much as with external ones. Several key ingredients are likely to be needed in any campaign to fully engage others:

- linking in with business planning;
- consulting with key stakeholders (at least once annually);
- using the right communication approach, eg restricting e-mails to brief announcements and information sharing but not when enquiring about which current business applications might be right for coaching;

- finding audience 'hot buttons' and knowing when to press them, eg speaking in terms of monetary savings when talking about coaching with a finance director;
- promoting coaching achievements with confidence, but remembering that a 'softly, softly' strategy sometimes works best;
- remembering that coachees and coaches themselves drive the initiative and won't allow it to drift if it's helping and seen as being beneficial, saving time and assisting with daily pressures.

Linking in with business planning

Tying into business planning, linking training outcomes with business drivers and critical success factors and showing how specific coaching interventions enhance the prospect of achieving performance targets create a regular opportunity for demonstrating what coaching is intended to deliver and agreeing what its new priorities should be. By becoming a cohesive element in business planning, coaching shouldn't then become seen as a subject for tactical planning to be addressed once strategic plans have been put in place.

Consulting with key stakeholders (at least once annually)

Talking to managers and executives, ideally face to face, is essential to understand their plans, targets and priorities as well as what hopes and expectations they have of what coaching can provide. Direct interaction allows for probing on specific points when needed, raising questions to clarify understanding and making proposals about coaching initiatives that can then be followed through.

Using the right communication approach

As we've noted, knowing which communication approach works best for different stakeholders is a key to pitching responses that will engage their interest and – crucially – communicate a message that coaching investments are sound.

Finding audience 'hot buttons' and knowing when to press them

Understanding how and when business strategies, budgets and plans are formulated, what matters in both the long and the short term and what their priorities and sensitivities are should give a coaching leader the insight to know which 'hot buttons' to press and when to press them.

Promoting coaching achievements with confidence, but remembering that a 'softly, softly' strategy sometimes works best

It's of course important to promote the positive impacts and memorable stories resulting from coaching, but remember that there is a time and a place for getting others to change old ways. Bright new ideas to change existing inter-department information flows and knowledge sharing may fall on deaf ears if they're not presented in the right way. Sometimes it's worth remembering that 'less is [can be] more' and that coaches and coachees should themselves be powerful ambassadors for coaching. So too, occasional affirmation and acknowledgement of the contribution made by the coaches can go a long way to winning their support (especially important when coaching is undertaken by volunteers).

Continued promotion of support services for new coaches/managers

Given the many tasks, e-mails, requests and demands that are constantly competing for their attention, it's not surprising that many coaches and (in particular) managers can quickly forget that a range of support services and aids may be available to them to help with their coaching practice. Brief, simple and regular updates for former training delegates may help prompt memories, as may making known when significant new content is added to the coaching knowledge base. This proved to be very important in Jackie's experience of building a virtual team (or 'family') of coaches within the London Metropolitan Police Service.

Such reminders are likely to be most effective if they are kept low-key. A simple, well-designed e-mail newsletter may work well: for example, comprising just a sentence or two to describe each of its various contents, with hyperlinking to pages containing fuller detail. We've even heard that some individuals seem to be more receptive of e-mails marked with a low priority flag, perhaps because the sender recognizes that they're not likely to be well placed to decide on the priorities of those who receive their messages. However, we wouldn't want to suggest that coaching topics should ever take a low priority!

One helpful reminder that can be provided periodically is anonymous services such as intranet-based search facilities that allow managers and coaches to seek answers to any question, including those that they believe they should know the answer to or didn't feel comfortable raising during training. However, this common fear may be combated in other ways too. Amongst the activities that may help managers feel comfortable to come forward with 'dumb questions' are:

- co-coaching with managers from other parts of the organization or possibly from other organizations;
- mentor support from a professional/in-house coach or learning and development specialist;
- coaching circles;
- buddy (peer-level) coaching.

We'll refer to many of these are in later sections.

Informal networking

Practice can be hard. Self-doubt can quickly set in when an individual perceives that they are making many mistakes, perhaps when attempting to act against their natural style as they attempt to form 'good' coaching questions or when trying to exercise self-discipline to avoid their mind skipping on to another question while a coachee is still in mid-thought about the last question posed.

Despite the frustrations and disappointments that practice can sometimes entail, it's essential for individuals whose natural style is to tell and form quick conclusions based on what they hear. Only through practice can slipping into a coaching approach become less hard graft and more second nature.

Indeed, research using new technology in such areas as how we evolve linguistic skills has revealed that the brain is considerably more plastic than had previously been believed. In other words, patterns of neuronal activation change and become reinforced through new experiences. The actual physical structure and functional organization of the brain change over time, building stronger neural connections in response to positive thoughts, experiences and useful learnings, and pruning those that are no longer useful.[2]

Creating the conditions to encourage informal networks – in which training delegates can regularly share their learnings, raise and discuss possible answers to questions – is more easily described in theory than it is to put into practice. The problem is that to be sustained, the members of a network must be enthusiastic, committed and proactive in arranging regular meetings.

Back-up networks and points of contact for support may be offered as a selling point for some managers, for whom the ability to talk freely with others about personal learnings or pose questions about a staff development topic may be rare. But networking is also important for another reason: it enables coaching skills to be practised.

In spite of the difficulties of getting an informal network off of the ground, the concept is nevertheless one that's worth pursuing during a training course. Beyond just giving encouragement, individuals might be invited to commit to a network for at least a defined period of time following their training, and especially when such commitment can be made a part of the assessment carried out for an accredited programme. It may be helpful to suggest a possible focus for initial networking, such as to propose an action learning set.[3] We've also observed that individuals' commitment to smaller networks appears to be generally stronger than it is to larger groups (perhaps because members may have more of a sense of letting others down if they don't regularly support the group). Of smaller groups, the triad (group of three) pattern appears to have the greatest durability.

Thus networks in which there is commitment and in which members obtain short-term benefit in their roles as managers (or coaches) are likely to have longer lives than those that are sustained simply because there is a common view that this is the 'right' thing to do. But ultimately, of course, if a network isn't giving value to the majority of its members, then it will end.

Maintaining early-warning alerts for possible backsliding, and intervening when necessary

Especially in larger organizations, no one individual can be expected to keep an ongoing watch on how well and how much coaching is being practised. Even were unlimited time available, being able to observe how coaches and managers operate would often be impractical. Much coaching takes place behind closed doors, after all.

However, coaching project leaders can gain some clues as to how well coaching is being applied. Most obviously, the outcomes of evaluation and periodic staff/coachee surveys should give a strong indication of what is happening on the ground. Similarly, departmental manager feedback may be informative, when available. Additionally, regular non-attendance of significant numbers of past delegates at review days, masterclasses, follow-on training, networking groups and the like may suggest a fall-off of interest in coaching (although there may be many good reasons for non-participation in such activities other than merely wanting to avoid coaching).

Those responsible for a coaching initiative might want to pay attention to such indicators; however, we suggest that the most powerful early-warning mechanism for checking on how well coaching is being accepted is via follow-up conversations with as many past trainees as possible (and, if possible, a sample of their staff/coachees). Ideally, such conversations should be held within three months of a delegate's training. Telephoning each individual in turn may seem to be quite a chore, but other than using audit and evaluation, it's the only sure way that we know of revealing whether coaching is being successfully embedded or not.

Supporting the continued development of coach/manager coach skill

More than training

Training is, of course, only a part of what's required to help individuals develop and keep their coaching skills fresh, and doesn't need to be restricted to group-based classroom sessions or pre-scripted courseware material either.

The following can be especially useful for helping coaches' and line managers' development:

- coaching circles;
- masterclasses;
- informal networking (eg triads);
- informal information sharing;
- inter-organization knowledge sharing;
- participation in coaching associations;
- review days;
- co-coaching (with or without observation);
- reflective practice;
- self-coaching; and
- supervision.

We'll briefly consider each of these below.

Coaching circles

A 'coaching circle' comprises a small group of coaches, typically four or more, who meet periodically to consider a coaching challenge brought by one member of the group.

The approach taken is as follows:

1 The person bringing the issue briefly describes its nature and outlines the challenge that they are facing.

2 Each other member of the group in turn then asks a clarifying question to test their understanding of the situation, while helping the issue holder to deepen their own reflections about the situation.

3 Members of the group continue to ask one question in strict succession, but without offering a comment (the sequence for asking questions is simply passed over to the next person in the circle if an individual has no question to ask).

4 Each member in the circle gives an affirmation to the issue holder, again in sequence. If they can't identify an affirmation, they then just pass over

their turn; after 10 minutes or so, the round of questioning is brought to a close and the issue owner is invited to take time away from the group to reflect on what they've heard, being encouraged to turn their back on the group if they are comfortable doing this, but not engaging in or commenting on the ongoing conversation at this point.

5 The remaining members of the group then consider their own responses to what has been discussed, and identify possible courses of action that may help the issue holder move forward.

6 The issue holder then feeds back to the group what they found useful and describes anything that they've resolved to put into action as a result.

7 The reflections of the group are shared.

One of the appeals of this approach is that very little time is usually required for a meeting to produce very practical outcomes (20 minutes is usually sufficient for any one meeting). A circle also gives each individual in the group a fair chance to readily bring an issue that is of concern to them and obtain the variety of perspectives on how they might address this. Others in the group benefit through reflecting on helpful coaching questions that are raised and by contemplating the various perspectives that are offered regarding a topic that they may themselves encounter in future.

Masterclasses

We've heard it said that the idea of a 'master' class might preclude the entire multitude of great female coaches from demonstrating their skills, but of course this isn't the case! 'Masterclass' is just one of those wonderful old English words that hasn't yet fallen foul of political correctness, at least for most people. It certainly isn't our intention to imply any gender bias by using the term.

For us, a masterclass enables less experienced coaches to observe and learn from someone who has finely tuned their craft. To observe a highly proficient coach demonstrate their skill is inspiring. Most masters perform at their best in unrehearsed coaching demonstrations.

In leading the launch of the London Metropolitan Police Service's coaching programme, Jackie was keen to engage a series of well-regarded coaches to offer their wisdom in the masterclass workshops that she had been scheduled to run every three months or so. The classes focused on different aspects of coaching (eg coaching conundrums, Solutions Focus techniques), introduced material that was new to participants (eg learning models) and profiled highly experienced coaches from a diverse range of different backgrounds and with widely differing styles. The classes were credited by attendees as being very effective in helping their own development, as well as being inspiring and enjoyable to boot!

Masterclasses aren't necessarily cheap. Hence, when commissioning them, it usually make sense to encourage attendance by as many coaches as possible (subject to practicality, of course). However, faced with an ever-tighter budget, Jackie experimented with another approach: actually charging external coaches a fee for attending masterclasses. This seemed a fair trade, as these were coaches to the organization's senior leadership team!

Informal information sharing

Coaches can learn a lot from the experiences of others, including stories of what hasn't worked well and what individuals have found to be effective. Excepting the various means for face-to-face and video/teleconference knowledge sharing described above, a brief written record of such learnings can also serve a useful purpose, especially as it can be accessed at any time by anyone, at the time that it's required.

Documenting learnings may involve a little effort, although even the briefest note can be useful. Coaches and managers may also be more prepared to contribute to and make use of a shared knowledge base if they find that there is a wealth of materials that they can draw upon – in other words, they won't always find that the 'cupboard is bare' when they come to look for help. While ideally a knowledge base would be largely self-created, in practice coaching project leaders will need to play their part in helping to populate it initially. Responsibility will also need to be delegated to ensure that learnings captured through review days and the like are recorded.

Review days

Review days (or possibly half-days), sometimes combined with a masterclass or other structured training, provide opportunities for a previous training class to come back together to share their experiences, consolidate and build upon their learnings, and set fresh action plans for further developing their coaching practice. Such workshops can help boost confidence, refresh enthusiasm and inspire with new ideas and techniques. When included as part of an accredited programme, reviews can also serve as an important marker for individuals to report on their progress and for any challenges that they've faced as they've started to coach to be aired and responded to.

While we suggest that the agenda for review days should largely be determined by attendees, it may be useful to be able to propose some elements. Jackie typically adopted the following in her sessions:

- providing an update on the progress of the coaching initiative;
- reviewing previously set action plans;
- facilitating a Solutions Focus circle;
- facilitating a question and answer forum;
- engaging others to attend review days (looking inwardly for support from well-trained and skilled people, drawing on untapped potential).

Reflective practice

Reflective practice, described by Moon as 'a set of abilities and skills, to indicate the taking of a critical stance, an orientation to problem solving or state of mind' (Moon, 2000), promotes independent learning by developing an individual's understanding and critical-thinking skills. Techniques such as self- and peer assessment, problem-based learning, personal development planning and action learning sets can all help this approach.

Reflective practice can often involve seeing what might be done differently in future coaching conversations. As Biggs puts it, 'a reflection in a mirror is an exact replica of what is in front of it. Reflection in professional practice, however, gives back not what is, but what might be, an improvement on the original' (Biggs, 1999).

Managers and coaches who commit themselves to reflective practice are likely to deepen their understanding of the process that they often encourage coachees to engage in. The practice can be illuminating not only in helping a coach build awareness of themselves and the impact of their coaching, but in helping their coachees to gain insight and understanding too.

Self-coaching

While coaching others can be very satisfying, armed with coaching skills and by following a few simple principles it's very easy for a coach or manager to coach themselves as well. Self-coaching takes reflective practice a step beyond just reflecting to drawing conclusions and committing learnings – everything that coaching others aims to achieve.

Central to the discipline of self-coaching is having an ability to channel self-talk to act as a questioner, listener and constructive critic. Applying this 'double-loop thinking' means being able to let the brain settle on one stream of thought (eg thinking, planning, reflecting) while having a separate, more detached flow of ideas that poses the questions and helps process responses. It's the second, critical and supervisory type of thinking that ensures that the reflective brain doesn't get sucked into a narrow channel of thought, while facilitating the coaching process. Some find that keeping a journal or writing ideas down helps with their reflective process, offering a two-step process for generating thoughts and then objectively critiquing and challenging them.

Skill building and further coaching skill applications for coaches and managers – what next?

There's probably no simple answer to the question of what should come next after initial coaching training. Certainly it's the case that what will be relevant for one organization may not be a priority for another. For most, review days, masterclasses and opportunities to observe and practise the coaching skills that they've already learned are more important than extending knowledge of coaching techniques.

Defining an effective training path must start with an exploration of what's really needed (eg to address the actual situations that coaches and managers have faced as they start to coach), what's actually happening on the ground, and where there are differences of need. What this reveals may not always be what coaching enthusiasts are asking for, nor what might have been assumed to be a suitable next step.

A good starting point is to ask coaches and managers what they want – those who haven't participated in post-training support, as well as those who have – and also assessing what's really happening on the ground. Apart from considering new topics, advanced coaching techniques and less familiar models, psychology training and the like, this comes back to honestly questioning how effective the earlier training has been in equipping participants to grasp 'the basics'. It's very possible that training may have skimmed over some key topics, attendees may have switched off on topics they feel they were already expert in, and significant gaps may need to be filled.

In a recent article, Clive suggested that one area that might commonly benefit from more attention is listening skill (Johnson, 2009). Teaching deep listening is hard because it's seen by many managers as being such a basic practice. This, of course, is not the case: few regularly demonstrate what Whitworth *et al* term 'level 2 listening' (Whitworth *et al*, 1998), in which a coach picks up not only what a coachee is saying, but how they are saying it. Fewer still progress to 'level 3', at which a coach understands what a coachee is actually experiencing, as though being able to see the world through their eyes.

Development topics for coaches

The following are amongst possible second-step and follow-on training options for developing coaches/managers, although their relevance depends on the stage coaching has reached and what coaches/managers say they most need:

- emotional intelligence;
- non-violent communication;
- principles of learning;
- cognitive-behavioural coaching;
- neuro-linguistic programming;

- transformational coaching;

- psychological perspectives in coaching;

- active listening;

- clean language.[4]

Unless it's enforced, follow-on training is likely to engage only the small number of managers who feel motivated to continue their development. Willing coaches and managers will always search out further opportunities for developing their skill and knowledge, possibly expanding their reading and even joining a coaching association.

However, managers who've not taken coaching into their daily repertoires may be less convinced of the value of more training, feeling that they've already 'ticked the box' by attending a foundation module. This may be especially so if their understanding of what coaching is reduces to remembering a handful of models, being able to ask a few choice questions and making sure that their coachees agree to take on board a few new action points.

For these sceptics, second-stage training needs to be seen as being worthwhile, interesting and offering something new. Bringing in an expert to offer new perspectives and fresh insights, using actors in role-plays and showing managers how to use anecdotes and image metaphors in their coaching may all help to make training more memorable and appealing.

Keeping courses brief, perhaps restricted to short breakfast or lunch-break or 'espresso' sessions and imaginative titling or branding of courses, might also be a key for encouraging high levels of attendance.

Continuous professional development for coaches – supervision

Both to help determine a suitable path for continuous professional development (CPD) and as a vital element in an individual's CPD itself, for in-house coaches, supervision is essential. We'll consider what supervision means and why it's important in a coach's development in Chapter 10. However, it's worth mentioning now that as a part of sustaining good coaching practice, supervisors themselves need to be identified and their own professional development requirements need to be catered for.

Providing training and appropriate support for newcomers

Newcomers to an organization who are expected to take on a coaching role and who've not previously received appropriate training obviously need to be equipped to take on this responsibility.

However, where a need for training is identified, it may not necessarily be the case that the same training offered to others previously may still be available. A range of factors may limit what can be provided. Amongst examples are the non-availability of an (external) training facilitator, the need for a minimum class size to undertake exercises and role-plays, and tightened budgets.

Coaching project leaders may then need to consider possible alternative development support that can be provided to fill the gaps in an individual's knowledge and skill set, and in some cases, catering for just one person's training at a time. This may involve using a mix of self-taught material, specially arranged role-play exercises and dedicated one-to-one support. One possible aid that we suggest might usefully be included in newcomer training is a video recording of a previous masterclass or role-play demonstration.

Proactively seeking opportunities for individuals to practise coaching

Nothing is more critical for embedding coaching as a core management discipline or in maintaining acceptable levels of coaching competency than offering new coaches opportunities to practise playing the role of a coach. In particular, being able to target individuals who are not seen as 'soft touches' to be coachees serves to show that coaching is for those in front-line operational roles as much as for anyone else.

Ideally, practice should take the form of coaching individuals who've requested coaching voluntarily or for whom there is a clear benefit for coaching – in other words, working with genuine clients. For managers who are keen to apply coaching skill in conversations with their own staff, there should be ample opportunities in this regard. However, for newly trained (and sometimes not so newly trained) members of an in-house coach pool, such opportunities may not always be available. Moreover, some coaches may be selected by potential clients more regularly than are others, creating a risk that some coaches may need to wait a long time before they can put their skills to good use with 'real' clients.

Those who are responsible for matching coaches with coachees may occasionally be able to help promote coaches who seem to spend much of their time waiting for opportunities to coach, for example by reassuring prospective coachees that a coach's recent induction to the coach pool doesn't mean that they are any less able than others to act competently.

However, as we've seen, the decision of whom to select as a coach must ultimately rest with a coachee.

There would then seem to be a potential dilemma, both for underutilized coaches and for those who have greater demands put upon them: that ultimately both may want to opt out of the coaching pool. One possible response to this is to ensure that underused coaches continue to receive opportunities for practice, even when clients are few and far between. Two approaches that can help are co-coaching and buddy coaching, both of which involve the same application of skill and attention that might be expected in a client-initiated relationship.

Co-coaching

The principle of co-coaching is simple: individuals are paired up and then meet regularly to practise their coaching skills. Usually, this involves one of the pair acting as coach to the other in one session, with the roles being reversed in their subsequent conversation. As an option, both can also opt to allow a third party to observe their coaching, with the observer then providing feedback to the coach after the session (where the pair is extended to a triad, the roles of coach, coachee and observer may be alternated). An informal review and exchange of feedback may also be given between a co-coach pair at the end of coaching sessions.

Novice coaches who are able to receive coaching themselves are further advantaged. Not only does coming to coaching as a client allow an individual to appreciate the perspective of a coachee's experience and benefit from the deep-searching, insight and inspiration that coaching produces, but it also helps build a stronger appreciation of how the coaching process works. Especially for more cynical managers, the opportunity to be on the receiving end of coaching can be the straw that breaks the camel's back in their resistance.

Some may argue that co-coaching amongst novice coaches may encourage a low standard being set, lacking as it does input from an experienced coach. We would beg to differ. Not only are many new coaches very capable and want to improve their skills, but they are very able to offer constructive criticism when playing the role of a coachee or observer. What's more, robust foundation training, regular review, supervision and moderation (amongst other support activities) help ensure that strong standards are maintained and developed. Indeed, playing the role of an observer during networking activities and training exercises can often be as informative as playing the role of a coach or coachee.

Buddy (peer-level) coaching

Buddying is simply a variation of co-coaching, in which individuals commit to regularly coach each other. Buddy relationships are normally established at a peer level, although not invariably.

Continuing to promote the benefits of coaching and publicizing success stories

One of the main reasons why coaching programmes falter is that once trained, managers are inclined to return to their old ways of working. The benefits that coaching can bring that might have been recognized during a training course can quickly become a distant memory when attention becomes diverted to more pressing matters. For senior managers and other stakeholders too, enthusiasm for coaching may weaken once the decision to fund a training programme becomes a point in history.

An implication is that before, during and after training, the benefits of coaching for managers and for the organization need to be sold. Here, the common rules for making almost any major new initiative stick apply: piling on top team leadership and enthusiasm, presenting a programme as a positive for all rather than as a bright new idea that is being imposed, and sustaining a strong momentum of upbeat communication.

Coaching project leaders are likely to need to take the lead in continuing to promote the case for coaching, although their task should become easier as evidence of coaching impacts builds up (one reason why periodic evaluation is important). Enlisting genuine interest and support from senior-level sponsors should also become easier as evidence of what coaching has delivered accumulates. At the same time, coaches/managers who've themselves become coaching advocates can play a part in publicizing what coaching is achieving in their informal conversations with other managers.

Ensuring that the systems, processes and other infrastructure needed to support coaching practice work and are developed in line with changing needs

The support available to coaches/managers and the infrastructure needed to allow a coaching service to operate effectively obviously need to be maintained in step with users' needs. While careful implementation planning should ensure that the systems and processes that are put in place at the outset should stand the test of time, this can't be accepted as a foregone conclusion. It's then incumbent on any coaching project leader to ensure that the supporting infrastructure remains fit for purpose.

Sustaining coaching for organizational development

Coaching and HR policy

As we mentioned in Chapter 4, some objectives for implementing a coaching programme (eg the level of take-up by managers intended at a particular point in time) may be more readily achieved where coaching responsibilities or targets can be incorporated into an organization's formal control mechanisms. Reflecting responsibilities and expectations for coaching in such things as role descriptions, managers' annual targets and project quality plans may help to communicate what is expected and enforce participation.

Over time, HR policies may change, perhaps in step with changing people-management strategy or to reflect new ways of conducting staff appraisals, recruitment selection, managing performance and developing the organization's talent base, and more. The potential implications of changing HR policy for existing coaching applications therefore need to be kept in check, as well as ensuring that any resulting new demands on coaching can be met.

Coaching and learning and development strategy

Coaching may or may not be managed discretely from learning and development activities. For one thing, coaching isn't just used for developing people; as a management discipline, it should be part and parcel of a manager's skills repertoire. However, coaching can play a very significant role in any organization's learning and development strategy.

One such role is helping individuals to consolidate and apply learning in complementing other forms of training. The impact of such intervention can be striking: one US study cited combined coaching and training as improving an increase in productivity by 88 per cent, compared with a 22 per cent rise resulting from training alone (Olivero *et al*, 1997).

Even where coaching is managed discretely from a learning and development function, it's therefore important that its potential contribution is readily reviewed in line with changing training needs. This calls for leaders of coaching programmes to be proactive in liaising with training department manages, not just when planning implementation initially, but on a regular basis. Those responsible for learning strategy too need to fully appreciate the contribution that coaching may make towards achieving specific objectives set for their learning initiatives and to be open to the prospect of giving up responsibility for aspects of people development when coaching may offer a preferable alternative to other options.

Beyond company walls

Inter-organization knowledge sharing

Much can be gained from sharing experiences with other organizations. Learning from others formed an important part of Jackie's preparation for launching the coaching programme within the London Metropolitan Police Service, but knowledge sharing can benefit any organization at any stage in a coaching implementation.

Of course, just because something has worked in one organization doesn't mean that the same will necessarily apply elsewhere. Nevertheless, potential pitfalls may be highlighted, ideas to consider might be revealed that might not otherwise have been thought of, and confidence may be gained by talking with someone who has faced similar challenges.

Knowledge sharing between coaches and managers across organizations can play an important part too. Any of the networking activities that we've suggested can be extended to involve coach/managers from different employers. Some may prefer having the opportunity to share their experiences with individuals who are completely outside their peer-group and line management structure and who don't share the same organizational mindset. Co-coaching especially can work very well when individuals from different organizations come together.

Making contact with other organizations can usually be easily facilitated through a professional coaching body, HR/coaching forum (eg member groups created via LinkedIn or similar online social networking services), or by simply picking up the phone and approaching others who've shared their experiences in the coaching press.

Some inter-organizational networks have established a very strong grounding. For example, in the UK, many government departments and agencies have combined to form a cross-government coaching network, while several regional health trusts have established coaching networks of their own, complete with regular co-coaching events, newsletters and annual conferences.

CASE STUDY   The power of 1+1:
The Kent Coaching & Mentoring Network

Close to a dozen prominent organizations in England's 'garden county' benefit from free access to a network of around 180 coaches, all of whom come with the assurance of having undertaken a comprehensive training and accreditation scheme.

The Kent Coaching & Mentoring Network began as the brainchild of Coral Ingleton, Learning and Development Manager with Kent County Council, as a partnership between the Council and Kent Fire & Rescue Service in which both organizations pooled their resources to develop, train and support coaches. Now, more than five years after its launch, the Network operates without a specific budget, breaking even by charging new joiners a one-off fee to train their coaches.

Continuing training, supervision and biannual conferences are a part of the package available to members, and after initial funding of their coaches' training, organizations within the Network enjoy corporate membership of the Association for Coaching, have access to a newly implemented coach/coachee matching and support tool (Mye-Coach), and are also able to request coaching for anyone in their organization.

Coaching is offered on a reciprocal basis, and isn't restricted by a coachee's rank or desired use for coaching (although some organizations offer differing guidance on who may request coaching). Support for talent management, career development and leading staff through a divisional restructuring are amongst the themes that have been tackled by the Network's coaches.

Serena Cunningham, who jointly manages the Network, puts its success down to allowing the concept time to become established, working with just a single partner at the outset, and building the infrastructure needed to support coaches. She believes that avoiding over-promotion of the Network has been important for sustaining its growth, while offering a secondary benefit that coachees take responsibility for seeking out coaching for themselves.

Now, having recently accepted its 13th cohort of delegates into its accreditation programme and with a growing interest in membership, the networking concept has more than proven the value of combining '1+1'.

Participation in coaching associations

Professional bodies such as the International Coach Federation and Association for Coaching provide excellent opportunities for CPD, co-coaching and networking. In addition to providing another option for individuals to develop skills and practice with others, involvement in such organizations enables individuals to benefit from sharing experiences with coaches from many different backgrounds.

Information sources

In addition to home-grown materials, a wide variety of fact sheets, guidance notes, suggestions and insights are available in the public domain. Websites such as www.cipd.co.uk, www.shrm.org and www.coachingnetwork.org. uk offer a range of advice and materials for downloading, while we have included our own package of 'downloadables' on the website supporting this book, www.managingcoachingatwork.com.

Coaching topics are often in the news too, not just in the HR and training press but more generally. Dedicated magazines such as *Coaching at Work* and *Choice: The Magazine of Professional Coaching* offer a wide mix of articles, news features, case studies and practical tools for coaches and managers, both in printed and online versions, while professional coaching associations similarly publish their own newsletters and journals. Coaching is also the specific or a primary theme for a number of academic journals, several of which are listed in Appendix C2.

Summary

Keeping the passion for coaching alive in any organization is not a task to be taken lightly. In the period following training it is especially critical for managers and in-house coaches alike to be able to consolidate their learnings, and it is also the period in which confidence to coach may be challenged and first attempts that are perceived as 'failures' may lead to discouragement. The key premise on which a coach's motivation and competency must be built is – 'practise, practise, practise'.

Backsliding is a genuine problem at any stage, but is most likely to occur during the early months following an individual's coaching training. At the same time, people may come and go, sponsor priorities may change and clients for coaching won't necessarily always be available at the time novice coaches most need to be able to put their new skills into practice.

While there are usually likely to be advocates of coaching who will need little encouragement to make coaching a part of their mindset and there will often be a small minority who will quickly revert to old ways too, a range of practical steps can help ensure that the interest of others continues to be engaged. Amongst these, informal networking, co-coaching, review activities and supervision may all offer benefits to those who engage with them.

Notes

1 'Factor analysis': a statistical process in which the values of observed data items are organized according to a number of possible factors that could explain the pattern they reveal, from which the most prominent factors can be identified.

2 A useful summary of recent developments in neuroscience research and their implications for coaching is provided in David Rock and Linda J Page's excellent book, *Coaching with the Brain in Mind* (Rock and Page, 2009).

3 'Action learning set': an approach to learning based on determining actions to try, putting these into practice and then reflecting on what has been discovered. Usually involves group working in the reflection and action-planning activities.

4 'Clean language' is a concept pioneered in the 1980s by the late New Zealander psychologist David Grove, referring to giving attention to questioning that doesn't become contaminated by a therapist's [or coach's] world view. See Grove and Panzer (1989).

PART THREE
Outcomes

Auditing and evaluating coaching

Introduction

Proving the real returns of initiatives that often produce what are seen as 'soft outputs' has long proved a luckless task. This is especially the case when a range of influences other than the topic in focus (coaching) can come into play, and also when considering that much coaching takes place behind closed doors. To use an analogy we've introduced before – sometimes, evaluating coaching can be like nailing jelly to a wall!

However, if a jelly's consistency is thick enough and its flavour is what's desired, then this can be achieved. In the case of evaluation, we might think of this mix of right consistency and desired flavour as having a robust explanation for what's concluded, being properly aligned with the questions posed by a particular evaluation study and applying a proven methodology.

It may be easy for coaches and the people they coach to recognize the clear outcomes of their regular sessions. The ability to distinguish the results of coaching may not be such a worry if a coachee is him- or herself a sponsor or budget holder. However, for those outside coaching relationships, the impacts of coaching – the actual results of this special but often expensive relationship – may often remain a mystery, and one for which buyers of coaching services are likely to want assurances before signing off fresh purchase orders.

Where the impacts of executive coaching are concerned, some bold claims have certainly been made. Take the following as examples:

> 'Coaching produced intangible and monetary benefits for seven out of eight business impact areas; and ROI of $3,268,325 (689 percent)' (Parker-Wilkins, 2006).

'Even after adopting a conservative approach to determining the return on investment, we demonstrated a 700% return on the coaching initiative' (Anderson and Anderson, 2004).

and the often-quoted but also much-criticized *Manchester Review* offering:

'Coaching made a ROI of 545 per cent, or that for every dollar invested in coaching, executives estimated that it contributed $5.45 to the business' (McGovern *et al*, 2001).

There's little doubt that such studies have attempted to apply a rigorous method in reaching their conclusions, but inevitably, such studies are usually beset with problems (see 'Some common limitations of evaluation approaches', below).

Worryingly, while the number of organizations that have invested in coaching programmes has been increasing, the percentages that routinely evaluate coaching appear to be falling. Pointing to the 2010 Learning and Talent Development survey conducted by the Chartered Institute of Personnel and Development (CIPD), Dr John McGurk, senior advisor to the CIPD on learning and talent, notes that only a little more than a third (36 per cent) of responding companies say that they evaluate coaching in some way – and this figure doesn't give any indication of how robustly such evaluation is carried out (CIPD, 2010; McGurk, 2010a). Not a pretty picture of the state of coaching evaluation!

We've often referred to the importance of evaluation in preceding chapters. We doubt that few would argue that seeking to discover what any initiative that costs time, money and human resource is delivering and how effectively it is achieving this isn't a worthwhile pursuit. However, evaluation itself takes time and presents a number of challenges, as we'll see.

We consider evaluation to be of such importance that we dedicate this and much of the next chapter to it, as well as returning in Chapter 10 to consider how evaluation and audit outputs can be used to help inform the future course of coaching investments.

Audit or evaluation?

We define auditing as a 'comprehensive, objective process of taking stock of any or various aspects of a coaching implementation'. This might simply include knowing how many people receive coaching, what degree of effort is put into providing it, what continuing professional development of coaches is occurring, and the like. Our definition may also be extended to assessing the capability of an organization's coaching facility, how this measures up against a level of aspiration (eg one of the levels of the Coaching Focus model, described in Chapter 4) and whether or not coaching activity is aligned with business need. In other words, the term 'audit' can take on quite a broad meaning beyond just establishing a 'coaching balance sheet', something that can come close to what we might interpret as being 'evaluation', considering not just what exists but how it's being delivered and why it's delivering what's observed.

An audit or discovery exercise usually focuses on describing a situation at a point in time, perhaps covering a defined period, but nonetheless representing a snapshot. Evaluation usually does likewise, but may be more likely to consider the future implications of the current state. However, audits are often used to inform decision making too: again, the distinction can be blurred (note that we'll consider how to use results of audit in Chapter 10).

There may be considerable overlap in the types of data gathered and approaches used for analysis in evaluation and audit, and arguably, 'evaluation' might be seen to encompasses 'audit'. We therefore choose to consider both together, although our own preference is to talk about 'evaluation' when seeking to get to the *impacts*, the *why* and the *how* of a coaching implementation.

Definitions for some other common concepts

While we're wrestling with the meaning of audit and evaluation, we might usefully propose a few definitions for terms that commonly arise in relation to them. As always with definitions, some may beg to differ from our offerings, so be sure to understand what others mean when hearing these.

Return on investment (ROI) usually applies to the financial benefits of carrying out a particular course of action (eg a coaching programme). Expressed in absolute terms as a percentage, ROI = (total benefits — total costs) ÷ (total costs) × 100. Total benefits may include financial savings and money made as a result of the investment. Total costs will usually include the investment (eg training) costs, cost of participants' time, any physical materials used etc, sometimes also including departmental overheads.

Sometimes, measuring ROI in absolute financial or performance terms is achievable. This is especially the case when considering a one-time, specific skill-related area such as coaching call centre staff on how to gain most value from using a new IT system. In such cases, it should be possible to calculate tangible change (eg in productivity – such as the number of calls satisfactorily handled by the call centre within a particular period compared with the previous situation).

However, as one commentator observes, 'the idea of an absolute number that shows the exact value returned for an exact value invested in [coaching] is a seductive idea. In some cases, it's quite attainable. In others, it may simply be a seductive idea' (Flynn, 1998). In his guide to coaching evaluation, McGurk too challenges the overemphasis that's often placed on figuring out ROI, arguing that this can be an unhelpful distraction and seldom the answer for understanding what difference coaching may be making (McGurk, 2010b).

'ROI' may be used in a more general sense to refer to the recognized benefits that have resulted from a course of action – the 'soft' benefits such as improved staff morale as well as the 'hard', such as improvements in productivity.

To assess whether hard ROI is appropriate or possible, we suggest:

- understanding what can be measured, when and how;
- weighing the time and effort involved against the rewards;
- ensuring that the results can be acted on, making knowledge of ROI a focus for learning and improvement, not just historical analysis; and
- remembering that ROI is always just a snapshot – short-, mid- and long-term benefits accrue at different times and sometimes in unexpected ways.

Setting a minimum *ROI threshold* avoids a need to quantify benefits precisely in financial terms. The investment is judged to have given a positive return if a particular benefit target is achieved or if the cost of benefits has exceeded the costs of the investment. This may be most suitable when time is limited for calculating absolute ROI or where a 'yes or no' assessment of value is what's required.

Opportunity costs are the true costs of what is given up in order to achieve something else. These may be costs saved (or extra income generated) as a result of preferring one course of action to another. For example, if one group of individuals are coached but another performing the same role aren't, it should be possible to determine whether the productivity increases of coached staff (or whatever other cost benefits are hoped for) are greater than the time and costs that the coaching involved relative to an un-coached control group.

Return on expectations (ROE) refers to the extent to which an investment has delivered against what those sponsoring it and/or others expected of it. Note that 'ROE' can have another meaning for finance executives and venture capitalists, who may more commonly use the term when talking about 'return on equity'.

With ROE, sponsors and/or others involved in the initiative usually decide at the outset what they want to achieve from it (or at least will have a view of expected benefits if asked at another time). The decision to invest is satisfied if the ROE targets are reached, or as one commentator put it, 'when [an organization's] leaders stand up and say "we had a really good year, meeting [or exceeding] our business goals", then I know that the [coaching] has been successful' (Tobin, 1998).

Principles of audit and evaluation

We suggest that key principles for audit and evaluation are that they should:

- be objective, not prejudiced by an evaluator/auditor's opinions;
- protect the anonymity of contributors of data used in analysis;
- respect the privacy of what is discussed in coaching conversations (ie individuals should only disclose what they choose to disclose);
- use meaningful data inputs that put quality before quantity, and which are relevant, rationalized, insightful and representative

(sufficiently sized samples to be statistically significant, and using stratified samples when appropriate[1]);

- avoid unnecessary activity, unless this adds significant value: for example, by limiting the time expected of participants in an audit/evaluation study, limiting survey questions to strictly what needs to be known;

- quantify only what can reasonably be quantified without a need for excessive time, resource and assumption making (note: quantification might include performance contributions, costed benefits and savings); and

- use data gained from surveys to inform, not to conclude.

In addition, we believe that evaluation should provide a compelling explanation for what has resulted from coaching that:

- makes sense of a mix of different data inputs (eg perceptions, performance data, anecdotes);

- answers devil's advocate questions such as 'Why has coaching made a difference?';

- isolates the impacts of different influences and different initiatives;

- gets to the 'why?' as well as the 'what?'; and

- makes clear the relationship between the outcomes of coaching and the organization's needs and priorities.

What to evaluate (or audit)?

Various reasons may prompt a need for evaluation. In some cases, just a single point of focus may be relevant.

Evaluation is usually likely to focus on what coaching has achieved, how effectively it's being delivered and whether investment should be sustained at the current level. Additionally, in her comprehensive study of coaching evaluation undertaken at the UK's Institute for Employment Studies, Alison Carter emphasizes the importance of considering the perspectives of coach, coachee and organization, as well as examining the processes that enable a coaching function to work (Carter, 2007).

Carter believes that using a framework incorporating these different perspectives adds value in evaluation, but observes that the needs of these different audiences for evaluation must be considered in advance, with coaches and others being engaged in the process of measurement. She further suggests that assessing the impacts of coaching long after a coaching relationship ends is normally difficult in practice, while noting that evaluating up front what potential coaching is likely to have in any cultural or systematic change is not straightforward (Carter, 2007, p 50).

Typical questions that an evaluator might seek to answer include:

- What are the impacts of [our] coaching investment (now and over a longer term, financial and otherwise)?
- How can we be sure that these specifically result from coaching?
- What is making the difference?
- Are we doing the right thing?
- Are we doing it [coaching] right?
- Is there a better way?
- Are the benefits sticking and will they last the test of time?
- What is being contributed to the organization?
- What should we do next?
- What should we magnify – what's working and we should do more of?

More specific questions may apply. For example, a study of a manager coach training programme might consider:

- How has coaching impacted on individuals' skills, knowledge, confidence, career management and proficiency?
- What contribution has coaching made in the development of talent and in suitably equipping individuals for their roles?
- How do the impacts that are directly attributable to coaching translate into 'business impact' (eg through staff motivation and proficiency, self-initiative in career development, readiness of individuals for new roles, achievement of performance objectives)?

Similarly, questions that an evaluation of an in-house coach programme might explore include:

- Which aspects of the programme have proved to be most effective (eg in the choice of coach, sourcing of in-house/external coaches, nature of coaching discussions)?
- Which have given most benefit?
- What are the impacts on coachees' capabilities?
- Are clear performance differences apparent when comparing individuals who have received coaching with those who haven't?
- What direction (including any changes, if relevant) might be considered for sustaining in-house coaching talent and enhancing coaches' professional development?

Who wants to know and for what purpose?

Of course, the question of what to evaluate must be largely influenced by the needs of those who have a vested interest in the study's findings. Critical stakeholder interests are likely to include coaching programme leaders, sponsors and funders, HR and learning directors, line managers and finance executives. Each is likely to have differing perspectives and information priorities, for example:

- For those responsible for leading coaching initiatives, knowing what's really being delivered is critical for pinning down what is and isn't working.
- HR directors may look at whether the skill levels, talent pool and recognition of strengths required by the organization are being fulfilled.
- Executives may focus on the strategic fit of the capabilities that coaching delivers, and their relevance to the organization's external reputation and competitiveness.
- Finance directors may want to know whether a coaching investment is offering a profitable return, and what level of investment should be sustained in the initiative (if any).
- Business managers may put emphasis on performance, profit, productivity and levels of customer satisfaction.
- Project managers may concern themselves with how freeing individuals for coaching better enables them to achieve goals.
- Line managers may worry about the extent to which coaching is developing individuals and increasing their performance and contribution to a team.
- Employees may be most concerned with work satisfaction, personal progression, well-being or having a sense of being valued by the organization.

Why evaluating coaching is hard

Of the organizations that had implemented a coaching programme that we consulted, very few could say what their initiatives were really delivering beyond isolated examples of impact. Those who could had generally set very specific objectives for coaching at the outset and also tended to have access to a wealth of performance data – contact centres, mystery shopper surveys, sales team performance and the like. This finding was striking, but brought home to us the extent of the challenges of evaluation. The following are amongst the more common challenges that were reported in our consultations:

- privacy;
- uncertain objectives;
- differing objectives; and
- complicating factors.

Privacy

At least where what we call 'pure' coaching is concerned, most (if not all) coaching conversations take place behind closed doors. It's a primary tenet of a coaching relationship that confidentiality should be maintained between a coach and coachee, without which individuals would often feel reluctant to explore their thoughts and feelings openly.

On the surface then, an evaluator's task to establish what happens during a coaching dialogue might appear to be doomed from the outset. This would be true were it necessary to understand the specifics of what is discussed, but evaluation doesn't call for this. Rather, individuals may be asked to comment anonymously on how they perceive the coaching relationship to work. For example, a coachee might be asked to offer observations of their coach's effectiveness in contracting, their ability to ask appropriate questions and the like, but without needing to identify who the coach in question is or give specific examples of conversation dialogues that they've had with them. Similarly, a coachee may feel at liberty to talk about some quite specific results of coaching and be able to rationalize why coaching was significant in bringing about such outcomes without having to breach the principle of confidentiality in their relationship with their coach.

Talking in general terms about how a coach coaches and pointing to specific instances that have occurred outside coaching conversations should enable appropriate evidence to be collected for many of the questions that an evaluation seeks to answer. This said, we strongly recommend that any individual who is asked to take part in an evaluation or audit study is made aware that they should comment only on those things that they feel they have liberty to comment on and which in their view wouldn't compromise the contract that they have with their coach or coachee.

Uncertain objectives

It may not be possible to set clear goals for coaching when a coaching relationship is begun, or even desirable to do so. Even where the context for coaching is clear and desired outcomes can be articulated, the needs an individual has to address in moving towards such an outcome may often only become apparent once a coaching dialogue has begun. To evaluate impacts may therefore involve reference to a target outcome and the progress towards achieving this rather than achievement of a specific, measurable goal.

Differing objectives

While coaching may be used by some organizations only for specific applications (eg to support a change programme or help individuals to prepare for a new role), in other situations the topics that are brought to coaching may be as varied as the number of individuals participating in them.

In terms of both individual and organizational impacts, the effects of coaching may be relatively large or small and relate to different areas of change (eg in attitude, skill and self-awareness). Evaluation may therefore need to disentangle the significance of these differing effects and assess how they collectively contribute to performance measures that have relevance for an individual, group or organization as a whole.

Complicating factors

Coaching rarely occurs in a vacuum, independently of other potential influences on a coachee's thinking and behaviour. Both positive and negative factors may combine to help facilitate one person's progress towards achieving the outcomes they hoped that coaching would produce. For example, opportunities to put what has been planned in a coaching session into practice may or may not be available, managers and other colleagues may or may not be supportive of an individual's attempts to make changes, and other interventions designed to help a coachee (eg training and action learning sets) may be combined with their coaching.

The CIPD's John McGurk also points out that coaching may be just one of a number of different variables that can come into the mix of what makes a difference, albeit noting that the fewer variables that exist, the easier it may be to emphasize coaching's contribution (McGurk, 2010b).

All potential factors need to be taken into account when assessing the results of coaching. However, as we'll see, while this is a serious task, it's not necessarily one that has to be burdensome.

Challenges some of the preceding considerations may be, although these can usually be readily overcome. In our view, some approaches to evaluation accomplish this better than others. It's therefore appropriate for us now to turn our attention to their relative merits.

Some approaches to evaluation

Our main reference source for identifying approaches to evaluation that might be applied to coaching is the wealth of experience and insight that has accumulated regarding evaluating learning programmes. With their potential use for evaluating 'the intangible' as opposed to judging an unambiguous outcome intended in some forms of training (eg teaching a foreign language), we've singled out the following:

- Donald Kirkpatrick's 'four levels' model;
- return on expectations (paired interviews);
- benchmarking;
- control groups; and
- the Net Promoter's Score.

We'll briefly describe each of these below and in Chapter 9 we will introduce a further approach that's our particular favourite.

Donald Kirkpatrick's 'four levels' model

Donald Kirkpatrick's 'four levels' model (Kirkpatrick, 1998) is perhaps the best-known approach for evaluating training. This develops evaluation in four stages:

1 'reactions', captured during or immediately following training (ie the 'happy sheet' delegates are normally asked to complete at the end of a course);

2 'learnings', an assessment some weeks or months later of what delegates have actually learned;

3 'behaviour change', or what delegates have actually taken on board; and finally

4 'results', or what impact the training has had on individuals' performance and business contribution.

A fifth level ('returns') is sometimes added, advocated by Jack Phillips, a contemporary and student of Kirkpatrick. Phillips argued that assessing return on investment goes beyond examining an organization's results, involving different activities and delivering what is ultimately quantified information (Phillips, 1997). For some, his fifth level might be seen more as a breakdown of level 4 than a discrete level in its own right. A little tautology may be in play here; however, this probably isn't a very productive argument to concern ourselves with now.

Return on expectations (paired interviews)

Consultations with coaching sponsors and project leaders should normally form part of any evaluation, providing the critical knowledge of what the people who sponsor coaching believe has been delivered. In many ways, this is the key test for virtually all evaluation.

Sponsor judgements may be based on perception, feedback that they have received or 'hard evidence', depending on the nature of the initiative and their level of direct engagement with those affected by it.

For many, good feeling and perception are enough to justify ongoing investments. Sometimes, the weight of evidence that points in either a positive or negative direction is clear for everyone to see. For example, someone with an 'attitude problem' might emerge from a few sessions with a coach as a 'new' person, or a timid manager who didn't have the confidence to delegate might suddenly shows a new self-assurance. Such examples may please a sponsor; however, it's still important to know whether coaching alone has made the difference and whether what are believed to be the crucial influencing factors actually have been responsible for the change.

Understanding whether a sponsor's expectations are being achieved usually involves:

- clarifying what types of benefits were expected from the coaching;
- seeking anecdotal evidence of perceived impacts, which may reveal what a sponsor has witnessed directly rather than what he or she has been led to believe by others;
- pinning down a sponsor's real response to the question 'What's in it for me?' (ie what their payoff is); and
- identifying the period over which stakeholders would expect to see a payback, and the extent of payback they hope for in future.

Research conducted by Portsmouth University adopted an interesting variation on the ROE approach as a part of a CIPD Change Agenda study (Anderson, 2007a). The team's initial phase of research sought to understand what chief executives, other directors and learning and development managers felt about training evaluation, using paired interviews with each.[2] Separate interviews allowed any gaps between each interviewee's perception of value to be highlighted against their differing perspectives of achieving improved business performance and developing people. However, while return on expectation partner interviews may be helpful for obtaining different views, they remain the views of just two people. Where more than two stakeholders have a vested interest in a coaching initiative, pairing will never give a full picture of what is perceived.

Interestingly, the Portsmouth study also revealed that pinpointing exact financial ROI isn't uppermost amongst most CEOs' concerns. Rather, the research showed that ROE does play an important part. The study also pointed out the potential relevance of different approaches to evaluation depending on the extent to which an organization valued the short-term rather than long-term contribution of training and the extent of the trust that senior managers placed in the contribution of learning. A low level of trust and emphasis on achieving benefits in the short term might point to a need for metrics-based evaluation (for example), whereas a high level of trust and focus on the longer-term impacts might favour ROE as an approach (Anderson, 2007a, p 11).

While this may describe what sponsors might want from evaluation, we prefer to pose the question of whether everything needs to be quantifiable to be credible. For reasons that will become clear when we introduce the thinking behind our preferred approach to evaluation in Chapter 9 ('the balance of probabilities' approach), we strongly doubt that this is so.

Beyond paired interviews, a range of sponsors, managers or others might also be asked to estimate the financial value of the results of an investment. While this may be a somewhat crude approach, it can be very telling of the perceived value each places on it, especially if most individuals in a particular role offer similar views.

CASE STUDY   Learning, growing and believing:
Electricity Supply Board, Republic of Ireland

With a workforce of around 7,000 people, the Electricity Supply Board (ESB) is one of Ireland's largest employers. The company has never been a stranger to facing major challenges. It's post-war programme to connect the bulk of Ireland's rural population to the National Grid has been described as a 'quiet revolution' and it now faces the combined challenges of tough competition, satisfying regulators and meeting consumer demand. At the same time, the company is committed to playing its part in helping Ireland meet its obligations to reduce its carbon emissions under the Kyoto Protocol to the United Nations Framework Convention on Climate Change.

Retention of skilled and adaptable staff is seen as being vital to achieving these challenges. Coaching is a linchpin in the process. As ESB's Head of Coaching, Paddy Stapleton, explains, 'People want to know where they stand. Coaching achieves this by focusing on each individual's potential and how this relates to the business strategy... it helps close the gap between achieving potential and current performance, and this enables us to develop high-performing leaders capable of taking the company forward.'

By clarifying what the organization expects from its people, providing a means for evaluating performance and giving direct feedback, coaching helps to create self-awareness of the behavioural adjustments individuals may need to make. Coaching has now being mainstreamed into core HR processes like performance management, recruitment selection and training and development conversations.

The company launched its coaching programme in 2006, and now has a pool comprising 70 internal and six external coaches. Close attention is paid to coaches' professional development, with a wide variety of activities enabling coaches to gain further practice and feedback as well as contributing their own ideas regarding how the organization's coaching practice should be developed. Professional training, 'triad' coaching circles and an annual conference are included amongst these. Before being accepted into the pool, external coaches must undergo a rigorous selection process; a similar process is now used for recruiting internal coaches.

In introducing coaching, ESB adopted a strategy of progressive development, ensuring that lessons could be learned from earlier experiences to ensure that what was put in place was appropriate for the organization's needs. Now having achieved a level of maturity with a strong support infrastructure in place and wide-scale board-level acceptance of the vital contribution of coaching, Stapleton has been able to reflect on what has been most important in achieving the current state.

Amongst a variety of factors, he cites 'the quality of coaches, professional standards and the rigorous selection process used by the external coach panel' as being particularly significant, but also recognizes that it's important to 'coach the right people'. A case in point is the use of coaching as a part of the company's 'First 100 Days' programme, in which coaching helps newly promoted managers to adopt a positive focus and vision, to feel reassured as they settle into new roles and recognize that the company actively demonstrates a real commitment to invest in people. Such experiences have given coaching considerable traction and helped build its positive image.

Equally important, evaluation has been taken very seriously. Coaching activities are tracked on an ongoing basis, allowing important issues to be picked up and organizational learnings to be captured and acted upon. This has supported the implementation strategy to recognize 'what works' and to flex the implementation model accordingly. Managers at all levels have been engaged by the coaching team's attention to communicating what coaching is about (a recent independent evaluation revealed that 88 per cent of managers who have been coached value coaching highly).

At the same time, top-level management support has been ongoing (coaching was actively sponsored by the executive director of HR, Luke Shinnors). Some senior managers even engage in external coaching forums such as the European Mentoring and Coaching Council (EMCC) and some have become evangelical about coaching. For example, the chief executive frequently extols the benefits of coaching when speaking to external audiences. As such, coaching has been embraced with a genuine recognition of the role it plays within the organization, rather than paying lip service to something that it's believed the company should be doing. The appointment of a senior manager with significant experience and credibility to lead the coaching programme (Stapleton) has also been important in making sure that coaching has become seen as a mainstream activity rather than a project with a limited life.

Demand for coaching is likely to remain strong, since the company never stands still – change is a constant feature and challenge. In 2008, ESB committed a €22 billion investment programme in international growth and developing sustainable networks (including smart metering, renewable energy and energy conservation), with the goal of halving its carbon emissions by 2020. A need to cater for such demands mean that talent management, creativity, staff adaptability and further improvement in performance mean more than just fine words.

Luke Shinnors sadly passed away before the publication of this book. Luke kindly helped us during our consultations and we would like to pay tribute to him.

Benchmarking

Benchmarking is considered by some to be a form of evaluation, based on the premise that a benchmark standard should be widely accepted and verified as representing a suitable way to do things (eg the competency levels that coaches should demonstrate). By performing 'correctly' it might be argued that everything else should fall into place, including delivering benefit. Evaluation using this approach aims to assess how well the organization's coaching capability measures up against a predefined standard.

Comparing an organization's performance with another (similar) business isn't necessarily without value, neither is seeking to achieve a particular standard that's likely to become a worthy target to aim toward, be this internally driven, as per the Coaching Focus model, or against what is accepted elsewhere as being 'best practice'.[3]

However, how coaching is being applied, the sourcing of coaching, operational limitations on coachees' abilities to put what they resolve in coaching sessions into practice and more, make comparison against most benchmarks difficult and even meaningless. What's more, every organization's needs, people management systems and cultures are different – to succeed, any use of coaching must recognize and harness the differences to an organization's benefit.

It seems to us that despite some recent efforts (eg 'Measure for Measure', a conference co-hosted in London by the International Coach Federation and Institute for Employment Studies[4]), there's a long way to go before we'll have widespread agreement on what benchmarks should apply for every organization. To achieve this will require a large body of data built up from the experience of many different organizations operating in different circumstances and with different needs, in much the same way as so-called meta-studies of factors affecting performance in other areas have been able to isolate those variables that have most influence (studies of learning methods used in higher education provide one example[5]).

However, there's another challenge to overcome too, as Professor Robert Garvey of Sheffield Hallam's Business School observed after the London conference on coaching research that we mentioned above: individuals' ideas on what approach should be preferred are often coloured by their own particular perspectives. The problem, Garvey explains, 'is what discourse [a researcher] is connecting to' (Garvey, 2010).

Control groups

Evaluation may be able to point out clear differences when it's possible to compare an 'experimental' directly with a 'control' group, ie where the impacts felt by one group of (say) individuals who've received coaching in customer care can be compared with a group of peers performing the same role in more or less identical conditions but who've not been coached. Several of our clients have been able to use this approach reliably, while others have reported that impacts such as a more than threefold increase in sales were apparent in a group of salespeople who'd received coaching after a new training course over colleagues who'd received only the training (Carter and Mortlock, 2008).

Control group evaluation may be especially relevant when piloting a new initiative ahead of a fuller roll-out and where two or more alternative approaches for achieving the same end are being compared. For example, the approach might be used when considering whether to source in-house or external coaching. It can also be useful when comparing the 'before and after' states of the same group (ie assessing performance before coaching is introduced and again sometime after). However, this approach obviously depends on the ability to compare like with like.

Control groups may also take account of such factors as the passage of time since individuals received particular coaching or the effects of combining coaching with specific training, using coaching with one group while another receives classroom training intended to achieve the same end and the like.

The Net Promoter's Score

The Net Promoter's Score aims to obtain insights by posing just two questions:

1 How likely on a scale of 1–10 are you to recommend [coaching]? and

2 Why did you score as you did?

It's the second question that should be the more revealing, prompting respondents to really reflect on their response in the knowledge that this is all the time that the survey requests of them. The technique was developed by Fred Reichheld as an approach to be used in sales management for assessing how customers value a company (Reichheld, 2006). We've found that it can often uncover a wider range of informative qualitative data than might be achieved from using a lengthy questionnaire, and additionally, it forces the questionnaire designer to be very focused on what they want to know!

Common limitations of evaluation approaches

Evaluating interventions such as coaching that normally produce 'soft' outputs and which don't occur in a vacuum would seem to be far from a perfect science. Each of the methods described above suffers from a number of limitations, many of which are common to all. We've listed some of these below, with an intention of flagging some potential pitfalls of interpreting the results from evaluation with a narrow focus, rather than because we want to put a damper on their relative merits!

Common limitations of evaluation approaches

- Opinions offered by contributors are often not fully thought through or rationalized.

- Errors are made in interpretation (see 'Common fallacies in interpreting the outputs of evaluation' in Chapter 9).

- Too much emphasis is put on data obtained from a single source (eg from a survey or case study).

- Potential inferences other than the topic of study aren't given sufficient attention.

- Conclusions are drawn from samples that are too small or that don't reflect the differences seen in the population that they are meant to represent (eg differing departmental cultures, differing needs and conditions relating to the environments in which individuals operate).

- A 'one size fits all' principle is adopted (eg in benchmarking).

- The views of important stakeholders of coaching aren't taken into account.

- Control and experimental groups may not operate in exactly the same way, restricting the ability to compare like with like.

- Insufficient time is allowed following the launch of a coaching programme before impact evaluation is carried out; however, as Chapman and Carter point out, evaluation can also be started too late (Chapman and Carter, 2009).

- Following an initial commitment to evaluation, interest wanes once a programme has been active for perhaps six months or more or a new initiative begins to become a new 'flavour of the month'. A coaching programme may often be evaluated during its early months, but not as thoroughly thereafter when attention turns to other initiatives.

The balance of probabilities method

With the challenges previously described and the limitations that each approach that we've outlined presents, it might reasonably be asked whether any sensible conclusions on the effectiveness or impacts can be made of what is an essentially 'soft' intervention. Fortunately, identifying what has most likely directly resulted from coaching – both the specific and the general – is perfectly possible and readily accomplished with relatively little effort. Even where coaching has begun without a clear context or expectation of its contribution or where fresh topics are brought from conversation to conversation (depending on what is immediately relevant for the coachee), results can still be a clearly discerned.

The solution comes in the form of what we call 'the balance of probabilities' approach, a method that aims to combine some of the stronger elements of other evaluation approaches. Rather than attempting to prove absolutely what has resulted from coaching – an approach that would put the burden of proof firmly on the shoulders of an evaluator – this technique aims to build a strong argument in favour of what all the available evidence points to. We'll take a close look at this technique in the next chapter.

Gathering evidence (investigative inquiry)

What type of evidence should be sought?

Evidence to support evaluation may come in many forms, partly depending on the areas in which coaching is expected to have most impact and which question lines a study sets out to explore.

Primary data sources – data captured by those involved in the evaluation themselves or directly through the management processes and systems set up to support coaching – might include specially defined surveys, coachee reflection forms, coaching training records, 'happy sheets', coach/coachee engagement data and coach moderator reports (to name but a few).

Where appropriate, analysis may be extended to using any available secondary data as indicators of a coaching initiative's impacts. For example, staff satisfaction surveys might be expected to reveal an improvement in perceptions of managers' engagement with staff in the period following coaching or the retention of recent recruits might be expected to increase when coaching is used to support an induction programme.

Possible sources of secondary data might include:

- previously published surveys, eg staff satisfaction surveys;
- staff appraisal/performance scores;
- staff attrition, exit interview and sickness records;
- reduced number/nature of grievances raised, reduced incidence of unhealthy conflict;
- improved knowledge sharing (eg increased number of contributions to a company intranet);
- business performance data, for example:
  - labour savings achieved through reduced duplication of effort or better team working;
  - productivity increases (eg resulting from a new process, behaviour, mindset, skill, knowledge or method);
  - better customer management (eg fewer customers lost, better management of debt, reduced customer complaint handling, increased number of customers willing to offer testimonials, mystery shopper scores);
  - income generation (eg sales performance, better success in winning competitive pitches, sales referrals by non-sales staff);
  - new or improved product/process ideas and impacts of innovation.

Each potential source of data can offer powerful information in its own right, but is unlikely to prove the case for coaching by itself. Of course, in using such potential indicators, consideration must also be given to any other factors that may have significantly impacted on these data, eg a 'flu epidemic might significantly drive up sickness absence!

Apart from their relevance as potential indicators of coaching impact, the decision to use secondary data depends on a number of factors:

- the availability of the data without a need for significant manual processing or manipulation, and the evaluator's access to it (eg subject to its confidentiality or sensitivity);

- the timeliness of the data – whether the period covered by the data can be reasonably mapped to the period covered by the evaluation;
- whether or not it is appropriate to make historical comparisons between (eg) pre-coaching and current performance; for example, if a major business reorganization has occurred during the period.

Note that it may occasionally also be relevant to use published external data in analysis (eg benchmark data for comparable programmes in other organizations).

At a minimum, sufficient data must be collected to be statistically significant as a sample, and if appropriate it should be stratified to be representative of the desired population being studied.[6] For example, stratification might need to ensure adequate representation of such variables as coaching undertaken in different countries/regions, urban/rural-based workforces, large/small work groups, face-to-face/remote coaching, involvement of different partners/associate companies in coaching, differing practices of consulting/technical and administrative staff, differing needs and perspectives of HQ/branch office staff, and so on.

During investigation, it's sensible to keep track of what you actually know (ie what is factual), what you think you know and believe you need to know, and what isn't known (Figure 8.1). With this distinction in mind, it's then easier to consider the importance of attempting to establish or confirm what hasn't yet been established to be fact.

Evidence-gathering methods

Various methods may be used for primary data gathering, but most common are:

- 180°/360° or other questionnaire surveys;
- facilitated focus group workshops; and
- interviews with representatives of discrete stakeholder groups.

FIGURE 8.1 Validating evidence

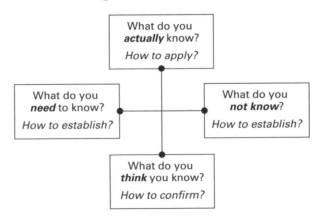

Combining at least two of these methods is recommended.

Whichever data collection methods are used, assurance of anonymity is needed to encourage candour. For example, participants need to feel confident that the comments of a line manager and a staff member can't easily be related. However, the prospect that a comment will never be recognized can't be guaranteed: some experiences that are related may be quite widely known. What's more, some duplication in responses captured via different means or through different individuals relating the same experience may occasionally result.

180°/360° or other questionnaire surveys

Surveys usually aim to understand perceptions on a variety of questions that the evaluation seeks to explore. From our experience, surveys are most useful for informing specific areas to explore further in focus group workshops and interviews and for establishing general perceptions of how different stakeholder groups rate the effectiveness and impacts of coaching across a broad sample. This may be especially useful where a large number of variables characterize the population base, and so a stratified sample of opinions is called for.

In an 180° or 360° survey,[7] multiple-choice or ranking questions are usually presented in mirror form to different stakeholder groups, allowing a gap analysis[8] to be made on their responses. Multiple-choice questions may use a four-point (or other even number) basis for responder scores to avoid the possibility of mid-point score 'opt-out' responses that odd numbers of options can produce. Deliberately brief (typically comprising just 10–15 questions), surveys should normally be designed to be completed in a matter of minutes and so encourage wider take-up and completion, as well as being easier to administer manually for respondents who do not have computer access.

Care is needed to avoid ambiguity when designing multiple-choice or ranking questions. However, even when questions are well framed, we've found that after reflection in interviews and focus group workshops, participants' views may sometimes differ significantly from impressions given in a survey. Asking for unnecessary demographic details and 'for interest' questions that aren't relevant to the study should be avoided.

We suggest that survey responses should require no more than 3–5 minutes per participant, increasing the prospect of a good completion rate and respecting the limited time that individuals can usually devote to them. Between 30 and 50 per cent of the study population should usually be invited to participate, although response rates of 10–15 per cent may be sufficient for analysis, depending on the population size (interviews and focus group workshops are invariably far more important for gathering qualitative data over surveys).

Surveys don't generally yield a good base of qualitative data and tend to be biased by how individuals feel at the time they take the survey and their desire to complete their response quickly, rather than being thought through and rationalized. Meaningful qualitative data are usually needed for rationalizing impacts, which surveys often fail to provide.

Sample sets of 180°/360° survey questions for coaching evaluation can be downloaded from the website supporting this book, www.managingcoachingatwork.com.

Facilitated focus group workshops

Focus group workshops involving a sample of stakeholders can be an especially effective way of eliciting anecdotes, quickly understanding general perceptions and exploring what difference coaching has made (and why). That's assuming, of course, that it has.

As with interviews, focus group workshops might be sequenced after a 180°/360° survey, allowing exploratory themes to be informed by survey responses such as identifying reasons for any apparent conflicts in survey responses.

A small group size should be preferred to limit the dominance of specific themes or individual views, and each group should ideally be restricted to a random sample of participants from a specific stakeholder group, usually excluding other stakeholder groups being spoken about (eg when supervisors reflect on coaches). This should encourage open discussion. Groups of five to eight participants are ideal, with workshops typically requiring 30–45 minutes each. The number of groups required will vary depending on the population size and stratification needs; however, between five and 10 workshops are usually sufficient to gather a strong base of representative data.

If possible and relevant, we recommend running at least two workshops with different representatives from each stakeholder group, to guard against the possible influence of a dominant 'group think' taking over and to be representative of different environments and groups. Facilitation by an independent person should help to protect the anonymity of individuals in the group and encourage candid discussion.

Interviews with representatives of discrete stakeholder groups

Given the private nature of coaching conversations, interviews are often preferred by coaches and coachees over group-based conversations, and it may also be relevant to schedule them with sponsors and representatives of other stakeholder groups. Executives too tend to prefer one-to-one conversations, and may be more inclined to be candid when talking out of earshot of their fellow directors.

Well-planned interviews that focus on a limited number of topics and that allow for probing when appropriate should minimize the amount of time needed for each interview, so increasing the number of interviews that can be scheduled in the time allowed for them.

As with surveys, better participation is likely if interviews are kept brief. This requires skill on the part of the interviewer to address and probe the right questions, sensitivity to possible contradictions, etc. Furthermore, by taking a random sample and not ascribing comments to any named individual, interviews should aim to protect anonymity and so encourage honest responses.

Caveats and cautionary notes

In planning evidence gathering, it's perhaps pertinent to remember an old truth often relayed by the computing fraternity – 'garbage in = garbage out'. The quality of conclusions that result from any evaluation necessarily relies on how meaningful and representative the data used for analysis are.

Some crucial points to be aware of when collecting/interpreting evidence are:

- questioning who needs to be asked to contribute their views, bearing in mind the potential impacts of the coaching on a team, organization and individual;
- recognizing whether the coaching is intended to improve performance, support career transition, is Solution-focused, etc – and exploring the extent to which its intended focus has applied in reality;
- when considering mixed forms of coaching, making clear which questions relate to (eg) coaching as a management style as opposed to formally contracted coaching;
- questioning whether case studies and examples are representative of general experiences or 'one-offs'; and
- understanding what other potential influences may have contributed to changes claimed to result from coaching, and identifying any significant factors that may have played a part when 'before and after' comparisons are made (eg a significant organizational change or change in role for a coachee).

Summary

The task of evaluating coaching presents a number of challenges that might discourage attempts to make sense of what has been delivered and why. One reason that coaching is often considered to be too hard to evaluate is that too limited an interpretation is put on the meaning of the term 'return on investment'.

To assess the impacts and effectiveness of a coaching initiative, it shouldn't be necessary to pinpoint how much has been spent or saved at a particular point in time. Rather, the real value of evaluation is to help inform future decision making and to give sponsors confidence that an investment in coaching is worth continuing. As one observer has put it, 'The 'R' [in 'ROI'] is no longer the famous bottom line and the 'I' is more likely a subscription fee rather than a one-time payment' (Cross, 2001).

Despite some of the limitations of common approaches to evaluation, the balance of probabilities method aims to limit the challenges and offer a readily extensible approach for gaining real insight into the results of coaching. We'll develop our consideration of this approach in the next chapter, examining how data from a wide range of sources can be brought together and presented as a compelling explanation for coaching performance.

Notes

1 Stratification ensures adequate representation amongst the data sample for each of the different types of group that a researcher wants to account for (eg ensuring that both headquarters and regional office staff are included or to guarantee that views from individuals at a number of different grades are picked up). Purely random sampling does not offer this guarantee.

2 The paired interview approach is fully described in Valerie Anderson's book that followed her Portsmouth University study, *Value of Learning: From return on investment to return on expectation* (Anderson, 2007b).

3 'Best practice': what is commonly regarded as a model or most effective process, technique, method or any other basis for carrying out a task for which a standard may be set. We are not the biggest fans of what we believe has become a very hackneyed term and one for which a subjective judgement may often have been involved in deciding what is 'commonly known' to be the best way of doing things. Nevertheless, it's a concept that perseveres and can have utility.

4 The conference, held in December 2009, was intended to encourage coaching researchers to work towards creating consistent measures for their work, not just in evaluation.

5 For an overview of meta-study approaches and their application in higher education, see Petty (2009).

6 A 'population' may be an entire organization, all individuals who have received coaching, all managers at a particular rank, etc. In other words, a population represents the entire group that is the subject audience for an evaluation.

7 A 180° survey may take account of just two or three perspectives (eg a coach and coachee), whereas a 360° survey aims to gather the all-round views of a wide range of people, such as peers, line managers and observers of coaches.

8 In the context of a stakeholder survey, a gap analysis shows the difference in perceptions reported by different stakeholder groups (eg if in response to a survey statement 'All individuals I know who've received coaching have achieved the goals that they set', 80 per cent of all coaches responding to the survey fully agree with this view whereas only 40 per cent of coaching sponsors share this view, a significant gap between these two groups would be apparent, ie twice as many coaches as sponsors give the statement their full thumbs-up). The value of gap analysis is that it highlights such significant differences and prompts inquiry into why these arise.

Making and continuing the case for coaching

Introduction

In the last chapter we considered a range of different approaches that might be used for evaluating what a coaching initiative is delivering, each having differing merits but also limitations. We referred to a range of types of data that might be relevant to use as inputs to an evaluation study and we described the more common methods for gathering primary data.

In this chapter, we'll describe how our preferred approach to evaluation, the 'balance of probabilities' method, can be applied. We'll focus especially on how to analyse the range of data that may be available to an evaluator and in turn how to draw insights from this.

Jackie's eyes used to glaze over whenever the topic of evaluation was mentioned. Clive, by contrast, has always been an enthusiast, but then again he's also a keen member of the All England Seagull Fanciers' Club! Jackie is now a firm convert, and the balance of probabilities approach has all the more appeal for her since it draws on many of the same principles that are applied in police detective work.

Evaluation can be a dry topic to gain a handle on at first, and this chapter may give a taste of that. But stick with us, all will fall into place and make sense!

To turn away from approaching evaluation is all too easy, but neglect may have dramatic cost implications for any organization. Through evaluation, several leading organizations are showing that informed decisions can be taken that set a profitable course for coaching, often making some surprising discoveries in the process.

At the supermarket giant Tesco, for example, former Head of Leadership Development Maxine Dolan said she was shocked to find what lay behind the secrecy of the external coaching that had been taking place, remarking that 'there were instances where a dependency had been created – some people had had a coach for more than two years and there was no measurement and no alignment with the business' (Hall, 2009). Sadly, many are still following this example.

Common fallacies in interpreting the outputs of evaluation

Let's now return to consider some fallacies that can be overlooked by the unwary evaluator, before moving on to explore how the balance of probabilities method attempts to avoid these. The following are amongst the more common misconceptions.

'Learning [or changed behaviour] has bedded in – this proves a positive return'

Of course, it's reassuring to know that an individual is still applying a change resulting from coaching some time after a coaching dialogue has completed. However, this doesn't invariably equate to a positive impact or return. On its own, simply knowing that someone has adopted a new way of thinking or changed the way they respond tells us nothing about how this is actually making a difference: we're still at level 2 in Kirkpatrick's model.

'Delegates who took action after being coached say that they can see value for themselves'

It's of course entirely normal for individuals to commit to actions during their coaching. Actions may well be intended to be useful and some may be capable of being quantified in terms of the benefits or savings they generate, but these again may fall short of achieving any tangible impact or organizational benefit.

'There's broad evidence that the training has had some impact – just listen to these great stories'

This one may be seen as a compromise to show that something has happened for the good, but a selection of positive stories and good feeling may simply be just that and not add up to overwhelming proof of positive impact.

Anecdotes need to be rationalized to ensure that they aren't just extreme examples, exceptions that prove the rule or wishful exaggerations.

At the same time, any quantified benefits need to be balanced against the costs of coaching to ensure that the effort was worthwhile. Being able to point to positive outcomes should be a minimum expectation for any coaching initiative. However, this shouldn't obscure the scale of any disappointments if coaching has failed to deliver in other cases.

'People perceive a positive difference'

Perceptions such as those collected from a 360° survey may be interesting to know and may or may not be useful, but despite the popular cliché, the perception of some isn't necessarily a reality for all. Amongst other factors that might suggest otherwise, perceptions may cloud views, be biased by specific rather than common experiences, be too limited in focus, or not tie an impact to a specific intervention.

That said, a common pattern of similar perceptions from a significant number of individuals might be a strong indicator of impact. But if we're serious about understanding impacts, we'll need to know more.

'The facts speak for themselves'

This might be a popular assertion for a lawyer to make, but many miscarriages of justice show that comments of this kind are just not true, however well an argument is presented! Even where clear and seemingly related changes are apparent some time after coaching (eg the productivity of coached staff reaches an all-time high), there remains an all too often thorny problem in analysis: how to isolate what coaching has specifically contributed. Claims that a particular initiative has made the big difference will be weak unless they can be rationalized and pitted against the devil's advocate argument that a number of possible factors may have played a part in bringing about a change.

'One good story often reveals the whole story'

Isolated stories may be significant, but they may not tell the whole story of what's happening on the ground.

How the balance of probabilities approach aims to address some common limitations of evaluation

The balance of probabilities method aims to limit the challenges of evaluation that we've outlined. At the same time, the method aims to be simple to understand and capable of being applied quickly, without an unreasonable demand on anyone's time nor needing to master particular techniques (eg to become a dab hand in statistics).

We sought to create an approach that would be sufficiently flexible to use irrespective of whether 'before and after' or control group comparisons could be made, and to be capable of making good use of whatever data could be obtained for analysis (including a restriction to anecdotal input only, if need be).

So how does the method achieve this? First, we need to define what we mean by 'evidence'.

What constitutes valid evidence?

In normal parlance, evidence may refer to anything that points to a particular conclusion being true. Possible candidates that might be presented to support an argument include published data, documents and verbal testimonies.

Individually such items may not always point to a clear proposition. Even when considered collectively, it won't always be the case that an explanation for the evidence that is put forward will be 100 per cent watertight. In the case of a criminal case, this will be left for a judge or jury to decide. The same applies to evidence presented to support the conclusion of an evaluation report. Ultimately it's a report's intended audience who need to be persuaded of the validity of its conclusion.

Even when an individual is on trial for a serious crime, judgements may be made that convict a defendant without the full facts of the case having been proven. A conclusion based on a burden of proof requires that those with whom judgement sits are as sure as they can be that the burden has been demonstrated beyond reasonable doubt. This may not always be a cut-and-dried conviction.

Judgements based on a balance of probabilities, common in civil law cases, take account of a range of evidence that points to the same interpretation and which most people should be able to accept, even if 'the facts' haven't been absolutely proven.

To distinguish a burden of proof from a balance of probabilities conclusion, Jackie likes to relate the following illustration. Seeing a man wearing a white sweatshirt with red piping and the words 'Red Sox' emblazoned across the chest, it might be reasonable, considering the balance of probabilities, to assume that he is a Red Sox supporter. Seeing the same man amongst the crowd at Fenway Park, cheering on the Red Sox and excitedly applauding each time they score a run, it might however be thought beyond reasonable doubt that he is a genuine fan of the Boston side.

Cases presented using the balance of possibilities method are obviously strengthened if the quality of evidence supporting them and the rigour of the arguments they present are robust. This is a key aim of our approach to evaluation – to answer questions about the performance of a coaching initiative as logically and with the strongest support from procured evidence as possible, given the time and resources available for conducting the study.

Inference and logic

In addition to primary evidence such as testimonies offered in interviews and focus group workshops, further evidence can be identified by applying logical arguments to what is known or has been said. In addition to abstracting further points in this way, the balance of probabilities approach stresses the importance of applying inference to justify its conclusions.

The philosopher Ben Dupré (Dupré, 2007) neatly summarizes the essence of what we are aiming to achieve, distinguishing the purpose of inference and logic along the way:

> An argument is a rationally sanctioned move from accepted foundations (premises) to a point that is to be proved or demonstrated (the conclusion)... The move from premises to conclusion is a matter of inference, the strength of which determines the robustness of the argument. The business of distinguishing good inferences from bad is the central task of logic.

Two forms of inferential reasoning may be used in the process – deductive and inductive. In the case of deductive reasoning, something is concluded to be true if several other premises apply. To paraphrase a popular explanation that Aristotle might have proposed, 'If it's true that all men are mortal and it's also true that Socrates is a man, then we must conclude that Socrates is mortal.' Or, to give another example:

1 The sun always rises in the east and sets in the west.
2 The sun is disappearing over the western horizon.
3 Therefore: daylight will soon be fading.

Of course, deductive reasoning depends on the strength of the premises it uses. Weak premises will not support a convincing conclusion.

Meanwhile, inductive reasoning involves reaching a view based on a series of corroborating points. To look at this another way, induction shows how a number of specific points support a generalized conclusion. For example:

1 Brazil has won the World Cup five times before now.
2 Almost all observers say that Brazil's team is one of the best they've ever fielded.
3 In the tournament's qualifying stage, Brazil is selected to play three sides that struggled to make the grade in their regional confederations.
4 Therefore: the odds are high for Brazil making it through the qualifying stages.

Closer to our focus of interest, examples of deductive and inductive reasoning that might apply in a coaching context are illustrated in Figure 9.1.

FIGURE 9.1 Deductive and inductive reasoning

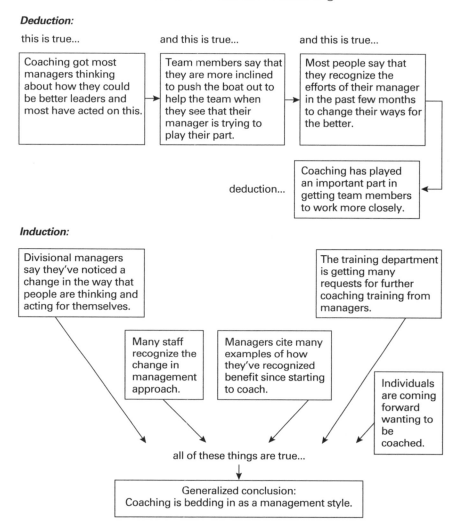

The five steps of the balance of probabilities method

Appreciating the meaning of evidence and treatment of applied logic outlined above, we're now well placed to introduce the balance of probabilities method for evaluation. The approach involves five main steps:

1 Defining the scope of evaluation.

2 Investigation.

3 Sorting and classifying the evidence – the case for and the case against a working premise.

4 Assessing the evidence – adding inference.

5 Presenting a balance of probabilities argument.

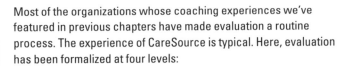

Making evaluation a routine

Most of the organizations whose coaching experiences we've featured in previous chapters have made evaluation a routine process. The experience of CareSource is typical. Here, evaluation has been formalized at four levels:

1 Coachees' satisfaction ratings are sought following the end of a coaching relationship, accounting for the effectiveness of the coaching process, the benefits obtained and referring to pre-coaching expectations.

2 Monthly evaluation is undertaken during the progress of a coaching relationship, considering how coaching has helped a coachee achieve their recent accomplishments and keeping check on progress against their expectations.

3 Structured 'value conversations' with coachees are conducted by the Director of CareSource University (CSU) or VP of HR three months after the end of a coaching relationship, exploring which insights have been gained and identifying evidence of the intangible impacts of such things as improved communication and better management of conflict.

4 'Value conversations' with clients designed to quantify the impacts of the changes they have made, including conversion of this value into annualized monetary benefits, weighted to account for clients' appraisal of the contribution that coaching has made in creating this.

This attention to understanding what contribution coaching has made has clearly revealed that coaching has helped new managers integrate into CareSource's culture, coming to grips with the organization's processes and the like far more quickly than had previously been the case.

Interpersonal coaching especially has yielded some dramatic impacts. For example, individuals who were struggling to make an impact and who were moving towards presenting a possible performance concern have completely turned around to become high performers. In at least one case, an individual moved to being groomed on a succession path and another achieved promotion.

Step 1 – Defining the scope of evaluation

The scope of an evaluation study should be described by one or more lines of inquiry that we seek to answer. Typical question lines include:

- Impact
  - What impact (if any) has coaching had?
  - How can we be sure that this is the case?
  - Why hasn't something else had an influence (or what else has had impact and how)?
- Investment return/opportunity cost
  - Are we getting as much back as we can in return for our coaching spend?
  - Could we be spending the money put into coaching more wisely elsewhere?
- Effectiveness
  - Is our coaching service fit for purpose?
  - Is our coaching service being delivered most effectively?

Note, of course, that the subject for each question may vary. For example, we may want to explore the effectiveness of coaching training provided for managers rather than to look at how well a coaching practice is operating. However, the general themes of each of these lines of inquiry are likely to be similar irrespective of the target for investigation.

We should note too that when defining the scope of evaluation, our concern is to identify the question or questions that we want to answer. This stage is not the time for developing any theories that we believe might be true; hypothesis testing is a task for analysis.

Step 2 – Investigation

Investigation covers the task of choosing what types of data may be useful for analysis, deciding who to consult with and how, and the physical task of gathering evidence. You might recall that we considered these concerns in Chapter 8.

Step 3 – Sorting and classifying the evidence – the case for and case against a working premise

Having completed an objective investigation, now is the point at which we aim to distinguish data that support a possible theory or 'working premise' from data that don't.

For example, one working premise under which to categorize data in the 'for' category might be 'the coaching service is fit for purpose'. Or, concerning the impacts of coaching, a possible premise that might be tested could be 'coaching has delivered qualified benefits whose value outweighs the time, effort and money spent on it'.

The task of considering which data either favour or oppose a working premise involves sorting each of item of evidence at hand under one of these two headings (see Figure 9.2). In fact, we may need to add a third heading to list any data that may not readily fall under either heading. Such items may be separately listed, even though they have relevance to the line of enquiry being explored. But before setting about this task, we must first decide which of the data we've gathered are relevant to each of the questions that our evaluation study seeks to answer.

FIGURE 9.2 Evidence sorting

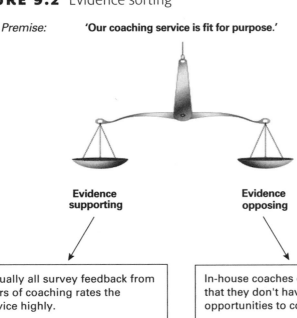

Premise: **'Our coaching service is fit for purpose.'**

Evidence supporting

Evidence opposing

Virtually all survey feedback from users of coaching rates the service highly.	In-house coaches often complain that they don't have enough opportunities to coach.
Both coaches and coachees typically say that they were well matched.	It's not clear whether some coaching relationships continue long after they should really end.
A strong pool of external coaches can be drawn upon to meet executives' demands.	Uses of coaching aren't tied to what matters most to the organization.
Coach networking events continue to be well attended more than two years after coaches were first trained.	Few coaches ever receive supervision.
(etc)	(etc)

Deciding which data are relevant

Our concern now is to decide which data available at our disposal are likely to be relevant and which we probably don't need to know about. Running down a list of comments collected from an interview may reveal a range of points that were incidental to the discussion but were recorded as they might provide useful information for purposes other than evaluation at some future date. For example, a finance director may have mentioned aspects of the organization's investment plan that could have a bearing on where coaching may or may not be used in future, although such information doesn't contribute to an understanding of how coaching is impacting currently.

Such items can usually be quickly filtered out from a list, a task that can be made easier by using a computer spreadsheet or database, so streamlining the filtering process and making it easy to keep track of changes as the task proceeds.

Optionally, and especially when dealing with long lists of data, it may help later analysis to attempt to group or classify each item in some way. Amongst possible categories that might apply in a list of impact-related items, example categories might include such things as 'improved motivation' or 'change in personal behaviour' (see Figure 9.3).

Identifying the sources of each data item

We should also label our data to show which items of evidence were presented by particular individuals or groups (assuming this hasn't been done already). Labels may be adopted to identify respondents uniquely, while protecting their anonymity. This referencing task is important to enable us to pick out in later analysis when one person has made many observations that effectively say the same thing. Comments such as 'coaching opened my eyes to what I need to do next', 'through coaching, I could see a way forward' and 'the big thing for me was getting a sense of direction' might add greater weight to an argument if they are offered by three different people rather than just one.

Reviewing apparently contradicting items

One further issue that occasionally arises at this stage is the question of how to deal with apparently contradicting data items. In the case of differing opinions or perceptions, the reasons for the differences may have been explored in discussion with individuals who contributed to the study; however, differences don't necessarily mean contradictions. Not everyone's experience of coaching may have led to a dramatic improvement in his or her personal effectiveness, for example.

FIGURE 9.3 Classifying data inputs

Item #	Evidence	Source	Classification	Include in analysis?
1	I stopped following everyone else's pattern of working late when I realized that this was making me resentful and less productive than I am now.	Workshop	Self-insight and changed behaviour	Yes
2	Coaching has inspired me to play to my strengths.	Survey	Motivation	Yes
3	My coach always seems to understand what I'm saying.	Workshop	Coach's attention	Yes
4	Coaching leaves me feeling uplifted in a way that most other things don't.	Workshop	Motivation to carry a commitment through	Yes
5	The questions my coach asks me strike a chord and get me to think differently about situations.	Workshop	Self-insight and changed behaviour	Yes
6	My coach has helped me appreciate that I don't always need to be moving on into new roles to keep developing.	Workshop	Self-insight and changed behaviour	Yes
7	The practical guidance given in the course on how to spot what a coachee may be saying has proved to be really useful in practice.	Workshop	Coach's attention	Yes
8	Coaching is the best thing that happens every week.	Survey	Unclassified	No
9	The coaching circle opened my eyes to possible ways for best dealing with [a difficult coaching situation].	Workshop	Opportunity to reflect on coaching experience	Yes
10	It was clear to both me and my coach when our sessions had reached their natural end.	Workshop	Effective contracting	Yes
11	I'm still keeping up with the approach to keeping meetings brief that I committed to when being coached over a year ago.	Workshop	Self-insight and changed behaviour	Yes
12	Three sessions with my supervisor made all the difference to me seeing the way forward [out of a blockage in a coaching dialogue].	Workshop	Opportunity to reflect on coaching experience	Yes
13	The time is well spent on coaching.	Survey	Unclassified	No
14	I'd say that the organization has definitely seen benefits since the coaching programme was introduced.	Interview	Unclassified	No
15	Customer complaints have gone down by 50% since all agents were put through the coaching programme. Last year, we only saw a drop of 15% after training our agents in how to deal with customers on the phone.	Workshop	Self-insight and changed behaviour	Yes
16	Coaching makes me stop and think about alternative ways of doing things.	Survey	Self-insight and changed behaviour	Yes
17	If I can see that there may be a better way to do things, I'm prepared to give it a try.	Workshop	Self-insight and changed behaviour	Yes
18	My relationship with the team turned around after I realized that I didn't have to act like a tyrant all the time. Now everyone is pulling their weight and we regularly hit our targets. It was only through coaching that I got to see myself as others do.	Interview	Self-insight and changed behviour	Yes
19	Including a number of different coaching models in the training course gave me confidence to coach in different situations when I first started to coach for real.	Workshop	Confidence to coach	Yes

Moreover, small contradictions need not detract from the important insights that can be drawn nor assessment of the outcomes that coaching has produced. We've rarely encountered situations where apparent contradictions can't be readily explained. Where this is the case, unless there's a fundamental impact on the argument, we suggests that it's usually sufficient just to note that a question mark exists against what can be interpreted from the items in question.

Step 4 – Assessing the evidence – adding inference

Taking our 'for' and 'against' lists in turn, out next task is to use this primary evidence to construct logical inferences. As we've mentioned before, we can use a mix of inductive and deductive reasoning to show how different items of evidence relate to each other. So if we were testing a working premise that 'coaching training for managers has brought about a tangible return for our investment', we might expect to see inferences being made that are similar to those listed in Table 9.1.

Any number of new items of inferred evidence many be added to the lists created under the 'for' and 'against' headings. To make clear the rationale for each, and showing whether deductive or inductive project logic has been applied, we suggest adopting the format shown in Figure 9.4.

Step 5 – Presenting a balance of probabilities argument

Having scrutinized available evidence to identify further inferences, the lists favouring and opposing the working premise may then be compared and reported upon. Essentially our interest here is to determine whether one list weighs significantly more heavily than the other, much like the content of one pan on a weighing scale might obviously outweigh the other.

Note that neither at this stage nor when sorting individual items of evidence do we attempt to score or otherwise qualify a weighting for each item. Since such an assessment would be necessarily subjective, it would leave us open to criticism by someone who was cynical about our argument. Our conclusion rests on the strength of our reasoning and the quality of evidence that we present; in most cases, others will be able to see for themselves which evidence seems to be more significant than others.

Sometimes it may be sufficient just to allow others to draw their own conclusions simply by observing the weight of an argument in one direction or the other (not only or necessarily by the number of items that are included in one list relative to the other, but also in the quality of evidence presented). See for example Figure 9.5.

More often than not, however, a narrative will be required to pull out the main conclusions and further rationalize why (say) the case for the working premise is favoured, applying further inference where necessary to explain our conclusion.

TABLE 9.1 Inferred evidence

Inference	Deduced/ inducted	Inferred by
Coaching training has made a difference.	Inducted	Many individuals specifically mention their manager's use of coaching when explaining what made the penny drop for them. Many managers who've coached team members have been impressed by the dramatic changes they've seen. In the period since their managers received coaching training, all but a small minority of individuals say that they've taken much bigger steps to improve their game than ever before.
Less time is being spent resolving grievances since managers started coaching. Most grievances against managers have traditionally related to a feeling of being ignored.	Deducted	Staff grievances against their manager are down 50% since the 'manager as coach' programme launched. Coaching shows real commitment to a person's views. Coaching is playing a role in cutting down on grievances. On average, each grievance takes around five days of effort to resolve.
Coaching isn't yet a habitual management style.	Inducted	Forty per cent of managers sampled say they often struggle to know how to use the 'GROW' model in unplanned, brief conversations. Fifty per cent of sampled managers say that they can rarely find the time to coach their staff. Few managers say that they've changed their approach when running team meetings to take on more of a coaching style.

FIGURE 9.4 Reporting primary and inferred evidence

Premise:	**'Our coaching service is fit for purpose.'**

Evidence supporting

> **Primary evidence:**
> ★ item # 1
> ★ item # 2
> ★ item # 3
> (etc)

Inferred evidence: inference	deduced/ inducted	inferred by
★ item # 1	inducted	item #'s or other points
★ item # 2	deduced	item #'s or other points
★ item # 3	inducted	item #'s or other points
(etc)		

Evidence opposing

> **Primary evidence:**
> ★ item # 1
> ★ item # 2
> ★ item # 3
> (etc)

Inferred evidence: inference	deduced/ inducted	inferred by
★ item # 1	inducted	item #'s or other points
★ item # 2	deduced	item #'s or other points
★ item # 3	inducted	item #'s or other points
(etc)		

Clearly, the more items of evidence that can be presented to support a particular point, the more convincing the argument is likely to be. This isn't to say that specific examples of an individual's experience might be referred to that isn't representative of others' experiences but may still be useful to report upon. This may be desirable, for example, when referring to one individual's specific experience that has had an exceptional personal impact as well as having a strong bearing on their working life too. Similarly, the insight that might be gained from a single well-articulated experience may be greater than the explanation offered by many more casual observations.

FIGURE 9.5 The balance of probabilities

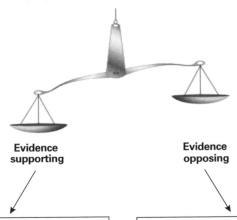

Premise: **'Coaching has transformed the way people work across the organization.'**

Evidence supporting

Evidence opposing

Individuals have stronger self-insight of their strengths.
Individuals better appreciate the organization's needs and priorities.
Individuals feel more confident to take decisions.
Staff whose managers came into their posts after the coaching training programme report lower scores in the Staff Satisfaction Review against questions relating to personal empowerment.
Staff who receive coaching responded positively to the recent restructuring while others feared it.

Many managers claim that they've simply been spending more time with their staff.
Some senior managers remain sceptical about the influence of coaching.

Of course, it won't always be the case that one list tips the scales much more strongly than the other. In such cases, where a clear argument can't be made in favour or against the working premise, our conclusion may simply be that the case for our working hypothesis 'hangs in the balance'.

Similarly, some key evidence might point towards a mixed conclusion. For example, an overwhelming impact of coaching may appear to be demonstrated in some areas while other influences such as the support of line managers or a new bonus scheme may also have played an important part in bringing about the kind of change that coaching was intended for. A mixed conclusion that might run along the line of 'on the one hand, [this] is clear, but on the other, [this] is also apparent...' is a perfectly valid conclusion for evaluation.

To take the definition that we introduced earlier, a balance of probabilities conclusion need not be decisive, but should take comprehensive account of all the information that's available to an evaluator. Highlighting the conclusions drawn and options recommended for acting on these provides a clear conclusion for any evaluation report or presentation.

Report presentation

We've found the following to be a particularly useful way of presenting findings:

- introducing the evaluation;
- for each of the lines of inquiry investigated, presenting the 'for', 'against' and 'balance of probability' arguments;
- drawing out suggested implications and recommending possible options for action.

We believe that this format usually provides everything that a reader might want to know: a robust, to-the-point conclusion that can be rationalized in more detail if required, a clear appreciation of the logic that has led to this conclusion and the data that supports it and an answer to the devil's advocate questions that might be raised. Additionally, we also like to incorporate a graphical presentation of how strongly available evidence bears out the strength of each working premise examined by the evaluation, drawing on a technique used in police detective work.

An *evidence grid* categorizes the quality of evidence offered by individuals and maps this against each premise. By 'quality' in this context, we mean the extent to which all presented evidence has been confidently claimed, rationalized or perceived. The concept is best explained with the help of Figure 9.6.

Note that in the example, the number of items of evidence offered as potential support or to oppose each working premise is noted, and similarly the number of items which falls under each category is shown. The overall impression created by the grid should usefully support the weightings applied in a 'balance of probabilities' argument.

Colour coding may optionally be applied to show the extent to which evidence backs up each broken-down indicator of the premise. For example, green shading might be used where there are significant items supporting an indicator (as in the case of coachees having confidence to 'have a go' in our example), yellow where the evidence is inconclusive and red where it is contradictory. In this way, gaps in supporting evidence for the premise are also highlighted. Summarizing information in this way also allows a simple, one-page summary to be presented to readers of the report who don't want to read through all the detail.

FIGURE 9.6 Evidence grid

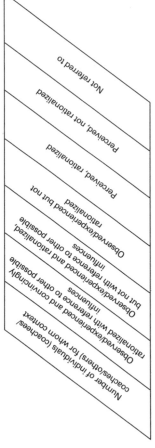

	Number of individuals (coaches/coachees/others) for whom context	Observed/experienced and convincingly rationalized with reference to other possible influences	Observed/experienced and rationalized but not with reference to other possible influences	Observed/experienced but not rationalized	Perceived, rationalized	Perceived, not rationalized	Not referred to
Coaching has given individuals the confidence to push out of comfort zones.	Through individuals having confidence to 'have a go', fewer matters have been escalated than before coaching began.	50	30	5	5	1	1	8
	Individuals have tried out ways of interacting with others that they weren't comfortable trying before.	50	5	5	5	2	3	30
	Individuals have said that they've felt proud that they've tried out things that they'd previously feared.	50	10	15	15	n/a	n/a	10

Number of individuals consulted: **50**

Supports premise.
Limited supporting perceptions/experiences.
Contradicts premise.

As an aside, the categories used in a grid during a crime investigation are usually a little different. To illustrate, imagine a robbery investigation in which a man has been identified as a possible suspect. A detective's concern will be to identify which witnesses saw the suspect actually commit a robbery, what was heard, what else was observed and so on.

Using a grid, this information might then be categorized to show the numbers of witnesses who saw the man, saw the robbery, heard shouts, observed a man fleeing in a red coat, saw him turn the coat inside out to show a black coat, flee the scene, etc. The method we apply in coaching evaluation might use different categories, but the technique is the same as a detective might adopt. Perhaps it might be clear why Jackie's eyes now light up when talk turns to evaluation!

One further reporting method that we've found to be particularly effective is the *impact chain*. This shows how the items of evidence gathered by a study combine to produce a series of sequential knock-on effects that together illustrate the impact chains or ways in which these combine to contribute to individual and business performance.

Constructing an impact chain follows a similar process to that used when compiling 'for' and 'against' evidence lists, but starts by considering the ultimate outcomes of coaching that have been achieved (or the 'business results', to use Kirkpatrick's language). These are depicted on the right-hand side of the chain.

Where a balanced scorecard or key performance indicators are used for measuring organizational performance, the 'outcome' boxes of an impact chain may often be mapped onto the specific measures used by such instruments.

Once the outcomes have been identified, the construction process then works backwards to show how these have resulted from direct outputs of coaching (the boxes on the left-hand side of the diagram).

In between, further consequences of the direct result of coaching are represented, including any impacts that result from combining several preceding elements in the chain. As usual, a picture can speak more than a thousand words to help explain what we've tried to describe (Figure 9.7).

Note that, in the diagram, each labelled category (eg 'Individuals have moved outside previous comfort zones', labelled 'C') is supported by at least five items of evidence. Factors that are external to the initiative but impact on its intended outcomes may also be represented in the diagram, eg prerequisite or critical success factors for coachees to be able to succeed.

The labels used to identify supporting data are optional when presenting a report; however, we've found that they are useful for an evaluator's own reference.

FIGURE 9.7 Impact chain

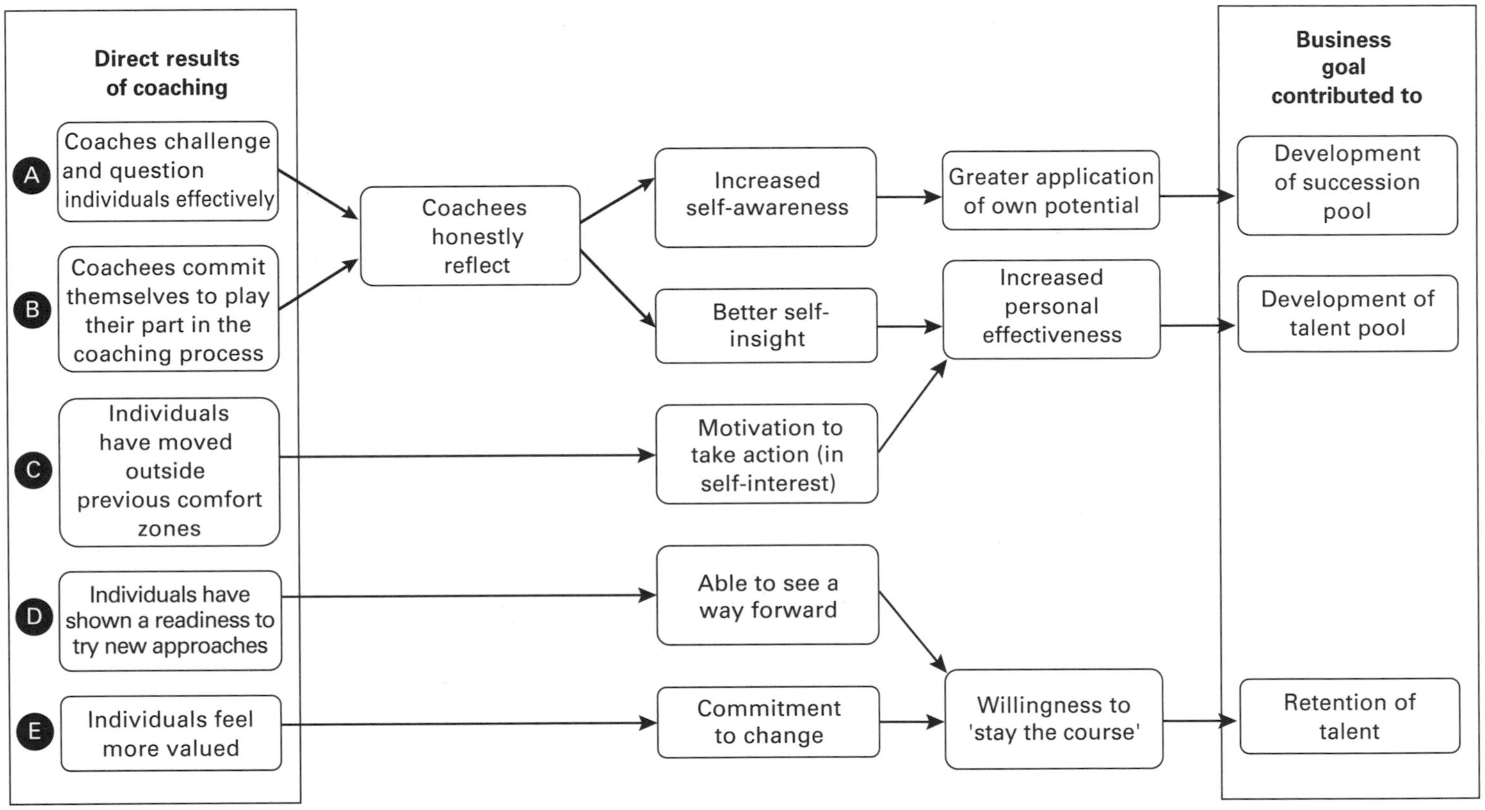

CASE STUDY
Not just down to chance: team turnaround at National Australia Bank

When Ian Gibson took on the role of leading a business account management sub-group in National Australia Bank's Technology Division, relationships between the group and the rest of the business had reached a new low. Even within the Melbourne-based division itself, individuals were often in conflict with each other rather than working towards a common cause. Consequently, when the newly appointed chief information officer (CIO) created a new Business Solutions Management (BSM) group, Ian and fellow executives took on the task of figuring out how to make a dysfunctional team functional.

Ian decided that coaching might have some role to play in changing behaviours, having observed the positive change that his own manager had shown after working with an executive coach. Even without understanding much about the theory of coaching and being sceptical of something that didn't apply the same sort of logic that kept the bank's machinery working, Ian and his fellow managers agreed that this mysterious practice was nonetheless worth a try.

The Melbourne-based consultancy Point Ahead was brought on board to help with the task (the company had already been working with the bank to support the grooming of the next generation of leaders, in which Ian's coach, Michael Fahie, had played a substantial role).

Following executive coaching himself, Ian quickly began to focus on the relational aspects in the team's dynamic and resolved to take the regular grumblings that were directed at him on the chin rather than normally feeling a need to defend against such criticisms. A three-day off-site team event facilitated by Michael allowed individuals to air their frustrations openly, after which a range of tools and techniques was introduced to help the team move forward.

Since it was very apparent what wasn't working, attention was put on how the team wanted to work together – taking a rounded Gestalt[1] rather than 'doctor diagnosing a disease' perspective. In turn, a set of dimensions that could be clearly measured was identified, such as 'we share responsibility for members' welfare'. As with Ian's own focus from coaching, emphasis in the group was put on resolving the team's own performance and relational difficulties first, before tackling how it worked in other parts of the business.

Following the workshop, monthly surveys were conducted to assess progress and identify any areas that needed improvement. Amongst the activities that were identified to help close the gap between what the team felt it had achieved and where it wanted to be, twice-monthly events were introduced. In addition, one-to-one coaching was offered for anyone that requested it. Virtually every team member took up this offer to a greater or lesser extent.

Through regular meeting, individuals got to know which skills and backgrounds their colleagues brought to the team and barriers began to be broken down. As had been Ian's experience, much emphasis in coaching and the team activities that interspersed with this focused on relational rather than mechanistic matters. In a strongly disciplined and target-focused environment such as a bank, confronting interpersonal and emotional matters in the workplace had for many until then been anathema.

The dimensions that had been identified at the earlier off-site workshop were reviewed in the team's twice-monthly events. Within just six to nine months of starting the process, the outcomes were striking. For example, the team's own perception of its overall performance had increased from 34 to nearly 75 per cent, while the number of the division's business unit clients that invited the team to have a presence in their executive teams had increased from three to 15. Suddenly, a team that had had difficulty attracting people from within the bank to join its number was increasingly receiving unsolicited requests from prospective job candidates.

The positive impression that was being radiated to others found further expression too as other teams began to call upon Ian and Michael's support to help them work through a similar process of transformation. Even when the bank underwent a major restructuring, the team's performance experienced only a temporary blip in its surveys before reverting to a pattern of extremely positive results, proving the resilience that the team had built up.

A part of the strength that the team had acquired lay with the fact that the process had given total clarity about what it wanted to achieve rather than leaving this open to individual interpretation. For Michael too, being able to work at both individual and team levels and so understand the team's interrelationships was important to help him be more effective in his coaching. That said, Ian believes that it is critical to engage the right person or people to act as coaches, and Michael had fitted the bill exactly in this regard.

Even though the well-defined dimensions that the team had set itself allowed for robust measurement, the question still remained – had coaching itself made the difference in bringing about the change that was apparent to all? To help answer this, Ian engaged a Six Sigma consultant to analyse the survey results statistically, and this confirmed that the improvements were statistically significant.[2]

Such independent analysis combined with the responses of others showed that the division's remarkable turnaround wasn't just due to chance. Ian and his fellow managers' ability to suspend their disbelief about something that they didn't fully understand at the start of the process had been justly rewarded.

Ian Gibson is co-founder of the GMDR group. He may be contacted at ian.gibson@gmdrgroup.com.au.

A word about using anecdotes as input in evaluation

Anecdotes are very important for gaining understanding and for telling the story of a coaching intervention. Stories can not only powerfully illustrate the consequence of an intervention, but they can also make clear why coaching, rather than something else, has made a difference.

Analysed systematically using a structured approach such as the balance of probabilities method, anecdotes can have a significant part to play in understanding reality, as well as giving assurance that a particular course of action is valid. Used to tell a story, they can engage an audience and leave a powerful impact. However, it's important to remember that a hand-picked story may be an example that doesn't fit the rule. Still, quality is almost always preferable to quantity where data inputs are concerned: a few well-rationalized anecdotes may offer far stronger insight than 100 unqualified ones.

In our experience, many academics have traditionally derided anecdotal evidence as not fitting with what they see as being 'the scientific method'.[3] But scientists have always been split on this matter – and necessarily so – since the disciplines of some don't always lend themselves to neat, empirical analysis. Many themes in human psychology and animal ethology provide examples.

Indeed, anecdotes are occasionally the only means for making sense of a situation, with other data not being available or possible to collect. As the economist Peter G Klein, associate professor at the University of Missouri, puts it: 'often all we have is anecdotes… a well informed anecdote is better than quantitative data that proxy only very crudely for the underlying phenomenon of interest' (Klein, 2007).

The ethologist Marc Bekoff comments that 'anecdotes and stories drive much of science although they are not enough on their own. But to claim they aren't a useful heuristic flies in the face of how hard science and soft science are conducted' (Bekoff, 2006).

When categorizing an anecdote, it may be useful to reflect on the possible commonality of a group of comments taken together at one time. For example, the following comments fed back at a focus group workshop might be related:

1 'I'm not sure whether I should be making suggestions when coaching.'

2 'The coaching training I received was perfect for my needs.'

3 'I'm not sure if I should be coaching at times.'

4 'I'm not good at making up questions on the spot.'

5 'Coaching for real isn't quite as easy as it was on the training course.'

6 'I often wish I could turn to someone for guidance when coaching.'

7 'I now find myself coaching all the time.'

8 'I find I want to advise but can't do this in coaching.'

9 'Coaching takes up so much time.'

In this example, the following categories might be applied:

- uncertainty about coaching boundaries (1, 3, 7 – possibly inferred);
- coaching training was fully adequate (2);
- coaching isn't something I always feel adept at (4, 5, 6);
- uncertainty about using a non-directive style and sometimes being able to give a gentle nudge; having confidence to use metaphor or stories (3, 8);
- seeing coaching as a bolt-on approach (3, 8, 9).

A wide range of articles on coaching evaluation can be downloaded from the companion website to this book, www.managingcoachingatwork.com.

Assessing counter-arguments

The balance of probabilities approach lends itself very well to addressing the question of why coaching has been specifically responsible for any impacts that are claimed as well as why it may not be able to make such claims. The distinction of evidence that favours, opposes or is inconclusive in supporting an argument that forms a core part of analysis clearly integrates this requirement.

Unlike when presenting to a jury as would a barrister in a criminal law case, an evaluator doesn't play the role of just prosecutor or just defence. Were this the case, possible lines of argument that an opponent to their view could put forward might be easily overlooked. It's vital that an evaluator retains an open mind and approaches evaluation objectively.

This may not be as easy as it seems. In particular, most people are predisposed to making unconscious judgements most of the time. If you think that you're not one of the majority, we recommend trying your hand at one of the online tests of implicit association[4] created by Project Implicit, a research initiative of Harvard University, the University of Virginia and the University of Washington to explore the influence of unconscious bias in human psychology (see the website https://implicit.harvard.edu/implicit/).

The temptation for most of us to draw premature conclusions while gathering evidence is very real. But any argument that is based only on selective information is unlikely to hold water with others.

One way in which the temptation to rush to conclusions might be avoided is to separate out evidence gathering (or investigation) from analysis and assessment. These are, of course, discrete steps in the balance of probabilities approach.

Ideally too, an evaluator should have no personal agenda that might influence the course of their investigation. Someone who is not otherwise engaged with the coaching process should bring the desired level of objectivity. However, where a coaching project leader undertakes evaluation themselves, it's incumbent on them to set aside personal feelings or beliefs about the initiative being evaluated.

The onus is, of course, on an evaluator to ensure that devil's advocate questions can be answered during their consultations with study participants. We always include the 'Why coaching?' and 'Why not something else?' questions in data-gathering activities. Such questions invite individuals not only to reflect carefully on what it is about their coaching experiences that is unique or significant, but also to keep an open mind on the range of other factors that may play a part in the changes they've noticed.

From an evaluator's point of view, this provides insight and highlights what else is happening outside the 'coaching vacuum'. Just as any good detective sets about an investigation, this means making sure that they stay aware of Suzuki's observation that 'in a beginner's mind,[5] there are many choices, in an expert's few' (Suzuki, 2010). In keeping a beginner's mind, an evaluator should expect to be surprised and find new insight along every new path that they follow.

Comparison with Kirkpatrick's 'four levels' model

You may be wondering how the balance of probabilities approach might fit with the 'four levels' model created by Donald Kirkpatrick, which after all has built up a strong pedigree over several decades.

Kirkpatrick's model has undoubted value. However, what is open to question is the sequential order that is presented for assessing these outputs. In the model, getting to the real nub of what a coaching programme is intended to deliver seems to be held off like some nervous 'dance of the seven veils'. Yet starting an evaluation exercise by considering these key outcomes may actually save effort over Kirkpatrick's traditional approach.

For a start, there's no good reason why evaluating learning, behaviour and results for an organization (levels 2 to 4) have procedurally to follow the customer satisfaction 'happy sheet' exercise that commonly concludes a training course. This might suggest that we can't begin to make sense of whether, say, a lack of change in behaviour (level 3) is due to learning objectives (level 2) being missed.

Of course, cause-and-effect relationships between the different levels should exist. However, these may not be the only or even the main reasons why performance at a succeeding level in the Kirkpatrick sequence falls short of, exceeds or achieves what was hoped for. For example, behavioural change may be influenced by individuals' confidence to push out of comfort zones, having opportunities to practise new skills or being supported after their training by a coach or mentor, amongst other factors. As we've noted already, coaching rarely occurs in a vacuum.

An alternative, time-effective approach may then be to start at 'the top end' – in other words, first question whether business impacts have been felt, and then look back if expected outcomes haven't been achieved. This is, of course, what we advocate in the balance of probabilities approach.

It's also relevant to look back to understand what underpins the results that are observed, with a view to isolating the vital contribution of coaching. Without a clear rationale, it's impossible to validate why specific impacts have occurred, an imperative that is played down in Kirkpatrick's approach.

In practice, identifying what business results and behavioural changes have occurred can happen at the same time as data gathering. There seems to us to be no need to physically separate these as different levels, even if they are logically distinct.

Our methodology doesn't then contradict Kirkpatrick's approach, but takes a different starting point. In fact, this actually mirrors one example of an adaptation of his model cited by Kirkpatrick himself adopted by the computer company Intel (Kirkpatrick, 1998).

Making evaluation a routine process

Evaluation need not be a clunky process, but inevitably it does involve a commitment of time, not just from the people carrying out a study but from those with whom they need to consult too. This is one reason why it's important to be well prepared when speaking with study participants, respecting that their time is precious. To make unreasonable demands on participants is a policy that's unlikely to encourage their further participation in future studies.

Given the time involved, the question then arises – how often should coaching evaluation be conducted? Unfortunately, there's no simple or right or wrong answer to this question. Evaluation may be especially relevant during the early stages of a new programme's roll-out. For example, it might be used to assess whether training delivered to early delegate groups has been effective, while allowing sufficient time to make any necessary changes for the benefit of others. In this case, a study may have a very specific focus ('Is training achieving its objectives?').

Evaluation studies that seek to explore the impacts of coaching must allow sufficient time for coaching to take place and impacts to be felt. We suggest that this might typically require a minimum elapsed period of six months since the start of live coaching or nine to 12 months following the launch of a coaching programme, and where practical, involve individuals whose coaching engagements were completed some months previously too.

Studies may, of course, focus on quite specific things and at different times, not necessarily setting out to conduct an end-to-end review of a coaching implementation. The effectiveness of support provided to internal coaches, the factors that encourage managers to embrace coaching after being trained and an attempt to quantify the return on investment that coaching is delivering are examples.[6]

Evaluation of implementation programmes may quite reasonably only be required for a definite period (eg many programmes have an active life of perhaps just one or two years). However, evaluation of what coaching is delivering and the continuing effectiveness or otherwise of the processes, infrastructure and support mechanisms for operating a coaching service are of course ongoing needs and shouldn't be sacrificed as attention becomes diverted to new change initiatives.

Crucially, evaluation can indicate whether the ways in which coaching is currently being used remain relevant for the organization's people management strategy and business need, and whether investment in it was and continues to be worthwhile, representing value for money. Here there is considerable overlap with what a snapshot audit might reveal. We'll come back to consider how coaching can be kept in step with the needs of an organization in the final chapter.

This need alone stresses the value of conducting evaluation (or an audit) routinely, perhaps at least once each year.

Promoting coaching

Leaders in organizations that have achieved a level of maturity in their adoption of coaching may need less convincing of the continuing value of sustaining a coaching investment than others. However, for most, an interest in and support for coaching may begin to wane unless its relevance can be kept as a visible item on the business agenda.

One of the critical goals of evaluation is to provide both the evidence that an organization's commitment to coaching remains relevant and to remind others that this continues to be so. For many, the greatest interest in any investment must be to see a return. This can only be accessed through effective evaluation.

In the next chapter, we'll consider the types of decision that may need to be taken based on what an evaluation study (or audit) reveals. For now, we might usefully conclude our discussion of the balance of probabilities method by reflecting on its value for keeping a passion for coaching alive.

To discover that coaching really is making a transformative difference in people's lives and in ways that benefit their teams and organizations is genuinely a cause for wanting to continue to promote the value of coaching with a vengeance. The difference in being able to do this on the back of tangible experience of what has actually been delivered rather than on its potential alone can't be overstated.

Summary

In this chapter, we've explored how the balance of probabilities method can be used in evaluation to analyse data and present a conclusion. The method aims to isolate the significance of the initiative being studied as a contributor to the financial performance or other impacts that are apparent while disassociating its impacts from other potential influences.

Development of logical arguments that support or oppose a working premise forces rigorous thinking about how different types of data (anecdotes, performance measures, etc) may relate and why. Inductive and deductive reasoning may be used to achieve this.

The same logical approach taken to explain how different data inputs to analysis contribute to a study's overall conclusion also provides an effective way to structure an evaluation report.

Notes

1 A Gestalt perspective takes account of the whole form and nature of something or someone, assuming that 'the whole is greater than the sum of its parts'. For example, a person's thinking on a particular topic may be better understood by taking account of their character, personality and background (amongst other things) together rather than just homing in on what influence each of these has individually.

2 'Statistically significant': a result produced during statistical analysis that is unlikely to have occurred by chance.

3 'Scientific method': a process of observing, experimenting and collecting measurable empirical data, analysing the collected data and using sound reasoning to substantiate a theory.

4 The concept of 'implicit association' refers to the conscious and unconscious preferences of individuals in relation to such things as gender, ethnicity and politics. We often make snap judgements based on associations that are deep rooted. For example, on first glance, some people may more readily see someone who has a facial disfigurement as being less attractive than someone whose face is not disfigured. Project Implicit, a research collaboration between Harvard University, the University of Virginia and the University of Washington, offers online tests covering a wide range of themes for association (see https://implicit.harvard.edu/implicit/).

5 'Beginner's mind': approaching a task or investigation as free of assumption and prejudice as possible, ready to accept novelty and not being biased by pre-existing views.

6 It's not normally the case that hard financial savings can be calculated as a part of an evaluation study, although ballpark savings that relate to the 'business results' that a study reveals can often be estimated with reasonable confidence. The costs of coaching are usually much easier to determine, and often without a need to make too many assumptions. When attempting to quantify the cost/benefit of coaching, we prefer to take a prudent approach: quantifying only what we believe can be assessed with confidence, even if this is a minimum return rather than the most likely or most optimistic calculation.

Learnings, change and new directions

Introduction

Coaching programmes that are launched on the basis of being 'a good idea' to try or brought in to follow a fashion are unlikely to deliver against their potential over the long term, and as many are likely to falter once an organization turns its attention to new ventures. The same might be said of training for front-line managers in coaching skill, and the enthusiasm for coaching showed by senior stakeholders and the commitment of coaches too, especially when appropriate support and suitable opportunities for coaching aren't readily available.

Notwithstanding the changing priorities that preoccupy the minds of those who may once have been keen sponsors of coaching, budget constraints and the promise of new initiatives to deliver the same benefits expected of coaching, as we've seen, a wide range of factors may intervene to push a coaching initiative off course. Sustaining competency and enthusiasm amongst coaches, managers and sponsors is a common need, but so too is ensuring that the day-to-day management of a coaching function doesn't fall through the gaps as organizations experience change.

We've seen examples of coaching initiatives that lost their momentum as a result of an evangelical and high-energy coaching project leader changing roles (though methodical and grounded types often make the best ongoing managers). Sadly, we've also quite often witnessed an onset of complacency amongst long-ago trained and well-practised coaches who believe that their days for benefiting from further training, support and development are long over.

So too, it's not uncommon for the simple task of occasionally acknowledging the contribution of internal coach volunteers to become neglected, and so goodwill is gradually lost. We've unfortunately also seen what should be self-sustaining programmes falter because excessive demands were made without appreciating the coaching pool's capacity to deliver on these.

What's more, as we've mentioned repeatedly, organizational needs change, and so too do the topics that coaching might most benefit. If one thing can be guaranteed, it's that a coaching function can never be left to stand still while an organization's people and business contexts are frequently in a state of flux.

In this chapter, we'll explore the crucial task of keeping step with change and ensuring that coaching maintains its place as a priority in the minds of those who lead organizations through change as well as with those who support and provide coaching. We'll consider the value of audit and evaluation for informing decisions about which direction a coaching initiative might take, and give attention to the relevance of continuing development of coaching practice, including what we consider to be the essential role of supervision. But even were it not for a changing backdrop of organizational change that should help keep coaches on their toes, there's usually much that can be gained and applied from the learnings that accrue from coaching practice itself.

Learnings and responses

What can be learned from coaching experience?

Organizational learning (or what we like to describe as 'living needs analysis') is a topic that's often bandied about but which in our observation isn't always given the serious attention it deserves.

Many organizations make a fair attempt to capture learnings, but the task of putting into practice what the learnings suggest should be adopted can prove to be an elusive task. Beyond appreciating what has been achieved and building a snapshot of the current state of a coaching implementation, other than to justify new budget proposals there seems to be little point in auditing or evaluating a coaching programme unless what is learned can help inform future decisions.

Learnings may bring advantages in different ways – improving the effectiveness of support given to coaches, managers, supervisors and coachees, identifying gaps where additional developmental support might be directed, streamlining and improving the processes for administering coaching or pointing out ways that departments, projects and partners might benefit from taking different approaches.

While working with the London Metropolitan Police Service, Jackie recognized an opportunity for her organization to make significant savings simply by enhancing the training given to staff managers and officers. A peer-to-peer approach with the individuals responsible for effecting such changes met with polite acknowledgement but no clear commitment to shake up an established and largely well-regarded training programme. It was therefore only through an escalated recommendation to consider the cross-organizational value of making a range of changes that Jackie's proposal was seized upon.

Perseverance, belief in the value of making a change and a concerted effort to evidence the benefits of taking a recommendation on board may well be needed to ensure that suggestions don't become confined to the archive. This may mean being selective and (if necessary) pushing hard to raise the case of perhaps just a few key recommendations. It also implies that activity and drive on the part of a coaching project leader and/or their sponsor are vital – a key proponent must remain determined to promote their cause, not just in submitting a written report or considering this responsibility as just another role requirement.

Applying learning

The process of learnings capture, analysis and application shouldn't be onerous: it should be welcomed and can actually be fun! Feedback mechanisms used in training courses, questionnaire surveys, documents to support coaching conversations (eg action forms completed by coachees), supervision and review activities should fuel an ongoing supply of information. At the same time, individuals can be encouraged and advised how to pass on informal feedback when they believe this may be appropriate.

A simple database or spreadsheet table may then be used to capture information (an example Microsoft Excel template may be downloaded from our website, www.managingcoachingatwork.com), and a regular review of new contributions to this list should enable points that need to be clarified or where fuller information might be sought to be identified before they are forgotten by originators.

Perhaps once each quarter or even annually, this list can be more closely scrutinized and each item categorized according to type (eg reviewing the effectiveness of current training approaches for achieving desired learning objectives, process gaps and support infrastructure weaknesses; holding combined workshops involving both internal and external coaches working within the same organization).

Where possible recommendations for influencing change are implied, an attempt might be made to indicate whether the recommendation is likely to be something that can be implemented quite easily, is likely to involve consultation with others and the expected impact that making changes might have. In turn, this should allow priority recommendations to be made.

Of course, learnings capture need not just occur at an organizational level. As we've seen and will discuss again later in this chapter, individual coaches' and manager coaches' development of practice are crucially underpinned through their own reflective practice and ability to share and learn from each other (through review activities, co-coaching, supervision and the like).

So too, much can be gained by sharing learnings with other organizations and keeping abreast of new thinking in professional coaching circles. Individual or corporate membership of a professional coaching body, participating in conferences and other events targeted at coaches and leaders of coaching programmes, and subscribing to relevant journals all provide ways of staying in touch.

Audit

A suggested role for auditing coaching was introduced in the previous chapter, in which we also distinguished 'audit' from 'evaluation' by reference to the former being most concerned with 'taking stock' and the latter adding an assessment dimension and typically being combined with quite specific recommendations.

At the most basic level, an audit may simply describe what is currently happening on the ground – how many people have been coached, how many coaching conversations have taken place, how many have been put through training, and the like – without remarking on whether this is more or less than had been planned for, desirable or otherwise. Evaluation, by contrast, may focus on quite specific topics of inquiry and attempt to quantify the value that coaching is delivering.

For our current purpose, it doesn't matter significantly that we need distinguish between these two. Our interest is in how the outputs of an audit or evaluation study may be used. The snapshot picture of an audit can be revealing in itself, especially if the picture that's described can be compared with a previously defined set of expectations.

However, as we've emphasized in the preceding chapters, what really makes the difference in deciding how to move a coaching initiative forward is having an understanding of not just what's happening but *why* this is so. A comprehensive evaluation study will answer the question 'Why coaching?' as opposed to some other intervention that has had an impact, so allowing decisions on the continued or changed use of coaching to be made with reference to other possible ways that an organization might want to spend its money.

An audit may prompt areas to explore – for example, to understand why something may not be working quite as effectively as had been hoped or identify the reason why something may unexpectedly be working significantly better than anyone ever imagined. If conducted using a framework similar to the Coaching Focus model described in Chapter 4, an audit can also prompt an exploration of what may be required to step up to a higher level of application of coaching than what is currently being achieved.

Both audit and evaluation therefore go hand-in-hand to provide information and point out areas where further understanding may be needed to inform effective decision making. In the context of planning the development of a coaching service, determining the training and support provided to those affected by coaching and in selecting the people management and business areas in which coaching is applied, both play a significant part.

Developing coaching

'Developing coaching' means more than just building up the competencies of coaches, important though this may be. It is a concept that applies to all who play a part in delivering and who benefit from coaching – managers, coachees, supervisors and others. Of course, it also refers to the improvement and possible expansion of the coaching service provided to an organization (improving access to coaching, increasing the types of applications for which coaching may be offered and continuing to make sure that what is on offer remains fit for purpose).

We might then consider the distinct needs for developing different aspects of coaching practice, including the role of supervision of coaches and sustaining motivation.

Developing coaching skill proficiency and continuous professional development for coaches

In Chapter 7, we posed the question 'What next?', considering the skill development needs of both coaches and managers who'd already been introduced to coaching. In both cases, we suggested a range of possible themes that might feature in ongoing training, but also pointed out the importance of supporting development in a way that is relevant for both the organization and the individuals concerned.

In the case of coaches' professional development, this implies that development needs should be routinely reviewed. For the manager as coach too, consideration of coaching should feature in periodic personal development discussions.

As we saw in Chapter 7, professional development should not rely solely on providing additional training. Indeed, some of the most effective means for developing awareness, knowledge and ability are found in buddy-coaching, coaching circles and reflective practice. Such activities allow individuals to relate to real experiences of coaching and to home in on a wide range of very specific topics that a training curriculum alone would be hard pressed to cover.

Quite apart from encouraging reflections on experience and providing opportunities for learning, these informal activities may serve the purpose of bringing coaches who may otherwise feel isolated together from time to time and also help sustain an interest in coaching amongst managers. Encouraging individuals to commit to continuous professional development also helps to guard against complacency, especially amongst coaches who have accrued many hundreds of hours of coaching practice.

In our view, 'professional development' shouldn't just be about getting better or learning more, but is about staying grounded in the things that make a person a 'great coach' – often what may be a simple principle to recognize but require acute emotional intelligence and discipline to put into practice. We are convinced that the best coaches – those who are best able to work most effectively with individuals to achieve both their needs and those of their organization, to permanently shift mindsets when relevant, inspire and motivate to action – are those who have the humility to admit their own weaknesses, and the discipline to continue to work on improving what many may regard as quite basic skills. As we've seen, the bedrocks for effective coaching include intent listening, sensitive reflection, using sensitive language, and the like. No end of reading of academic papers, producing impressive dissertations or training programme certificates can substitute for a coach's honest desire to continue to be their very best and to be mindful of their influence in any situation.

All of this points to a need for coaches to have an opportunity to reflect carefully on their own practice, and (ideally) to be able to do this with a degree of objectivity. Often too, coaches may want to stop and reflect on how they are approaching a coaching dialogue with a client – especially if a client's progress appears to be slow or if roadblocks are readily being encountered. Both of these needs might suggest that it would be useful for coaches to receive coaching themselves, and in a sense, this is a part of what supervision provides, as we'll see later.

Developing a coaching service

Invariably, a coaching practice may need to change some aspects of its operation to align with the changing demands that are put upon it. For example, integration with project plans and training course syllabuses is likely to be needed when coaching is to be used to support a new change project or development programme.

Expanding the reach of coaching to support new areas of business need or to give access to a wider base of people are perhaps amongst the more obvious ways in which a coaching service may develop over time. Where this involves an increase in the task of administering and managing the service, the need for robust quality management processes and support systems becomes more pertinent, as well as possibly requiring an increased amount of effort from those charged with responsibility for monitoring the coaching process.

An ambition to step up the extent to which an organization embraces coaching might also call for a review of the capability of existing management practice. In general, this is likely to involve investment in infrastructure and standardizing on processes that have previously been applied on an informal piecemeal basis. For example, criteria for achieving higher levels in the Coaching Focus model include such things as the presence of a universal system for matching coaches and coachees, incorporating measures of coaching competency in manager role profiles, and assessment criteria and formal procedures for planning for future coaching needs.

The biggest impetus for change is likely to be changing business need. By ensuring that routine evaluation takes account of evolving business strategy and people management priorities, and by maintaining effective ongoing communication with heads of department, learning and development managers and others who may have responsibility for initiatives in which coaching may play a part, it should be possible to keep abreast of such changing contexts and so be able to respond in an appropriate way when needed. Coaching performance that is directly linked into balanced scorecard or similar frameworks for measuring organizational performance offers an especially effective way of ensuring that coaching continues to be aligned with what matters for a business, although, as we've seen, such frameworks aren't always in place nor are they necessarily easy to integrate with.

Even without a desire to grow or a need to change focus, it's unlikely that any coaching service will lack any scope for improvement. Lessons learnt through experience and feedback offered by service users should normally be sufficient to indicate possible areas for change. These may in turn be assessed for the potential benefits they may bring in exchange for the costs of making a change.

Supervision

The practice of supervision is well established in medical and academic circles, amongst other professions. With the clear precedent of its value shown in psychotherapy and other 'helping services', it's perhaps not surprising that the notion has been readily embraced by the coaching profession.

In the context of coaching, supervision has been variously defined as '[a] process by which a coach with the help of a supervisor, who is not working directly with the client, can attend to understanding better both the client system and themselves as part of the client–coach system, and transform their work' (Hawkins and Smith, 2006), 'a formal process of professional support, which ensures continuing development of the coach and effectiveness of his/her coaching practice through interactive reflection, interpretative evaluation and the sharing of expertise' (Bachkirova et al, 2005) and our personal favourite, 'an opportunity to bring someone home to their own mind, to show them how good they can be' (Kline, 1999).

A more detailed way of defining the nature of supervision might follow an idea described by Proctor (1986), that supervision is:

- normative – a supervisor accepts (or more accurately shares with a supervisee) responsibility for ensuring that the supervisee's work is professional and ethical, operating within whatever codes, laws and organizational norms apply;

- formative – a supervisor acts to provide feedback or direction that enables a supervisee to develop the skills, theoretical knowledge, personal attributes and so on that will mean the supervisee becomes an increasingly competent practitioner; and

- supportive (Proctor calls this 'restorative') – a supervisor is there to listen, support and confront the supervisee when inevitable personal issues, doubts and insecurities arise – and when client issues are picked up by the supervisee.

What is apparent from each of these descriptions is that supervision is designed to help a coach make sense of their own experience, to see how they can better help their clients. This might be contrary to a more generalized use of the term, which might usually suggest a managerial-type role: someone who has a vested interest in the outcome, and is in some way 'above' the individual they are supervising, empowered to direct them. When training coach supervisors, we sometimes hyphenate the term (as 'super-vision') to emphasize that this is not its intended meaning in the context that we're concerned with, but rather an objective non-hierarchical overseer or 'professional guardian'.

Nonetheless, our reference to the term does imply that a supervisor needs to have a sound grasp of the professional standard that a coach should adhere to (ie to core competencies, ethics and practice) as well as the skill to help a coach reflect upon and gain insights into their current coaching performance. It's been argued too that coaches may benefit from being able to call upon a range of supervision and mentoring services, from both within and outside their own organization (Gray, 2010), although we've yet to see how effectively this might work in practice.

A supervisor needs to be objective, sensitive to cues offered by the coach and totally focused on the coach's (and their coachees') interests. As such, a supervisor often needs to employ similar skills and have similar attributes to a coach; in particular, they need strong emotional intelligence, an ability to provide objective oversight and acute listening skill.

Time spent in supervision preparing for a coaching dialogue can pay dividends many times over. While it may be hard to quantify, many coaches to whom we've spoken believed that they had been saved many hours of possibly difficult conversation with coachees by giving over a few hours to hard reflection with a supervisor. Supervision helps attend to a coach's continuing development needs, provides a check on whether matters like contracting have been undertaken satisfactorily and enables a coach to reflect on whether it may be appropriate to propose closing out a dialogue with a coachee.

Benefits may also accrue in the enhanced learning and developing competency (and so impact) of coaches, in sustaining coach motivation and better equipping coaches to consider how best to help their coachees move forward. But there are positive impacts for coachees, the organization and supervisors themselves too. Coachees should receive greater benefit from the impact of two minds considering their situation and have greater assurance that their coach will observe safe coaching boundaries; organizations may capture learnings from supervision and have similar reassurance of a coach's 'safety'. Furthermore, supervisors themselves have much to learn through the scenarios that arise in their conversations with coaches.

Supervision conversations may be approached systematically. Several models have been proposed as references for supervisors, including Hawkins and Shohet's 'Seven-eyed' model (Hawkins and Shohet, 2006), which reminds a supervisor to consider a range of factors such as the impact of a coach's relationship with their client, the interventions they use and the supervisory relationship itself, and Bluesky International's 'REFLECT©' model, which recognizes the importance of reflective practice (Lewis, 2008).

We've adopted a model of our own, putting an emphasis on what a supervisor might help a coach to work through. We call the model 'STOP':

- Stepping back: putting a distance between the coach and whatever they are involved with at the moment – from the momentum of action, emotion and thinking.

- Thinking: shifting thinking, disengaging thoughts in order to either rest or engage in a different level of thinking.

- Organizing thoughts: pulling thinking together, bringing coherence to a plan, considering priorities and providing a sequence for actions, making sense of an experience.

- Proceeding: when the purpose and the next step are clear and the coach feels more connected with themselves, their motivations and needs.

As with coaching, not all supervision sessions will include identical elements. For example, sometimes a focus on a coach's development may be of more interest; at others, the emphasis may be on considering a potentially challenging topic in a coaching dialogue.

Similarly, the frequency of supervision sessions that are needed may vary from coach to coach and from time to time, depending on the stage a coach has reached, the stage a coaching dialogue has attained, and current need. However, in the absence of other guidance, a guideline adopted by many coaches we know is that coaches should commit to at least one hour of supervision for every 20 hours of coaching that they undertake. But this really should be seen as being a minimum base line.

Developing a supervision capability

Supervisors require training, support and opportunities for shared reflection as much as do coaches. So too, matching a coach with a potential supervisor is not something that can be left to chance. As with establishing a coaching service, a decision needs to be taken on whether supervisors should be sourced internally, externally or using a mix of both.

The same considerations for establishing a coaching practice that we've discussed in previous chapters also apply when building up a supervision capability. Similarly, attention needs to be given to forecasting the future demand for supervision, taking account of the fact that calls on supervisors may not be determined just by the size of a coach population alone, but by the (unpredictable) nature of issues that are brought to supervision, some of which will be more demanding and time consuming than others. In other words, it's prudent to over-plan slightly for future supervision needs.

When initially launching a coaching service, there may be few (if any) suitable potential candidates to canvas as supervisors, given that a reasonable level of coaching experience is a normal prerequisite for this role. Organizations that are in this position may therefore have no option but to look outside, calling on support from professional supervisors or possibly from other organizations in a partner network.

Sooner or later however, it's likely that most organizations will want to build their own supervision capability, and this calls for a recruitment and development process that has a similar rigor to that involved when engaging coaches. We suggest possible topics that might be included in the essential training for supervisors in Table 10.1, and have also included a suggested Supervisor Role Profile amongst the downloads available from our website, www.managingcoachingatwork.com.

TABLE 10.1 Suggested scope of training for supervisors

- Defining supervision and the role of the supervisor
- Outcomes and benefits of super-vision -- for coach, coachee, supervisor and organization
- systematic super-vision (using a model as a framework for supervision, eg 'STOP');
- The progress of coaching: contracting, boundaries, the stage coaching has reached, the individual and the organization (private and public goals, contexts for objectives)
- Understanding people in the coaching relationship (psychological models, eg theory of mind, transactional analysis)
- Listening between the words, uncovering the unseen (eg language of the eyes)
- Self-understanding: assumptions, personality, prejudice, language impacts, cross-cultural conversations, transference
- Overcoming jams and difficult coaching scenarios
- The coach–supervisor relationship
- Reflective practice: self-awareness and self-management
- Continuous professional development for coaches

Sustaining interest and commitment

We've touched on the need to sustain interest and engagement in coaching before, suggesting some possible ways of keeping passion alive. Re-engagement and reselling of coaching may become all the more relevant when a change is planned in the direction of a coaching service: for example, by extending its reach to new applications. At a minimum, relevant audiences need to be made aware of the change and the reason for adopting a new focus needs to be made clear to avoid target sponsors and beneficiaries developing a possibly false perception that the coaching service is still trying to find its way.

Reporting on an audit or evaluation exercise provides a good opportunity to point out what an organization has achieved from coaching. As we suggested in the last chapter, promoting the findings of an evaluation study should normally be routine, and there can be few better ways to sell a case for a new focus for coaching than to be able to highlight what has already been achieved.

Planning for future need

The ability to provide a coaching service that remains fit for purpose means that the audiences who are sought out to support coaching and to be coached, the people made available to coach and the uses to which coaching is put need to remain relevant for emerging business need. At the same time, to avoid disappointing potential clients for coaching and so also endangering the credibility of the coaching function, a reasonable attempt must be made to match the likely demand for coaching in the foreseeable future with the supply of suitably qualified coaches. That's not to mention keeping a watch on the infrastructure, development support and cadre of supervisors needed to facilitate their needs too.

CASE STUDY Singular focus: bringing coaching to the Humberside Police Constabulary

The Humberside Police Force wasn't the first UK constabulary to seize on the benefits of coaching, but when it launched its programme in 2008 it had formed a clear view of where coaching would fit in and quickly be able to make its impact felt.

Police officers and staff alike engaged with the programme, with several from amongst the senior ranks signing up to join the first cohort of coach trainees. Emphasizing 'what coaching gives' (and why coaching achieves this rather than alternatives) was a key to this, observes Superintendent Judi Heaton, one of the programme's early champions.

The programme adopted a phased implementation approach, with externally led training, training of in-house trainers and later of coach supervisors following in a planned sequence. Superintendent Heaton maintains that getting the design of training right is critical to ensure that coaches are properly equipped for the specific role that they're expected to perform. In the Force's experience, the ability to draw upon a structured training programme that fitted the needs of the organization was a significant advantage. Within one year of launching the programme, the Force had created a self-sustaining coaching team, with coaches continuing to balance coaching assignments with busy workloads.

The Force insisted on a robust interview process when recruiting coaches to the in-house pool, supported by experienced internal coaches who had been identified when preparing the programme as well as others drafted in from a neighbouring force. Recruiting the right people to be coached was also important.

Following initial training, coaches received regular practice, even when not engaging with coaching clients, meaning that their skills remained fresh. As Superintendent Heaton comments, 'the capability of coaches is extremely important, and this requires them to maintain professional practice'. These so-called 'coaches under construction' were supported through supervision and co-coaching, while review days and a biannual joint meeting involving all coaches and supervisors became a part of what is now a regular calendar. Supervisors also continue to meet regularly to share generic learnings and develop their own practice.

Superintendent Heaton believes that factors that should underpin the introduction of an in-house programme include:

- having an appropriate infrastructure in place;

- coordinating all coaching activities;

- appointing a coaching coordinator who is a coach and able to really drive the coaching function, ensuring that support is provided for all involved in its delivery;

- directing where coaching is needed and focusing on individuals' development; and

- mandating supervision.

Humberside Police Force saw coaching as a developmental opportunity, and have employed it widely to help potentially talented officers and staff in such areas as achieving higher potential, supporting those put on a fast track and preparing individuals for promotion. Some remedial and directive coaching has also been used, working in cooperation with coachees' line managers, while the Force has also recently started using coaching to help women police constables and sergeants (who still form a minority amongst the uniformed ranks). The Women's Integrated Network, a voluntary group of officers and other personnel, has encouraged coaching as an integral part of new officer induction. This intervention is already proving to be helpful for newcomers as they face their new roles.

Coaching has especially helped to challenge viewpoints and allow individuals to see things from different perspectives. An independent audit praised the Force's commitment and appropriate balance of rigour, broad subject matter and focus on relevant themes and coaching competencies.

Coaching may not always be an easy sell for organizations that often rely on swift decision making for effective command and control, but Humberside Police Force has shown that there's not only a place for coaching within their service, but a useful one too.

Note: as lead consultant to this project, Jackie would like to acknowledge Andrea Wood and Superintendent Heaton for their contribution to driving the implementation at Humberside Police Force and making it happen.

Planning supply to meet demand

As many of the case studies featured in this book show, a controlled roll-out of an in-house practice has been a critical factor in the successful uptake of coaching within the organizations who've shared their experiences with us. The cautionary note that this implies is that organizations may do well to ensure that they can walk before they try to run, initially restricting access to coaching and limiting its promotion before being able to cater for genuine demand.

At the other extreme, organizations that offer coaching to any individual have succeeded by ensuring that their contracting process for coaching is robust. Typically this has involved having not just evidence that a coachee is aware of what coaching aims to achieve and can demonstrate their commitment to play their part to make it work, but also involving active sponsorship from coachees' line managers and a careful assessment of whether coaching is the most appropriate intervention for helping individuals' needs. Without such safeguards being in place, an organization that promotes access to coaching too widely is likely to find that its money is not being spent to best advantage, with coaching relationships striking up without a necessary purpose and continuing ad infinitum without consideration of their usefulness.

An attempt to estimate future coaching demand is relevant whether adopting a controlled roll-out or 'big bang' approach to implementation, enabling planning for adequate numbers of coaches, supervisors, administrators and others being available to satisfy the need, not to mention that those providing the service will have received relevant training. Historical analysis provides one useful input to forecasting. With all things being equal, reasonable judgements on likely future loading requirements can be made based on the previous levels of demand. In addition, plans to grow or reduce access to coaching can be factored in, with forecasts being projected from past experience (the number of coaching hours, averaged elapsed time periods for coaching engagements and the like).

Plans may be further developed based on usually well-defined requirements of change projects, training programmes and other initiatives that coaching is intended to support. Such initiatives are likely to prescribe a minimum quota for coaching and affect a defined number of people.

However, a problem arises in forecasting because not all things usually remain equal over time. Quite specific demands for coaching arise in response to possibly unforeseen circumstances as well as some that might be anticipated, such as an increase in the number of individuals who want to know how best to position themselves when an organization passes through periods of disruption and rapid change. There's no set formula that can be called upon to determine how many sessions or what period may be required to give a coachee most value, especially when a dialogue begins based on exploring what's needed to achieve a general desired outcome rather than a specific goal (as is often the case and is often desirable).

We therefore suggest that, budget provision allowing, the golden rule that we've mentioned several times before is applied in this case – that forecasts of coaching demand should assume a little more than might be foreseen, but not significantly more that might mean that coaches don't have regular opportunities to put their skills into practice. Of course, a level of backfill may be provided by external coaches engaged on short-term contracts when necessary, although budget provision for such eventuality still usually needs to be planned. Forecasting coach resource loading may be assisted by using project planning software or a spreadsheet application.

One dilemma that may confront leaders of coaching practices is not having sufficient budget to cater for future needs. We wish that we could offer a simple solution to this unsatisfactory but not uncommon scenario; however, short of selling in-house coaching services externally, fresh funding can't just be summoned out of thin air! Some enterprising coaching leaders have managed to generate additional funding for the services they offer, for example by charging external coaches to take part in masterclasses and other CPD activities, as well as by earning revenue from pooled coaching training and services (see Kent Coaching & Mentoring Network case study, pp 156–7).

What may often be possible is to review how available budget is currently being spent with a view to considering whether there are effective alternative means for achieving similar end results. For example, it may be possible to source manager training internally more cost-effectively than by using an external supplier, or some classroom-based training might be suitably substituted with activities such as coaching circles and buddy coaching. Sharing knowledge, expertise and resources with other organizations in a partner network may also offer opportunities for making the best use of limited budgets.

Ultimately, a strong and enduring coaching service can be accomplished on a shoestring. Jackie managed to put coaches through a rigorous programme of development and accreditation as well as setting in place a strong infrastructure for managing coaching practice within one of her final roles as lead consultant at the London Metropolitan Police Service, with Martin Tiplady, the Met's Director of HR, being very much on board as lead sponsor of the programme too. The passion of those who sponsor and lead coaching initiatives, combined with the enthusiasm and commitment of coaches to focus on developing their essential skills through self-reflection and shared experience, costs very little in financial terms.

Changing aspiration and transition

It might seem a natural tendency to want to aspire to achieve more from coaching, or to move 'up a level', to use the language that we adopted earlier. However, it's reasonable to question whether such aspirations are always most appropriate, given the situation an organization may find itself in. For example, it may be foolhardy to commit to a programme of changes that will involve a large investment of time and resource when an organization is passing through a period of uncertainty and when the existing coaching practice seems to be serving its needs well.

Similarly, the desire to foster a 'coaching culture' may be less well received at a time when a command and control style of leadership is called for. This has often been the case when organizations and even nations are in times of crisis. For example, the no-nonsense, strongly directive wartime British Prime Minister Winston Churchill lived up to the proverb 'cometh the hour, cometh the man' at a time when a more participative style of leadership might have exposed the country's vulnerability.

Aspiration must therefore be aligned with a sense of purpose. There can be little point aiming to expand and make radical change when an organization may not be ready to adopt coaching more fully than it has to date, nor when this doesn't fit with what's most needed in the moment. Similarly, those who are set on keeping up with the neighbours or with organizations that they see as setting a benchmark in coaching maturity may easily miss the point.

When the reasons for a significant shift in coaching have been thought through and justified, transition must be carefully planned. While much of the initial groundwork may already have been done, the same matters that we discussed in Chapter 5 when considering planning for an initial implementation will apply. Amongst these will be explaining the need for change and engaging participation, considering skill development and infrastructure support needs, and deciding whether a rapid roll-out or some other approach is most appropriate (possibly informed by what has been learnt from implementation experience so far).

Summary

In this chapter and throughout the book, we've endeavoured to stress that coaching implementation is an ongoing task that can't just be signed off as a 'completed project' once a final round of delegates have been put through training, processes and systems for managing coaching have been put in place and an inaugural audit or evaluation study has concluded that all is progressing well. Organizational priorities change, and so too do people's needs and the potential contribution that coaching can make if it is properly aligned with current need.

It's always possible that evaluation may reveal that the current focus of coaching may not be quite as relevant as it might once have been. Indeed, evaluators and auditors must always aim to remain objective when carrying out their task, mindful that company resources must be spent wisely and that any preconceptions that coaching will always deliver the best 'bang for buck' may be misguided.

This said, we've yet to come across any evaluation or audit report that indicated that an organization's use of coaching had passed its sell-by date. Coaching is no passing fad or just a good idea to try but is what many have discovered is what sets their organization's achievements apart from others. We sincerely hope that you may number amongst them.

APPENDIX A
Templates and micro-tools

Recruiting internal coaches, advertisement for candidates

WANTED! COACHES FOR CONSTRUCTION

Candidates are invited to join a new internal coaching practice. Coaching will be performed on a voluntary, as required and as available basis, in addition to candidates' current responsibilities.

In return for giving (typically) three hours of time each month, successful applicants will develop a valuable professional competency, gain skills that can be usefully applied in everyday conversations and be a part of a closely knit team that is committed to helping others achieve their best.

Prior coaching experience is not required as full training and support will be provided. Most importantly, candidates must be committed to learning and developing coaching skill, and be receptive to constructive feedback. Candidates must be ready to commit to a strict ethical code that respects individuals' privacy, be ready to learn and have a genuine interest in helping others to achieve their objectives.

To find out more or to express a possible interest in this unique opportunity please contact [CONTACT INFORMATION] before [DEADLINE DATE]. Should you then wish to apply, we will require a brief CV from you, accompanied by a cover note explaining what you believe you can bring to a coaching role and what motivates you to apply for this opportunity. Candidates who are shortlisted will then be asked to attend interview.

Please note that we expect that interest in this opportunity will be high, although we are able to accommodate only a limited number of applicants at this time. Line manager approval for release for initial training and to coach will be required before applications move to the interview stage.

Role profile – coach

Role

The role of a coach is to aid another individual ('client') in their appreciation of and response to a topic of their interest, including but not restricted to their self-development, performance, leadership, interpersonal, career or role needs. The nature of assistance offered by a coach puts emphasis on helping clients to draw insights and determine actions for themselves. Nevertheless, a coach may encourage, challenge and feed back to their clients as appropriate. Coaching involves a co-active relationship between coach and client, based on trust, mutual appreciation and a joint commitment to work with the client's best interest at heart.

Responsibilities

Responsibilities include, but aren't restricted to:

- acting as ambassadors for coaching when required, explaining its purpose, benefits and approach (for example to potential coaching clients);
- participating in occasional knowledge-sharing, co-coaching and professional development activities with other coaches;
- operating with the procedures, systems and policies defined by the organization's coaching practice;
- engaging and contracting with new clients;
- preparing for, conducting and (when appropriate) following up on coaching conversations;
- participating in coaching evaluation activities.

Attributes

Coaches should display the following attributes:

- humility, including a readiness to be challenged, accept and respond to feedback, and learn from others;
- avoidance of making assumptions;
- ability to avoid directing or influencing others' thinking;
- honesty;
- openness;
- patience;
- strong self-awareness (having high emotional intelligence);

- be non-judgemental;
- be unprejudiced towards others (on any basis).

Competencies

Coaches should display the following competencies:

1 Ability to communicate effectively with others:
   - able to listen intently, including appreciating what may lie behind an individual's words;
   - able to articulate ideas effectively, for example using meaningful metaphors and analogies;
   - able to use questions that are appropriate, free of bias, non-judgemental and useful to the person being questioned;
   - know when to remain silent;
   - be able to replay back what has been heard, using language that the recipient is likely to be most responsive to;
   - able to adapt communication style as appropriate for the person being coached and the current circumstance.

2 Ability to assess what may best assist another individual move forward at any point in a conversation:
   - able to identify possibly related themes that have been mentioned;
   - able to maintain a clear oversight of the course of a conversation and the course of a coaching dialogue (relationship/process) as a whole;
   - know which interpersonal intervention is most appropriate for the stage a conversation has reached (eg when to probe for more detail and when not to);
   - know when and how to challenge;
   - know when and how to encourage (eg by affirming client actions);
   - able to bring a coachee to make a clear agreement on their next steps and feeling motivated to see these through;
   - able to recognize when support resources or tools may be appropriate for helping a client in a particular situation and know how to use these;
   - knowledge of and ability to effectively apply (according to context) one or more coaching models.

3 Ability to build relationship:
   - able to create and sustain rapport;
   - able to instil trust from others;
   - able to work with clients as people rather than as 'subjects';

- able to appropriately receive client emotion;
- able to manage within the boundaries of a coaching relationship, knowing when and being able to refer a client on matters that fall outside these;
- ability to appreciate the contexts in which the client operates;*
- ability to maintain confidentiality in a coaching relationship.

4 Ability to start and end a coaching relationship effectively:

- able to contract effectively with a new client, agreeing ground-rules to guide the relationship and defining what the coaching aims to achieve;
- able to recognize when it may be most appropriate to close out a coaching relationship or to suggest a referral to another coach.

5 Commitments:

- respectful of commitments made to coachees (eg maintaining agreed meeting times unless extreme circumstances prevent this);
- commitment to regular supervision and continuing personal development (as a coach);
- commitment to be guided by [ORGANIZATION's] ethical code, in spirit as well as by rote.

* Appreciation of a client's context doesn't imply a need to comprehensively understand the requirements of their role, share their level of technical competency or experience, etc. This competency is more or less relevant depending on the context of the coaching (eg most leadership coaching requires a general appreciation of the types of challenge faced by individuals operating at a senior level).

A copy of this template and a template role profile for SUPERVISORS can be downloaded from the companion website to this book, www.managingcoachingatwork.com.

Recruiting internal coaches, candidate selection criteria

FIGURE A.1 Template for internal coach recruitment

Candidate Assessment (In-house Coach):

Cohort/Project:			
Candidate:		**First pass:** (Accept/Long list/Exclude)	
		Interview: (Accept/Long list/Exclude)	
		Manager Approval: (Yes/No)	

First Pass (application sift):

Application shows evidence of the following:	Max. score (max.= strongly demonstrated; 0 = not demonstrated)	Score	Comment / Examples
Clear and reasonable motivation to apply	6		
Appreciation of what commitments coaching may involve	4		
Appreciation of what attributes are required for role	4		
Appreciation of what competencies are required for role	4		
No indication of ulterior motive or false expectation	2		
SCORE *(out of a maximum of 20)*	20		

Interview:

Candidate shows evidence of the following:	Max. score (max.= strongly demonstrated; 0 = not demonstrated)	Score	Comment / Examples
Has good motivation to apply for role	5		
Explains motivation to apply in context with their current role and career aspirations	4		
Has investigated/read material to familiarize with the expectations of coaching	5		
Has thought through time and effort implications of coaching	3		
Shows commitment horizon of more than one year	3		
Body language matches words spoken	3		
Demonstrates good potential to develop essential coaching skills (eg active listening, reflective responses)	5		
Is positive and enthusiastic about the opportunity	4		
A SCORE *(out of a maximum of 32)*	32		

Candidate shows evidence of the following:	Max. score (max.= strongly demonstrated; 0 = not demonstrated)	Score	Comment / Examples
Presentation is inconsistent with points made in application	5		
Inclined to interrupt frequently before a point/ question has been made	4		
Inclined to base statements on assumptions	3		
Misrepresents what interviewer has said (eg 'What you're really saying is..')	2		
Passes judgement	3		
Positions self as controller/ leader of the conversation	3		
B SCORE (out of a maximum of 20)	20		

A – B		
Other comments: (include here any comment that explains your assessment and scores and that may be of particular relevance to the candidate when giving interview feedback, eg specific examples of your observation)		

Note: maximum scores shown above are examples only.

A copy of this template and a template offering checklist criteria when assessing EXTERNAL COACHES can be downloaded from this book's companion website, www.managingcoachingatwork.com.

Request for coaching

FIGURE A.2 Request for coaching

REQUEST FOR COACHING			
Name of person for whom coaching is requested:		**Location:**	
Team/Department:		**Tel #:**	
Line Manager:		**E-mail address:**	
Requester:		**Date of Request:**	
Subject area (Please indicate the topic(s) that the coaching is intended to address)			
Objectives (If either specific or general objectives or expected outcomes have already been identified for the coaching, please indicate these here)			
Why is coaching expected to be most appropriate for meeting this need? (Please indicate if other interventions have been considered/attempted)			
Is face-to-face or telephone coaching preferred?	Face-to-face ☐ Telephone ☐ No preference ☐		
When would you prefer the coaching to commence?		**If possible to identify, which regular days/times are likely to be most suitable for coaching?**	
Signature (individual for whom coaching is requested)	Date...............		
Signature (line manager of individual for whom coaching is requested)	Date...............		

Coachee reflection

FIGURE A.3 Coachee reflection

COACHING/REFLECTIVE THOUGHTS			
Name:			
Subject of coaching in last session(s):		**Date(s) of session(s):**	
Subject of coaching proposed for next session:		**Date of next scheduled session:**	
Objectives for next session: (What do you hope to achieve when next meeting your coach?)			
Learnings and Insights: (What have you learned/considered anew as a result of your last coaching session?)			
Resolutions: (What did you resolve to do as a result of this session? Indicate when these have been achieved or attempted for the first time)	*Resolution*		*Achieved/Attempted*
Points for discussion: (List any points that you think you might like to consider at your next coaching session)			

Coaching management process

We suggest that a Process Guide for managing a coaching service might include the following sub-processes:

TABLE A.1 Coaching management process

Sub-process	Purpose	Scope
Strategic alignment	Ensure orientation of the coaching service remains in line with organizational need.	Aligning coaching with corporate strategy, people management strategy, learning and development planning and training design.
Stakeholder communication	Ensure appropriate, routine communication of need-to-know issues to relevant stakeholders; continue to maintain active and supportive engagement of stakeholders.	Nature, frequency and channels for communications.
Client–coach matching	Propose, oversee and monitor matching of clients with coaches; ensure appropriate engagement contracting and manager authorization; monitor effective close-out of engagements.	Matching client–coach needs and personalities; client's line manager authorization; client–coach contracting; client objective and expectation setting.
Coach selection (internal)	Ensure robust and consistent approach to selecting internal coach candidates.	Selection criteria; recruitment approach.
Coach selection (external)	Ensure robust and consistent approach to coach selection.	As above + criteria for supplier engagement.
Moderation	Ensure a consistency in the level of coaching competency delivered.	Moderation activities, frequency and approach; responses to handling inconsistencies in coaching delivery.

Evaluation (programme/ service level)	Routinely assess the effectiveness and impacts of the coaching service.	Scope of evaluation; method for data capture and analysis; reporting format and audiences; frequency of evaluation.
Organizational learning	Ensure that useful and relevant learnings gained from coaching are shared with others.	Capture, filtering and dissemination of organizational knowledge.
Coach development	Ensure ongoing, consistent provision of CPD for coaches.	CPD activity; calendar scheduling; coach accreditation; sharing coaching knowledge.
Client evaluation (engagement level)	Capture meaningful information from clients during and after coaching engagements that can be used to assess the effectiveness of the engagement and draw learnings for the coaching service as a whole.	Capture, analysis and application of learnings gained from coaching experience.
Demand forecasting	Identify expected demand for coaching and types of coaching; plan availability/ recruitment of coaches to meet anticipated demand.	Tracking of coach loadings/type of coaching undertaken; projection of demand; planning for coach and supervisor availability.
IT system management	Ensure that IT and knowledge system(s) and resources that are used for managing the coaching service, and for supporting coaches, clients and others, are kept operational and relevant.	Data backup, restore and capacity management; maintaining and enhancing knowledge base and portfolio of support resources.

A number of framework templates supporting a sample of these sub-processes can be downloaded from the companion website to this book, www.managingcoachingatwork.com.

Micro-tools: JaM

JaM ('Just a Minute') micro-tools are designed to help equip managers to use brief coaching conversations with team members and others. Several examples are included on this book's companion website, www.managingcoachingatwork.com.

APPENDIX B
Checklists for implementing, managing and developing a coaching service

The following checklists summarize some of the key activities that may need to be considered as a part of implementing, managing and developing a coaching service. Not all items may be relevant for every initiative, while some are only relevant during initial implementation. These distinctions should be obvious for most items.

TABLE B.1 Contexts for coaching

- ☐ How is/should coaching be defined within our organization?
- ☐ Is this definition universally understood?
- ☐ Where might coaching have a role to play in our organization rather than other interventions such as training?
- ☐ Is a coaching agenda appropriate for our organization?
- ☐ Is a scorecard approach appropriate to help define a coaching agenda?
- ☐ Have all available sources been checked to understand the organization's current plans, priorities and needs for which coaching may be relevant?
- ☐ Have the views of others regarding possible uses of coaching been sought and considered?
- ☐ When appropriate, are the activities that are planned for complementary initiatives dovetailed or integrated with the coaching initiative(s)?
- ☐ Is it appropriate to think in terms of achieving an aspiration level for coaching?
- ☐ Should differing aspiration levels apply for the different forms that coaching might take (eg providing coaching for executives, developing an in-house practice, 'manager as coach' initiatives)?
- ☐ Which aspiration level is appropriate to target first (for coaching as a whole or for each form of coaching)?
- ☐ How well does the organization match up to this aspired level(s)?
- ☐ Has the scope of work required to move to this aspired level(s) been assessed?
- ☐ Which type of implementation approach may be appropriate for achieving this aspiration(s)?

- ☐ Have the relative merits of each of the five implementation approaches been compared?
- ☐ Does/has the chosen implementation approach take account of any recent changes to organizational priorities, management structures and departmental responsibilities?
- ☐ Does/has the implementation approach take account of any insights available from an audit or evaluation study?
- ☐ Does the business case for coaching appeal to the interests of senior managers?

TABLE B.2 Planning and preparation

- ☐ Does the organization need to prepare the way for coaching, eg by making clear that it's OK for people to admit to a weakness?
- ☐ Has an attempt been made to describe the main elements and characteristics of the organization's cultural recipe?
- ☐ Is it possible and appropriate to attempt to influence the take-up of coaching?
- ☐ Do both the coaching project leader and sponsor(s) have the personal influence, passion and drive to 'make coaching happen'?
- ☐ If not, has help been identified/enlisted to ensure that others give proper commitment?
- ☐ Are the objectives of the coaching initiative realistic, capable of being achieved with available resources and time?
- ☐ Has a project plan been defined?
- ☐ Is this being followed?
- ☐ Is it still relevant?
- ☐ Have all preparatory activities relevant for the chosen implementation approach been identified?
- ☐ Does the plan allow flexibility to adapt to what is learned as the project proceeds?
- ☐ Does the plan dovetail/integrate with the organization's people development strategy and plan?
- ☐ Have these been informed by pilot project experience/earlier learnings?
- ☐ Have the relative merits for engaging external consultancy support been considered?
- ☐ Is the scope of external consultants'/trainers' assignments clearly defined?
- ☐ Have the relative merits of combining coaching with other initiatives been compared, eg integrating coaching with training that is focused on addressing a specific business need?
- ☐ Are the cultural differences of coaches and coachees taken account of by the target coaching service, eg considering multinational working?
- ☐ Have the implementation lessons/tips of others been considered and acted upon when appropriate?
- ☐ Is the intended implementation approach overly ambitious, ie putting pressure on individuals to run before they can walk?

TABLE B.3 Recruitment and matching

- ☐ Are coaches/trainee coachees being recruited in an appropriate and consistent way?
- ☐ Are necessary items in place to support recruitment, eg coach role profiles, a rationalized code of ethics?
- ☐ Have appropriate criteria for recruiting external coaches been defined, eg specifying the type of credentials that they should bring, the level of practical experience featuring in their coaching training, evidence of their commitment to supervision?
- ☐ Have appropriate criteria for recruiting internal coaches been defined, eg relating to candidates' attitude and motivation?
- ☐ Has the relevance of requiring accreditation for external coaches been considered?
- ☐ Are appropriate forms of contract in place for external coaches, eg considering short-term call-off needs, incentivizing loyalty?
- ☐ Is the progress of committed coaching contracts being monitored?
- ☐ Have the credentials of external coaches been verified?
- ☐ Are coaches continuing to be recruited and engaged based on forecasts of future demand?
- ☐ Does the process for coachee engagement involve line manager participation?
- ☐ Does the process for considering requests for coaching ensure that there is both a valid business case for each request and a genuine client for coaching?
- ☐ Are chemistry meetings held as a part of coach/coachee matching?
- ☐ Are managers of coachees committed to playing their part in helping individuals put what they take from coaching into action?

TABLE B.4 Training and development

- ☐ Has the required content for training been defined?
- ☐ Does the intended training adequately cover the required content?
- ☐ Does the intended training make use of appropriate learning methods and ones that are likely to engage trainees?
- ☐ Have the relative merits of staggering training been considered?
- ☐ Has the option of providing training to coachees been considered?
- ☐ Have the relative merits of customizing existing training materials, using a ready-made course or developing material from scratch been compared?
- ☐ Is the training planned appropriate and meaningful for the audience(s) it targets?
- ☐ Does the training give emphasis to topics that are appropriate for the current level of coaching experience of trainees, eg offering micro-tools for managers who are new to coaching?
- ☐ Have sourcing options for providing training been compared?

- [ ] Do training facilitators have appropriate experience and skill to facilitate coaching training?
- [ ] Are development activities other than training to help trainees build up their skills planned/happening?
- [ ] Does the training allow adequate opportunities for trainees to experiment, practise and reflect?
- [ ] Has proposed training been piloted and the learnings been acted upon?
- [ ] Is feedback received from trainees being acted upon?
- [ ] Has feedback from trainees been sought some months after they completed training rather than just via 'happy sheets' at the time of a course?
- [ ] Have the different approaches for supporting coaches' continuing development been considered and trialled if appropriate?
- [ ] Do managers have opportunities to practise coaching skills in supportive and non-judgemental environments?
- [ ] Do both coaches and coachees have opportunities to engage in reflective practice?
- [ ] Is adequate and appropriate provision made for developing coach/manager skills?
- [ ] Is knowledge sharing amongst coaches encouraged and facilitated?
- [ ] Are coaches, managers and supervisors being consulted with to identify their ongoing training and support needs?
- [ ] Is the sell case for second-stage training for managers being effectively promoted?
- [ ] Is training and support provision for supervisors adequate and appropriate?
- [ ] Does training and development provision cater for new managers, eg accounting for one-to-one tutoring?
- [ ] Are internal coaches receiving regular coaching practice, even when they may not regularly be matched with coaching clients?
- [ ] Are networking activities begun by coaches/managers being sustained?

TABLE B.5 Coach supervision

- [ ] Are coaches receiving supervision/mentoring?
- [ ] Is supervision being developed in line with the findings of evaluation studies?
- [ ] Is the role of a supervisor properly understood by both coaches and supervisors?
- [ ] Are supervisors recruited in a consistent and appropriate way?
- [ ] Are the qualifying/selection criteria for supervisors appropriate?
- [ ] Have the relative merits of using external or internal supervisors been compared?
- [ ] Are supervisors appropriately skilled, including having adequate coaching experience and training?
- [ ] Are the support and development opportunities provided for internal supervisors adequate and appropriate?
- [ ] Is expected future demand for supervision routinely forecast and catered for?

TABLE B.6 Communication

- ☐ Have all potential stakeholders of the coaching initiative been identified?
- ☐ Have they been properly engaged?
- ☐ Has a project communication plan been defined?
- ☐ Is this being acted upon?
- ☐ Does this allow and encourage two-way communication?
- ☐ Is this integrated with communications planned by others?
- ☐ Are leaders of complementary initiatives to coaching being consulted with on an ongoing basis?
- ☐ Have possible objections that might be met and counter-responses been identified?
- ☐ Has a 'lift test' explaining the coaching initiative been defined?
- ☐ Has the potential use of social networking been considered for supporting coaches/managers?
- ☐ Has the sell case for coaching been put to managers?
- ☐ Does this set realistic expectations about how coaching may help them in their essential tasks, eg considering whether what is proposed will equip them to coach in brief, ad hoc conversations?
- ☐ Have potential advocates for coaching been identified and targeted?
- ☐ Are these being supported effectively?
- ☐ Are their line managers supportive of their involvement?
- ☐ Are learnings, news and tips being regularly communicated to coaches and other interested stakeholders?
- ☐ Are new training offerings, relevant insights and quick tips being regularly communicated to coaches/managers?
- ☐ Are the summarized findings of audit/evaluation being communicated effectively to relevant audiences?

TABLE B.7 Accreditation

- ☐ Has the relevance of requiring accreditation for internal coaches been considered?
- ☐ Has the relevance of aligning with one of several alternative accrediting bodies been considered, as well as the option of providing internal accreditation?
- ☐ Has the relevance of requiring accreditation for the coaching programme been considered?

TABLE B.8 Service management

- ☐ Are sufficient numbers of appropriately skilled people engaged to train, administer and support forecast future demand for coaching and supervision?
- ☐ Does demand forecasting take account of historical data?
- ☐ Does demand forecasting take account of new change projects, training programmes and other initiatives that coaching might be expected to play a role in supporting?
- ☐ Can sudden high demands for coaching be met, eg by backfilling with external coaches on call-off contracts?
- ☐ Have revenue-earning opportunities for the coaching service been considered and trialled, eg charging external coaches to attend masterclasses?
- ☐ Does an early-warning system exist to point out possible backsliding?
- ☐ Is the process for managing coaching being kept in step with changing needs?
- ☐ Is the process for managing coaching being kept in step with changing HR policy, training strategy and people development plans?

TABLE B.9 Infrastructure

- ☐ Are appropriate information systems and intranet content to support the coaching process in place?
- ☐ Are these being properly maintained and developed in line with changing needs?
- ☐ Is a bulletin board or other 'question and answer' facility for coaches being maintained?
- ☐ Is knowledge of learnings and developments in the coaching world being maintained, communicated and acted upon when appropriate?
- ☐ Is a knowledge base for coaches being maintained?
- ☐ Are support tools available for coaches and being maintained?
- ☐ Are the knowledge base and toolset adequately populated, eg when they are initially set up?

TABLE B.10 Process

- ☐ Has a process for administering coaching requirements been defined?
- ☐ Is this written down?
- ☐ Is this being adopted?
- ☐ Has this been communicated to all who need to be aware of it?
- ☐ Does this include sub-processes covering all the relevant activities of coaching management, eg coach/coachee matching, demand forecasting, assessing requests for coaching?
- ☐ Is the process easy to understand and use?

TABLE B.11 Moderation, evaluation and audit

- [ ] Is the consistency of how coaching is being delivered being routinely moderated?
- [ ] Has consideration been given to how the benefits of coaching can be assessed?
- [ ] Does routine evaluation take account of this?
- [ ] Is the organization's coaching provision routinely audited or evaluated?
- [ ] Are audits or evaluation studies being carried out at appropriate times and time intervals?
- [ ] Do routine audits keep track of basic metrics such as how many people have been coached during a particular period, what is the average number of coaching hours per coaching relationship, etc?
- [ ] Have the relative merits of alternative approaches to evaluation been considered and is the most appropriate being applied?
- [ ] Are both the effectiveness and impacts of coaching routinely evaluated?
- [ ] Are sponsor and key stakeholder perceptions of coaching performance being routinely captured?
- [ ] Does audit/evaluation take account of all relevant, readily accessible data?
- [ ] Are all relevant, practical methods being used in data gathering for audit/evaluation?
- [ ] Are adequate data samples being used, eg in questionnaire surveys?
- [ ] Are data samples representative of the population base, eg appropriately stratified?
- [ ] Are the outputs of evaluation providing what's needed to inform future action?
- [ ] Are the outputs being acted upon?
- [ ] Is the process for drawing conclusions from audit/evaluation robust, eg catering for potential devil's advocate criticisms?
- [ ] Does evaluation take account of alternative explanations that might be put up against claims of coaching's impact?
- [ ] Does the evaluation approach avoid a need for an evaluator to make assumptions and subjective judgements?
- [ ] Is evaluation conducted by someone who doesn't have a vested interest in the success or otherwise of the coaching initiative (when practical)?
- [ ] Are the effectiveness and impacts of supervision being routinely evaluated?

TABLE B.12 Organizational learnings

- ☐ Are learnings from coaching experience being routinely captured, communicated and acted upon?
- ☐ Are organizational learnings and knowledge being shared with other organizations?
- ☐ Are external support resources and information sources being used, eg drawing insights from relevant coaching journals?
- ☐ Has the relevance of coach/organizational membership of professional coaching bodies been considered?
- ☐ If so, is the continuing relevance of any existing alignment routinely reviewed?

TABLE B.13 Developing the use of coaching

- ☐ Are the applications and results of coaching tied in with business planning, including key performance indices and balanced scorecards when appropriate?
- ☐ Are managers and executives being regularly consulted to understand their changing priorities and needs?
- ☐ Are target sponsors' hot buttons recognized and attended to when promoting coaching?
- ☐ Are potential ambassadors for coaching being identified and properly supported?
- ☐ Are the benefits of coaching being promoted on an ongoing basis, eg to point out success stories?
- ☐ Is the support that's available for coaches/managers being promoted on an ongoing basis?
- ☐ Are the readiness of the organization and the desirability to move the coaching initiative to a new aspiration level being reviewed following audit/evaluation?
- ☐ Is the relevance for potentially expanding or contracting the current coaching service being routinely reviewed in the light of audit/evaluation?
- ☐ Is development of coaching guided more by what other organizations are doing rather than in relation to what has been clearly articulated as being relevant for the business?

APPENDIX C1
Coaching associations

The following associations, institutes and other professional bodies provide a range of support services and accrediting/credentialling for coaches, as well as useful fora for those responsible for managing coaching within organizations. Most of the organizations listed operate internationally, although those with a specific geographical focus are indicated.

American Association of Professional Coaches (USA, Canada)
http://www.aapcoaches.com

The American Coaching Association (ACA) (USA)
www.americoach.org

American Psychological Association, Division 13 (USA)
www.apa.org/about/division/div13.html

Association for Coaching (AC)
www.associationforcoaching.com

The Association for Professional Executive Coaching and Supervision (APECS)
http://www.apecs.org

Association of Coach Training Organizations
www.acto1.com

Australasian Institute of Professional Coaches (AIPC) (Australia, New Zealand)
http://www.aipc.org.au

Australian Psychological Society Interest Group in Coaching Psychology (Australia)
www.psychology.org.au

The British Psychological Society Special Group in Coaching Psychology (UK)
www.bps.org.uk

China Coach Association (China)
www.ctca.cn

Coach Universe
www.coachuniverse.com

Coaches and Mentors of South Africa (COMENSA) (Republic of South Africa)
www.comensa.org.za

The Coaches Association of India (India)
www.coachesassociationofindia.com

The Coaching Commons.
www.coachingcommons.org

CoachLab, International Society of Professional Coaches
www.coachlab.net

Coachville
www.Coachville.com

The Conference Board (Council on Executive Coaching) (USA)
http://www.conference-board.org/councils/councilsDetailUS.
cfm?Council_ID=155

European Mentoring and Coaching Council (Europe)
www.emccouncil.org

The Executive Coaching Forum
www.theexecutivecoachingforum.com/index.htm

Global Executive Coaches (GEC)
www.globalexecutivecoaches.com

Hong Kong Coaching Community (Hong Kong)
www.coachinghk.com

The International Association of Coaches (IAC)
www.certifiedcoach.org

International Business Coach Institute (IBCI)
www.businesscoachinstitute.org

International Coach Federation (ICF)
www.coachfederation.org

International Coaching Community (ICC)
www.internationalcoachingcommunity.com

International Consortia of Business Coaches
www.i-cbc.com

International Consortium for Coaching in Organizations (ICCO)
www.coachingconsortium.org

International Institute of Coaching (IIC)
www.internationalinstituteofcoaching.org

Israel Coaching (Israel)
www.coaching.org.il

Japan Coach Association (Japan)
www.coach.or.jp

Life & Business Coaching Association of Ireland (Republic of Ireland)
http://www.lbcai.ie/index.php

Peer Resources Network (PRN)
www.peer.ca/coaching.html

Professional Coaches and Mentors Association (PCMA) (California)
www.pcmaonline.com

Society for Coaching Psychology
www.societyforcoachingpsychology.net

Solution Focus Consulting Inc. (Japan)
http://www.solutionfocus.jp

Worldwide Association of Business Coaches (WABC)
www.wabccoaches.com

APPENDIX C2
Coaching journals and periodicals

Choice: The Magazine of Professional Coaching
http://www.choice-online.com/about.html

Coaching at Work
http://www.coaching-at-work.com

Coaching: An International Journal of Theory, Research & Practice
www.InformaWorld.com/coaching

Consulting Psychology Journal: Practice and Research
www.apa.org/journals/cpb/description.html

International Coaching Psychology Review
http://www.sgcp.org.uk/sgcp/publications/publications_home.cfm

International Journal of Coaching in Organizations
http://www.ijco.info

International Journal of Evidence Based Coaching and Mentoring
www.brookes.ac.uk/schools/education/ijebcm

International Journal of Mentoring and Coaching
www.emccouncil.org/uk/ public/international_journal_of_mentoring_and_
coaching/volume_vii_issue_2_extract/index.html

The Coaching Psychologist
http://www.sgcp.org.uk/sgcp/publications/publications_home.cfm

The Journal of Coaching Education
http://www.tandf.co.uk/journals/authors/rcoaauth.asp

Training and Coaching Today
http://www.personneltoday.com/staticpages/trainingmagazine.htm

Many other journals and periodicals that are dedicated to organization
development, learning and HR also carry regular features or include sections
dedicated to coaching.

REFERENCES

Chapter 1

Anderson V, Rayner C and Schyns B (2009) *Coaching at the Sharp End: The role of line managers in coaching at work*, CIPD, London.

Brown, S F and Grant, A M (2010) From GROW to GROUP: theoretical issues and a practical model for group coaching in organizations, *Coaching: An International Journal of Theory, Research and Practice* 3 (1), pp 30–45.

Burn, G (ed) (2007) *Personal Development All-In-One For Dummies*, John Wiley & Sons, Chichester, p 33.

Caplan, J (2003) *Coaching for the Future: How smart companies use coaching and mentoring*, CIPD, London, p 20.

CIPD (2008) *Annual Survey Report 2008 – Learning and Development*, CIPD, London.

Dembkowski, S (2006) *The Seven Steps of Effective Executive Coaching*, Thorogood Publishing, London, p 11.

Garvey, R (2008), cited in Sparrow, S (2008) Coaching and mentoring: spot the difference, *Personnel Today*, 18 March.

Hersey, P and Blanchard K (1977) *Management of Organizational Behaviour: Utilizing Human Resources*, third edition, Prentice-Hall, New Jersey.

Howell, W C and Fleishman, E A (eds) (1982) *Human Performance and Productivity: Information Processing and Decision Making*, Volume 2, Erlbaum, Hillside, New Jersey.

Jay, M R (1999) *Coach 2 The Bottom Line: An executive guide to coaching performance, change and transformation in organizations*, Trafford Publishing, Bloomington, IN, p 19.

Kilburg (1996), cited in London, M (2001) *How People Evaluate Others in Organizations* (Series in Applied Psychology), Psychology Press, Hove, p 222.

Loehr, A and Emerson, B (2008) *A Manager's Guide to Coaching: Simple and effective ways to get the best get the best from your employees*, AMACOM, New York, p 2.

Luft, J and Ingham, H (1955) The Johari Window, a graphic model of interpersonal awareness, *Proceedings of the Western Training Laboratory in Group Development*, Los Angeles: UCLA.

Parsloe, E (1999) *The Manager as Coach and Mentor* (Management Shapers), CIPD, London, p.8.

Taylor, D (2007) *The Naked Coach: Business coaching made simple*, Capstone, Bloomington, MN, p 312.

Vint, A, Recaldin, C and Gould, D (1998) *Learning to Fly: Leadership & performance in the boardroom*, Kogan Page, London, pp 192–3.

Whitmore, J (2002) *Coaching for Performance*, 3rd edn, Nicholas Brealey, London.

Chapter 2

Carter, R (2009) *The Brain Book*, Dorling Kindersley, London.

Diesseroth, K (2010), interview cited in Thomson, H (2010) Brainbeat, *New Scientist*, 10 July, pp 28–31.

Gallwey, W T (1997) *The Inner Game of Tennis: The classic guide to the mental side of peak performance*, Random House, London.

Garvey, R (2010) Getting the measure of you, *Coaching At Work*, 5 (2), p 57.

Hattie, J A (2009) *Influences on Student Learning*, www.arts.auckland.ac.nz, accessed 2009.

Jarvis, J (2006) *The Case for Coaching: Making evidence-based decisions*, CIPD, London.

King Humphrey, E (2010) The mad artist's brain, *Scientific American Mind*, November/December, p 6.

Kolb, D (1984) *Experiential Learning: Experience as the source of learning and development*, Prentice-Hall, Englewood Cliffs, NJ.

Lewin, K (1951) *Field Theory in Social Science: Selected theoretical papers*, ed Dorwin Cartwright, Harper & Row, New York.

Lupyan, G (2009) Extracommunicative functions of language: verbal interference causes selective categorization impairments, *Psychonomic Bulletin & Review*, 16 (4), pp 711–18.

Marzano, R J (1998) A theory based meta analysis of research on instruction, cited in Petty, G (2009) *Evidence-Based Teaching: A practical approach*, 2nd edn, Nelson Thornes, Cheltenham, p 74.

McAuliffe, K (2009) They don't make Homo Sapiens like they used to, *Discover*, March.

Meteyard, L, Bahrami, B and Vigliocco, G (2007) Motion detection and motion verbs, language affects low-level visual perception, *Psychological Science*, 18 (11), pp 1007–13.

Ornstein, R (1998) *The Right Mind: Making sense of the hemispheres*, Harcourt Brace International, New York.

Peacock, F (2007) *Arrosez les fleurs, pas les mauvaises herbes!: Une stratégie qui révolutionne les relations professionnelles, amoureuses, familiales*, Les Editions de l'Homme, Paris.

Pinker, S (2007) The brain: the mystery of consciousness, *Time*, 19 January.

Qiu, J, Li, H, Jou, J, Liu, J, Luo, Y, Feng, T, Wu, Z, and Zhang Q (2010) Neural correlates of the 'aha' experiences: evidence from an fMRI study of insight problem solving, *Cortex*, 46 (3), pp 397–403.

Robson, D (2010) The voice of reason, *New Scientist*, 4 September, pp 30–3.

Rock, D and Page, L J (2009) *Coaching with the Brain in Mind: Foundations for practice*, Wiley, Chichester.

Rock, D and Schwartz, J M (2006) A brain-based approach to coaching, *International Journal of Coaching in Organizations*, 4 (2), pp 32–43.

Siegel, D J (2007) *A Mindful Brain: Reflection and attunement in the cultivation of well-being*, W W Norton, New York.

Sigman, M and Dehaene, S (2008) Brain mechanisms of serial and parallel processing during dual-task performance, *Journal of Neuroscience*, 28 (30), pp 7585–98.

Telford, C W (1931) The refractory phase of voluntary and associative responses, *Journal of Experimental Psychology*, 14, pp 1–36.

Thomson, H (2010) Brainbeat, *New Scientist*, 10 July, pp 28–31.

Zeus, P and Skiffington, S (2002) *The Coaching at Work Toolkit – a Complete Guide to Techniques and Practices*, McGraw-Hill, Sydney, Australia.

Zimmer, C (2009) The brain stop paying attention: zoning out is a crucial mental state, *Discover*, July/August.

Chapter 3

Baker, D, Greenberg, C and Hemingway, C (2006) *What Happy Companies Know: How the new science of happiness can change your company for the better*, Prentice Hall, Upper Saddle River, NJ.

Keddy, J and Johnson, C (May 2006) *Really Making a Difference: Insights from coaching implementation experience*, accessible at www.keddyconsultants.com.

National Mentoring and Coaching Benchmarking Study (South Africa) (2008), Benchmarking coaching and mentoring, *HR Highway* 2(3), pp. 10–11.

Scannell, E (2007) *The Race to $100 Billion*, redmondmag.com, 05/17/2007, http://redmondmag.com/articles/2007/05/17/the-race-to-100-billion.aspx, accessed June, 2010.

Weinstein, M (1997) *Managing to Have Fun: How fun at work can motivate your employees, inspire your co-workers and boost your bottom line*, Pocket Books, New York.

Chapter 4

Garvey, R (2010) Getting the measure of you, *Coaching at Work*, 5 (2), p 57.

Johnson, G, Scholes, K and Whittington, R (2007) *Exploring Corporate Strategy*, 8th edn, Financial Times/Prentice Hall, Harlow.

Kay, A (2010) *Fry the Monkeys Create a Solution: The manager's and facilitator's guide to accelerating change using Solution Focus* (volume 1), Create Space.

National Mentoring and Coaching Benchmarking Study (South Africa) (2008), Benchmarking coaching and mentoring, *HR Highway* 2(3), pp. 10–11.

Shekar, C, Best HR career advice, in six words or less, *Human Resources Professionals: The 'unofficial' forum for SHRM members (LinkedIn)*, accessed at http://www.linkedin.com/groupAnswers?viewQuestionAndAnswers=&discussionID=14224092&gid=120142&trk=EML_anet_qa_ttle-0Tt79xs2RVr6JBpnsJt7dBpSBA on 16 March 2010.

Chapter 5

Boyatis, R (2010) Should coaching be regulated?, *LinkedIn group post (Group: Coaching at Work)*, 27 March.

Hall, L (2009) Tesco goes shopping for new suppliers, *Coaching at Work*, January/February.

Handy, C (2000) *21 Ideas for Managers*, Jossey-Bass, San Francisco.

ICMF (2010) *Bully or Strong Manager?*, http://www.conflictmanagementforum. org/bullysurveymarch10v01.pdf, accessed 1 September 2010.

International Coaching Register (2010) http://www.internationalcoachingregister. org, accessed 22 March 2010.

Kirkpatrick, D (2006) *Evaluating Training Programs: The four levels*, 3rd edn, Berrett-Koehler, San Francisco, CA.

Luft, J and Ingham, H (1955) The Johari Window, a graphic model of interpersonal awareness, *Proceedings of the Western Training Laboratory in Group Development*, UCLA, Los Angeles, CA.

Owen, D (2009) *In Sickness and in Power: Illness in heads of government during the last 100 years*, Methuen, London, p 305.

Stuart, P (1993) Selling HR: how to get CEO support, *Personnel Journal*, **72** (5), pp 112–26. Accessible online at Workforce.com: http://www.workforce.com/ archive/feature/22/21/70/index.php, accessed 23 March 2010.

Yates, K and Kibbe, K (2010) Social media: transforming the way companies communicate change, *Workforce Management On-line*, January, http://www. workforce.com/archive/feature/26/97/21/index.php, accessed June 2010.

Chapter 6

Hjerth, M (2008) *Micro Tools and the PLUS model*, SOLWorld website, http:// solworld.ning.com/group/microtoolsandtheplusmodel, accessed July 2010.

Jackson, P and McKergow, M (2006) *The Solutions Focus – making coaching and change SIMPLE*, Nicholas Brealey International, London.

Jones G and Gorell R (2009) *50 Top Tools for Coaches: A complete toolkit for developing and empowering people*, Kogan Page, London.

Kolb, D A (1984) *Experiential Learning. Experience as the source of learning and development*, Prentice-Hall, Englewood Cliffs, NJ.

Lee, G (2003) *Leadership Coaching*, CIPD, London.

Lewin, K (1948) *Resolving Social Conflicts; Selected papers on group dynamics*, ed G W Lewin, Harper & Row, New York.

O'Neill, M B (2000) *Executive Coaching with Backbone and Heart: A Systems Approach to Engaging Leaders with their Challenges*, Jossey-Bass.

Rock, D and Page, L J (2009) *Coaching with the Brain in Mind: Foundations for practice*, John Wiley & Sons, Chichester.

Siegel, D J (1999) *The Developing Mind: Towards a neurobiology of interpersonal experience*, Guilford Press, New York.

Whitmore, J (2009) *Coaching for Performance: GROWing human potential and purpose – the principles and practice of coaching and leadership*, 4th edn, Nicholas Brealey, London.

Chapter 7

Anderson, V, Rayner, C and Schyns, B (2009) *Coaching at the Sharp End: The role of line managers in coaching at work*, CIPD, London.

Biggs, J (1999) *Teaching for Quality Learning at University*, Open University, Buckingham.

Grove, D J and Panzer, B I (1989) *Resolving Traumatic Memories: Metaphors and symbols in psychotherapy*, Irvington, New York.

Johnson, C (2009) One step beyond, *Coaching at Work*, CIPD, London.

Moon, J A (2000) *Reflection in Learning and Professional Development: Theory and practice*, Routledge, London.

Olivero, G, Bane, K, and Kopelman, R E (1997) Executive coaching as a transfer of training tool: effects on productivity in a public agency, *Public Personnel Management*, **26** (4), pp 461–9.

Rock, D and Page, L J (2009) *Coaching with the Brain in Mind: Foundations for practice*, John Wiley & Sons, Chichester.

Whitworth, L, Kimsey-House, H and Sandahl-Davies, P (1998) *Co-active Coaching – New Skills for Coaching People Toward Success in Work and Life*, Black Publishing, Palo Alto, CA.

Chapter 8

Anderson D and Anderson M (2004) *Coaching that Counts: Harnessing the power of leadership coaching to deliver strategic value*, Butterworth-Heinemann, Oxford.

Anderson, V (2007a) *Change Agenda: The value of learning – a new model of value and evaluation*, CIPD, London.

Anderson, V (2007b) *Value of Learning: From return on investment to return on expectation*, CIPD, London.

Carter, A (2007) *Practical Methods for Evaluating Coaching*, Institute for Employment Studies (Report 430), Brighton.

Carter, A and Mortlock, S (2008) *How Organisations Evaluate Whether Coaching Really Works*, Presentation to West Midlands Coaching Pool Conference 2008, Birmingham.

Chapman, M and Carter, A (2009) How to… evaluate coaching, *Coaching at Work*, **4** (2), pp 54–5.

CIPD (April 2010) *Learning and Talent Development 2010: Summary of key findings*, CIPD, London.

Cross, J (January 2001) *A Fresh Look at ROI*, Internet Time Group.

Flynn, G (1998) The nuts and bolts of value training, *Workforce*, **77** (11), pp 80–5.

Garvey, R (2010) Getting the measure of you, *Coaching At Work*, **5** (2), p 57.

Kirkpatrick, D L (1998) *Evaluating Training Programs: The four levels*, 2nd edn, Berrett-Koehler, San Francisco, CA.

McGovern, J, Lindeman, M, Vergara, M, Murphy, S, Baker, L and Warrenfeltz, R (2001) Maximising the impact of executive coaching: behavioural change, organizational outcomes and return on investment, *The Manchester Review*, **6** (1), pp. 1–9, quoted in Passmore J and Gibbes C (2007) The state of executive coaching research: what does the current literature tell us and what's next for coaching research?, *International Coaching Psychology Review*, **2** (2), p 119.

McGurk, J (2010a) *Let's Get Real About Coaching Evaluation*, Presentation to the CIPD Coaching Conference 2010, London, 28 September.

McGurk, J (2010b) *Real World Coaching Evaluation*, CIPD, London.

Parker-Wilkins, V (2006) Business impact of executive coaching: demonstrating monetary value, *Industrial and Commercial Training*, **38** (3), pp 122–7.

Petty, G (2009) *Evidence-Based Teaching: A practical approach*, 2nd edn, Nelson Thornes, Cheltenham.

Phillips, J J (1997) *Return on Investment in Training and Performance Improvement Programs: A step-by-step manual for calculating the financial return* (Improving Human Performance), Gulf Publishing, Houston, TX.

Reichheld, R (2006) *The Ultimate Question*, Harvard Business School Press, Boston, MA.

Tobin, D R (1998) *The Fallacy of ROI Calculations: Corporate Learning Strategies*.

Chapter 9

Bekoff, M in Turner, J and D' Silva, J (2006) *Animals, Ethics and Trade: The challenge of animal sentience*, Earthscan, London.

Dupré, B (2007) *50 Philosophy Ideas You Really Need to Know*, Quercus Publishing, London.

Hall, L (2009) Tesco goes shopping for new suppliers, *Coaching at Work*, January/February.

Kirkpatrick, D L (1998) *Evaluating Training Programs: The four levels*, 2nd edn, Berrett-Koehler Publishers, San Francisco, CA, p 186.

Klein, P G in Perfors, A (March 2007) The singular of data is anecdote, *Social Science Statistics Blog*, Harvard University, Cambridge, MA.

Suzuki, S (2010) *ZEN Mind, Beginner's Mind*, 40th Anniversary Edition, Shambhala Publications, Boston, MA.

Chapter 10

Bachkirova, T, Stevens, P and Willis, P (2005) *Coaching Supervision*, Oxford Brookes Coaching and Mentoring Society, Oxford.

Gray, D E (2010) Towards the lifelong skills and business development of coaches: an integrated model of supervision and mentoring, *Coaching: An International Journal of Theory, Research and Practice*, 3 (1), pp 60–72.

Hawkins, P and Shohet, R (2006) *Supervision in the Helping Professions*, 3rd edn, Open University Press/McGraw Hill Education, Maidenhead.

Hawkins, P and Smith, N (2006) *Coaching, Mentoring and Organizational Consultancy: Supervision and development*, Open University Press/McGraw-Hill Education, Maidenhead, p 147.

Johnson, C and Keddy, J (2010) *Managing Conflict at Work: Understanding and resolving conflict for productive working relationships*, Kogan Page, London.

Kline, N (1999) *A Time to Think*, Ward Lock, London.

Lewis, L (2008) *Certificate in Supervision Training Programme*, Bluesky International, www.blueskyinternational.com.

Proctor, B (1986) Supervision: a co-operative exercise in accountability, in *Enabling and Ensuring: Supervision in practice*, ed A Marken and M Payne, Leicester National Youth Bureau/Council for Education and Training in Youth and Community Work, Leicester.

INDEX

NB: page numbers in *italic* indicate figures or tables